Beginning Programming For Dummies, 3rd Edition

Cheat Sheet

S0-BZQ-391

Liberty BASIC subprogram structures

```
Main program instructions
GOSUB [subprogram]
Main program instructions
END

[subprogram]
Subprogram instructions
Subprogram instructions
RETURN

SUB SubroutineName Variable
 ' One or more instructions here
END SUB

FUNCTION FunctionName(Variable)
 Instructions
 FunctionName = value
END FUNCTION
```

Common programming filename extensions

Extension	Description
ASM	Assembly language source code
BAS	BASIC language source code
C	C language source code
CLA	Java class file (byte code format, short for CLASS)
CPP	C++ language source code
CS	C# language source code
EXE	Executable file (machine code format)
HTM	HyperText Markup Language file (short for HTML)
JAV	Java language source code (short for JAVA)
JS	JavaScript language source code
PAS	Pascal and Delphi language source code
PL	Perl language source code
PY	Python language source code
TXT	Text or ASCII file

Tips for writing programs

- ✔ Use descriptive variable names.
- ✔ Use appropriate data types.
- ✔ Write programs that are easy to read and understand.
- ✔ Use simple algorithms and data structures whenever possible.
- ✔ Comment your program liberally. (Or, as an alternative, make your code so clear and easy to read that you don't need comments in the first place.)
- ✔ Write modular programs by dividing a large program into several smaller programs that you isolate from one another.
- ✔ Test boundary conditions by giving your program extremely high and extremely low numbers.
- ✔ Choose the right algorithm and data structure for your program.
- ✔ Eliminate all unnecessary instructions or variables.
- ✔ Make your program work first; then worry about optimizing the program to make it smaller and faster. Remember that a slow, bloated program that works is preferable to a small, fast program that doesn't work.

Copyright © 2004 Wiley Publishing, Inc. All rights reserved.
Item 4997-9.
For more information about Wiley Publishing, call 1-800-762-2974.

Wiley, the Wiley Publishing logo, For Dummies, the Dummies Man logo, the For Dummies Bestselling Book Series logo and all related trade dress are trademarks or registered trademarks of John Wiley & Sons, Inc. and/or its affiliates. All other trademarks are property of their respective owners.

For Dummies: Bestselling Book Series for Beginners

Beginning Programming For Dummies, 3rd Edition

Cheat Sheet

Liberty BASIC control structures

```
IF Condition THEN Instructions
IF Condition THEN
 Instructions1
 Instructions2
END IF
IF Condition THEN
 Instructions1
ELSE
 Instructons2
END IF
SELECT CASE Variable
CASE Value1
 Instructions1
CASE Value2
 Instructions2
END SELECT
SELECT CASE Variable
CASE Value1, Value2, Value3
 Instructions1
CASE Value4, Value5
 Instructions2
END SELECT
SELECT CASE
CASE (Variable [<, >, <=, >=, =, <>] Value1)
 Instructions1
CASE (Variable [<, >, <=, >=, =, <>] Value2)
 Instructions2
END SELECT
```

Shortcut keys for Liberty BASIC

Key	What It Does
Ctrl+A	Select All
Ctrl+C	Copy
Ctrl+F	Find/Replace
Ctrl+G	Find Again
Ctrl+X	Cut
Ctrl+V	Paste
Ctrl+Z	Undo
Shift+F5	Run
Alt+F5	Debug
Del	Clear

Liberty BASIC mathematical operators

Mathematical Operation	Symbol to Use
Addition	+
Subtraction	−
Division	/ (forward slash)
Multiplication	*
Exponentiation	^

Liberty BASIC loop structures

```
WHILE Condition
 Instructions
WEND
FOR Counter = Start TO End
 Instructions
NEXT Counter
FOR Counter = Start TO End STEP Increment
 Instructions
NEXT Counter
```

For Dummies: Bestselling Book Series for Beginners

Beginning Programming
FOR
DUMMIES®
3RD EDITION

by Wallace Wang

510.78PG
W246
2004

WILEY

Wiley Publishing, Inc.

Beginning Programming For Dummies®, 3rd Edition

Published by
Wiley Publishing, Inc.
111 River Street
Hoboken, NJ 07030-5774

Copyright © 2004 by Wiley Publishing, Inc., Indianapolis, Indiana

Published by Wiley Publishing, Inc., Indianapolis, Indiana

Published simultaneously in Canada

No part of this publication may be reproduced, stored in a retrieval system or transmitted in any form or by any means, electronic, mechanical, photocopying, recording, scanning or otherwise, except as permitted under Sections 107 or 108 of the 1976 United States Copyright Act, without either the prior written permission of the Publisher, or authorization through payment of the appropriate per-copy fee to the Copyright Clearance Center, 222 Rosewood Drive, Danvers, MA 01923, (978) 750-8400, fax (978) 646-8600. Requests to the Publisher for permission should be addressed to the Legal Department, Wiley Publishing, Inc., 10475 Crosspoint Blvd., Indianapolis, IN 46256, (317) 572-3447, fax (317) 572-4447, e-mail: permcoordinator@ wiley.com.

Trademarks: Wiley, the Wiley Publishing logo, For Dummies, the Dummies Man logo, A Reference for the Rest of Us!, The Dummies Way, Dummies Daily, The Fun and Easy Way, Dummies.com, and related trade dress are trademarks or registered trademarks of John Wiley & Sons, Inc., and/or its affiliates in the United States and other countries, and may not be used without written permission. All other trademarks are the property of their respective owners. Wiley Publishing, Inc., is not associated with any product or vendor mentioned in this book.

LIMIT OF LIABILITY/DISCLAIMER OF WARRANTY: WHILE THE PUBLISHER AND AUTHOR HAVE USED THEIR BEST EFFORTS IN PREPARING THIS BOOK, THEY MAKE NO REPRESENTATIONS OR WAR-RANTIES WITH RESPECT TO THE ACCURACY OR COMPLETENESS OF THE CONTENTS OF THIS BOOK AND SPECIFICALLY DISCLAIM ANY IMPLIED WARRANTIES OF MERCHANTABILITY OR FITNESS FOR A PARTICULAR PURPOSE. NO WARRANTY MAY BE CREATED OR EXTENDED BY SALES REPRESENTATIVES OR WRITTEN SALES MATERIALS. THE ADVICE AND STRATEGIES CONTAINED HEREIN MAY NOT BE SUITABLE FOR YOUR SITUATION. YOU SHOULD CONSULT WITH A PROFESSIONAL WHERE APPROPRI-ATE. NEITHER THE PUBLISHER NOR AUTHOR SHALL BE LIABLE FOR ANY LOSS OF PROFIT OR ANY OTHER COMMERCIAL DAMAGES, INCLUDING BUT NOT LIMITED TO SPECIAL, INCIDENTAL, CONSE-QUENTIAL, OR OTHER DAMAGES.

For general information on our other products and services or to obtain technical support, please contact our Customer Care Department within the U.S. at 800-762-2974, outside the U.S. at 317-572-3993, or fax 317-572-4002.

Wiley also publishes its books in a variety of electronic formats. Some content that appears in print may not be available in electronic books.

Library of Congress Control Number: 2003114793

ISBN: 0-7645-4997-9

Manufactured in the United States of America

10 9 8 7 6 5 4 3 2 1

3B/SU/RR/QT

WILEY

About the Author

After spending his first two post-college years working for a dead-end corporation that encouraged its employees to use euphemisms to disguise the fact that they were manufacturing nuclear weapons with the potential to wipe out most forms of life on the planet, Wallace Wang decided that his life was meant to be spent doing something more exciting than existing in a corporate culture that stifled freedom and democracy while building missiles ostensibly to protect freedom and democracy. With the thought of escape in his mind, he bought one of the first IBM personal computers on the market — and quickly realized that the accompanying computer manuals were completely incomprehensible.

After deciphering the manuals and learning to master the arcane commands of the ancient MS-DOS version 1.25 operating system, Wallace decided to publish fragments of his notes in a local computer magazine for the amusement of others — and to provide an alternative source of income for his eventual departure from the mentally suffocating environment of the military-industrial complex.

After people began responding favorably to his introductory computer magazine articles, he continued writing more, eventually turning to writing full-time. For the first time, he managed to earn a living in a job that didn't involve developing something that could blow up people who happen to live in another part of the world.

Today, the author is happily pursuing a dual career in the book publishing industry and the stand-up comedy industry. His eventual goal is to convince people that enjoying yourself while learning is all right. In the meantime, he plans to continue making fun of any idiots and morons who happen to get in his way.

Dedication

This book is dedicated to all the wonderful people I've met along the path of life, including . . .

Cassandra (my wife), Jordan (my son), and Bo, Scraps, Tasha, and Nuit (our cats).

Lily Carnie, the only person I know who can truly see both sides of the story.

All the friendly folks I've met while performing at the Riviera Comedy Club, located at the Riviera Hotel & Casino in Las Vegas: Steve Schirripa (who also appears on the HBO show, *The Sopranos*, which you can read about at www.hbo.com/sopranos), Don Learned, Bob Zany, Gerry Bednob, Bruce Clark, Darrell Joyce, Tony Vicich, and Kip Addotta. The next time you're visiting Las Vegas, drop by the Riviera and watch a comedy show. Then dump some money in a slot machine on the way out to ensure that the Riviera Hotel & Casino continues making enough money to keep its comedy club open.

Patrick DeGuire, who helped me form Top Bananas (at www.topbananas.com), our company devoted to providing clean, quality stand-up comedy to the wonderful people in San Diego. Thanks must also go to Leo (the man, the myth, the legend) Fontaine, Chris (the Zooman) Clobber, and Dante (who gets excited just to see his name in a book).

Author's Acknowledgments

If it weren't for Matt Wagner and Bill Gladstone at Waterside Productions, I may never have written this book (and someone else may have). That's why I don't mind paying these guys 15 percent of the book royalties so that they can afford to buy their groceries.

Additional thanks go to Allen Wyatt (the technical reviewer) for making sure that everything in this book is accurate, and to Cassandra (my wife) for putting up with multiple computers that (from her point of view) seem to spontaneously appear and disappear from the house at random. Each time a computer disappears, a more advanced model appears that promises more speed and hard disk space but still never seems to have more speed or as much room as the previous computer model that it replaced.

A final note of thanks must go to the Chinese and Russians who've translated my other books, *Microsoft Office For Dummies* and *Visual Basic For Dummies*. The Chinese and Russian editions are the only foreign translations of my books ever to include my previously published references to General Dynamics as a "bomb factory." Whether translators in other countries purposely omitted this humorous reference or whether it's just a coincidence that only the Chinese and Russian editions included this reference is unknown.

Still, this fact alone provides an endless source of amusement to think that Chinese and Russian readers are privy to an American joking about his country's nuclear missile factories, while readers in other countries are not. For that reason alone, the Chinese and Russian translators of my books have my eternal gratitude and blessing, not because they happen to be Chinese or Russian, but because they appear to be able to appreciate a joke.

Publisher's Acknowledgments

We're proud of this book; please send us your comments through our online registration form located at www.dummies.com/register/.

Some of the people who helped bring this book to market include the following:

Acquisitions, Editorial, and Media Development

Project Editor: Andrea C. Boucher

  (Previous Edition: Linda Morris)

Acquisitions Editor: Bob Woerner

Technical Editor: Allen Wyatt

Editorial Manager: Carol Sheehan

Permissions Editor: Carmen Krikorian, Senior Permissions Editor

Media Development Specialist: Travis Silvers

Media Development Manager: Laura VanWinkle

Media Development Supervisor: Richard Graves

Editorial Assistant: Amanda Foxworth

Cartoons: Rich Tennant (www.the5thwave.com)

Production

Project Coordinator: Erin Smith

Layout and Graphics: Seth Conley, Michael Kruzil, Barry Offringa, Lynsey Osborne, Heather Ryan, Shae Wilson, Melanie Wolven

Proofreaders: TECHBOOKS Production Services, Carl William Pierce, Brian H. Walls

Indexer: TECHBOOKS Production Service

Publishing and Editorial for Technology Dummies

Richard Swadley, Vice President and Executive Group Publisher

Andy Cummings, Vice President and Publisher

Mary C. Corder, Editorial Director

Publishing for Consumer Dummies

Diane Graves Steele, Vice President and Publisher

Joyce Pepple, Acquisitions Director

Composition Services

Gerry Fahey, Vice President of Production Services

Debbie Stailey, Director of Composition Services

Contents at a Glance

Table of Contents

Introduction

*F*irst of all, *anyone* can learn to program a computer. Computer programming doesn't require a high IQ and an innate proficiency in advanced mathematics. Computer programming just requires a desire to learn and the patience never to give up.

Programming is a skill like swimming, dancing, and juggling. Some people are naturally better than others, but anyone can get better with constant practice. That's why so many kids become programming wizards at such an early age. The kids aren't necessarily brilliant; they're just willing to put in the time to learn a new skill, and they're not afraid of failing.

If you ever dreamed about writing your own programs, rest assured that you can. Programming can be lots of fun, but it can also be frustrating, annoying, and time-consuming. That's why Wiley publishes this particular book — to help you discover how to program a computer with the minimum amount of inconvenience and the maximum amount of enjoyment.

Whether you want to pick up computer programming for fun, to start a new career, or to help make your current job easier, consider this book your personal guide through the sometimes scary — and initially intimidating — world of computer programming.

After you finish this book, you can choose the best programming language to accomplish a particular task, understand the tools that programmers use, and even write your own programs for personal use or for sale to others.

And after you read *Beginning Programming For Dummies,* 3rd Edition, you can find more detailed information about specific languages by reading *Visual BASIC.NET For Windows For Dummies,* by Wallace Wang; *C For Dummies,* by Dan Gookin; *Visual C++ .NET For Dummies,* by Michael Hyman and Bob Arnson; *C++ For Dummies* and *C# For Dummies,* by Stephen R. Davis; *Beginning Programming with Java For Dummies,* by Barry Burd; *Windows Game Programming For Dummies,* by Andre LaMothe; or *Perl For Dummies,* by Paul Hoffman (all published by Wiley Publishing).

Who Should Buy This Book

Everyone should buy this book right now because you know the importance of stimulating the economy by spending as much money as possible so the current President can stay in office another four years. But you should especially buy this book if you want to know any of the following:

- How to write a computer program
- The best programming languages to use and why
- Shortcuts for programming a computer as simply and quickly as possible
- The evolution of computer programming languages
- How to program a Macintosh, Palm handheld, Linux, Windows 98/Me/NT/2000/XP, or PocketPC computer
- Whether to write your next computer program by using Visual BASIC, C++, Perl, SmallTalk, C#, or some other programming language

To help you start right away, this book shows you how to use a programming language by the name of *Liberty BASIC,* which is a shareware BASIC compiler that you can download from the Liberty BASIC Web site at www. libertybasic.com (or copy from the CD that comes with this book). By using this book and Liberty BASIC, you can start programming right away, and later, if you want, graduate to the other programming books in the popular *For Dummies* series.

How This Book Is Organized

This book follows the time-honored tradition of the printing industry by organizing consecutively numbered pages one after the other to form a book. To help you find what you need quickly, this book consists of seven parts, where each part covers a certain topic about programming a computer, as the following sections describe. Whenever you need help, just flip through the book, find the part that covers the topic you're looking for, and then keep the book at your side as you get back to work.

Part 1: Programming a Computer

If computer programming seems a mysterious arcane science, relax. This part of the book demystifies all the common myths about computer programming, shows you exactly how computer programs work, and explains why programming isn't as difficult as many people think.

To help you better understand programming, this part also shows you how programming has evolved, why so many different programming languages exist, and how programming follows easy-to-remember principles so you can start programming your own computer right away.

Part II: Learning Programming with Liberty BASIC

Trying to pick up programming from a book is like trying to learn judo by reading a pamphlet. In both cases, you may glean a theoretical understanding of the subject, but until you actually practice your skill, you don't know how much you really picked up.

To give you practical, hands-on experience in using an honest-to-goodness programming language, this part of the book explains how to install and use Liberty BASIC so that you can write real computer programs by using the BASIC programming language. Writing programs in Liberty BASIC helps you to better understand how programming really works as you work with programs and see the results right on your own computer.

Part III: Advanced Programming with Liberty BASIC

Liberty BASIC provides plenty of advanced features for displaying graphics, making sound, and debugging your programs. This part of the book shows you how to take advantage of these special features and shows you the principles behind writing programs in other languages at the same time.

Part IV: Dealing with Data Structures

As do people, computers need a place to store information. People usually dump their information in wallets, purses, filing cabinets, or garages, but computers don't have that luxury.

Instead, computers must store information in something known as a *data structure*. Every computer program uses data structures, and programmers invent all sorts of different data structures for various uses. So in this part of the book, I explain how every program uses data structures and provide hands-on examples you can try using Liberty BASIC.

Part V: Algorithms: Telling the Computer What to Do

Algorithms are a fancy way of telling a computer how to accomplish a specific task, step-by-step. Think of an algorithm as a recipe that the computer blindly follows without question.

One perfect algorithm doesn't exist for writing all computer programs, just as one perfect recipe doesn't exist for making all dinners. To make programming easier, programmers invent common algorithms for accomplishing certain tasks. This part of the book explains how those algorithms work and why you want to use them.

Part VI: Internet Programming

The Internet is an integral part of the computer world, so this part of the book introduces you to the basics of various Internet languages, including HTML (which designs the appearance of Web pages), JavaScript, and Java.

In this part, you also see how other people create cool Web pages that look good and can display forms and respond to users. You can use this information to create Web sites that interact with users.

Part VII: The Part of Tens

To help gently guide you toward writing your own programs, this part of the book provides information that you may find useful to take your programming education a step farther.

This part is where the book shows you many of the opportunities that a career in programming can offer. In this part, too, you discover where to find and use various free or commercial programming languages available on the Internet or on this book's enclosed CD. Many of these programming languages sport common names such as C++ and BASIC — or bizarre names such as LISP, Oberon, and Python.

How to Use This Book

Most people use this book to read, although a few are known to line their bookshelves with copies to give the room a more literary appearance. You're most likely to use this book as a reference, a tutorial, or a weapon (if you can throw it really hard at somebody you don't like).

Ideally, you want to use this book along with your computer. Read some of the book and then try what you just read on your computer so that you can see with your own eyes how programming works.

Foolish assumptions

To get the most out of this book, you need access to a computer (because trying to understand computer programming is tough if you can't get near a computer). To take full advantage of this book, you need a computer running Microsoft Windows 98, Windows Me, Windows NT, Windows 2000, or Windows XP.

If you don't feel comfortable with Windows 98, Windows Me, Windows 2000, or Windows XP, buy *Windows 98 For Dummies, Windows Me For Dummies,* or *Windows XP For Dummies,* all by Andy Rathbone (and published by Wiley Publishing). For more information about Windows NT or 2000, pick up a copy of *Windows NT 4 For Dummies* or *Windows 2000 Professional For Dummies,* both by Andy Rathbone and Sharon Crawford (also published by Wiley Publishing).

Icons used in this book

Icons highlight useful tips, important information to remember, or technical explanations that can amuse you for a moment before you forget all about them. Keep an eye open for the following icons throughout the book:

This icon highlights useful information that can save you time (as long as you remember it, of course).

This icon reminds you to do something or emphasizes an important point that you don't want to forget.

Watch out! This icon tells you how to avoid potential headaches and trouble.

This icon points out step-by-step explanations that show how the computer follows the instructions in a typical program.

This icon highlights information that's nice to know but that you can safely ignore if you choose. (If you want to become a real programmer, however, you need to cram your brain with as much technical information as possible so that you can fit in with the rest of the programmers in the world.)

Part I
Programming a Computer

The 5th Wave   By Rich Tennant

WANDA HAD THE DISTINCT FEELING HER HUSBAND'S NEW SOFTWARE PROGRAM WAS ABOUT TO BECOME INTERACTIVE.

In this part . . .

Figuring out how to program a computer may seem intimidating, so this part of the book gently guides you through the wonderful world of computer programming. First, you see exactly what programs do and how professionals write programs.

Next, you learn why so many different programming languages exist and why some are more popular than others. You get to know the different tools that programmers use to create, edit, and distribute a program from start to finish.

Finally, this part shows you what to consider if you decide to write a program. You see the pros and cons of using different programming languages and understand how people can write programs even though they may possess very little programming experience.

By the time that you finish this part of the book, you should have a better idea of how to write a program, what steps to follow, and how to convert your idea for a program into an actual working product that you can sell or give away for others to use. Who knows? With a little bit of imagination and a lot of persistence, you may create the next program that makes so much money that you can start your own software company and make a million bucks.

Chapter 1

Learning Computer Programming for the First Time

In This Chapter

▶ Learning computer programming

▶ Understanding how a computer program works

▶ Knowing how to program a computer

Despite what you may have heard, programming a computer isn't difficult. Computer programming is a skill that anyone can pick up, given enough practice, patience, and caffeinated beverages.

Although computers may seem like tremendously complex electronic beasts, relax. Few people know how an internal-combustion engine works, yet people still figure out how to drive a car. Similarly, anyone can pick up programming skills without worrying (too much) about the specific details that make a computer work.

Why Learn Computer Programming?

The first question that you (or your friends, co-workers, and relatives) may ask is, "Why bother learning to program a computer?" The answer depends on your ultimate goals, but the following list offers some common answers to consider:

✔ **For fun:** People learn skiing, dancing, gardening, scuba diving, and flower-arranging because they enjoy the experience. Similarly, programming a computer can prove fun because you can, for example, design simple programs that display your boss's ugly face on the computer. More complex programs may make you a million dollars so that you never again need to work for a boss with an ugly face. Figure 1-1 shows a program known as *Comedy Writer*, which prods users into creating funny ideas. A stand-up comedian wrote the program in BASIC for his own amusement, using a program known as *CA-Realizer*. Then he decided to sell the program to others.

✔ **To fill a need:** Many people learn programming with no intention of becoming a full-time, professional programmer. They just want a program that solves a particular problem, but they can't find a program that does it, so they write the program themselves. A psychologist who specialized in dream interpretation used his knowledge and a program known as ToolBook to create and sell *DreamScape,* a program that interprets the meaning of dreams, as shown in Figure 1-2. Whatever your interests, you can write a program to solve a specific problem that others may find useful as well.

✔ **For a new or second career:** With computers taking over the world, you're never unemployed for long if you know how to program a computer. Companies are always looking to create new programs, but you also find a growing market for programmers who can maintain and modify the millions of existing programs that do everything from storing hotel reservations to transferring bank deposits electronically. If you know how to program a computer, you're in a much better position to earn a lot of money and live wherever you want. You may still want to keep your current job, but programming gives you a new way to expand and share your knowledge. A group of alternative health-care practitioners, for example, wrote *IBIS,* a program that provides information for treating a variety of ailments by using acupuncture, massage, diet, and homeopathy (see Figure 1-3). They wrote IBIS by using a program known as MetaCard.

✔ **As an intellectual challenge:** Many people find the sheer complexity of computers as fascinating as studying a mathematical puzzle. Not surprisingly, computers tend to attract people of above-average intelligence who enjoy programming a computer to pry into the thought processes of their own minds. To help turn a computer into a thinking tool, one programmer created the *Axon Idea Processor* (see Figure 1-4) by using Prolog, a popular programming language used for researching artificial intelligence. The goal was to create a program to help people manipulate ideas, concepts, and facts so that they can devise a variety of possible solutions while better understanding their own way of thinking in the process. If using a computer normally seems boring, try writing your own program to help you use your brain more effectively.

Although you can make a decent living programming computers, you can also make a decent living selling paper clips, fixing leaky toilets, or raising farm animals. If you aren't doing what you truly enjoy, all the money in the world isn't going to make your life better. Choose to learn programming because you want to — not because you think that it's going to make you rich.

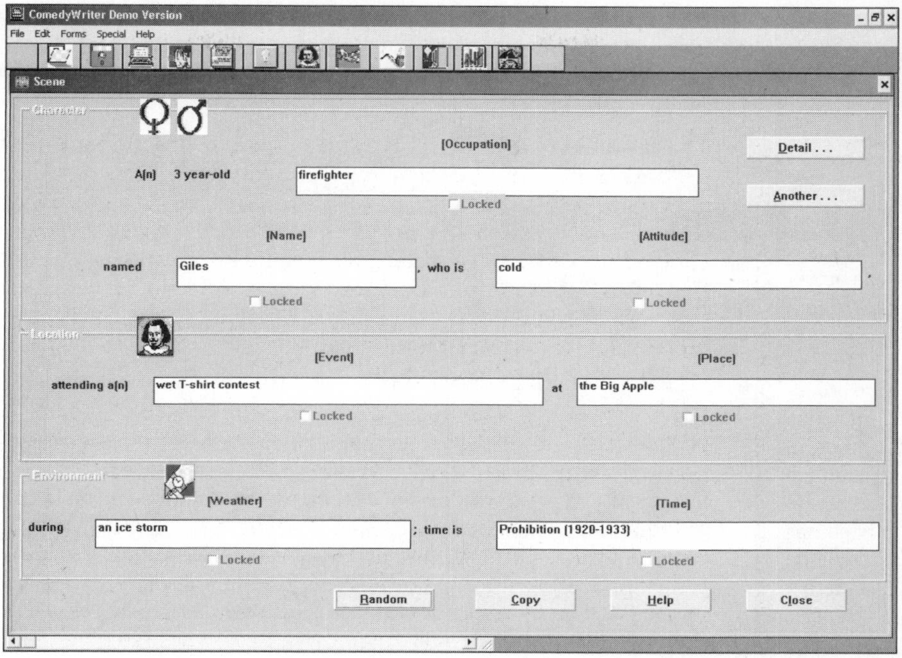

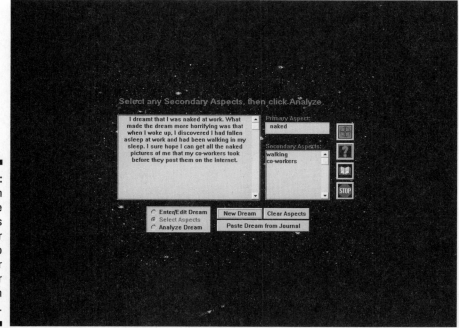

Figure 1-1:
Comedy
Writer is a
program
that can
help you
create funny
ideas.

Figure 1-2:
Dream
Scape
enables
your
computer to
analyze your
dreams for
hidden
meanings.

Figure 1-3:
IBIS
harnesses
the power
of your
computer to
help health-
care practi-
tioners find
a variety of
alternate
health-care
procedures
for curing
different
diseases.

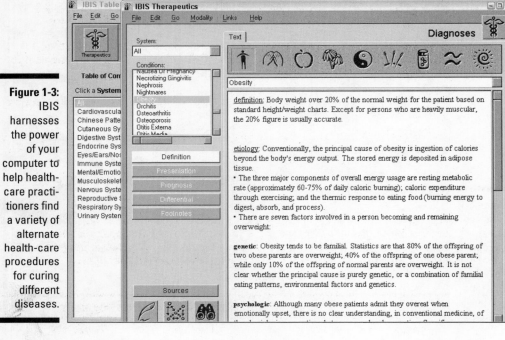

Figure 1-4:
The Axon
Idea
Processor
turns your
computer
screen into
a canvas for
organizing
and manipu-
lating ideas.

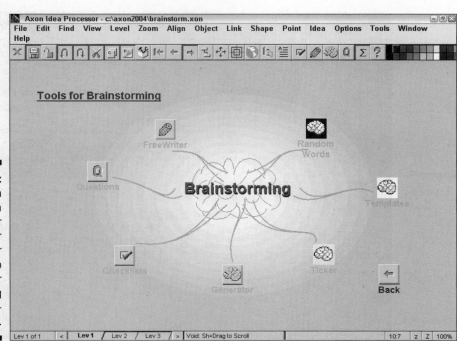

How Does a Computer Program Work?

Computers don't do anything without someone telling them what to do, much like the average teenager. To make the computer do something useful, you must give it instructions in either of the following two ways:

✔ Write a program, which tells a computer what to do, step-by-step, much as you write out a recipe.

✔ Buy a program that someone else has already written that tells the computer what to do.

Ultimately, to get a computer to do something useful, you (or somebody else) must write a program.

A program does nothing more than tell the computer how to accept some type of input, manipulate that input, and spit it back out again in some form that humans find useful. Table 1-1 lists some common types of programs, the type of input that they accept, and the output that they produce.

Table 1-1	Input and Output for Various Programs		
Type of Program	*Input*	*What the Program Does*	*Output*
Word processor	Characters you type from the keyboard	Formats the text; corrects spelling	Displays and prints neatly organized text
Game	Keystrokes or joystick movements	Calculates how fast and far to move a cartoon figure on-screen	Moves a cartoon figure on-screen
Stock-market predictor	Current and past prices for stocks	Tries to recognize trends in a stock's price fluctuations	Predicts the future price of a stock
Missile guidance program	Current location of the missile and the target	Calculates how to make the missile's location and the target's location coincide	Corrects the trajectory so that it stays aimed at the target

(continued)

Table 1-1 *(continued)*

Type of Program	Input	What the Program Does	Output
Optical character recognition (OCR)	Text from a scanner	Recognizes shapes of characters	Converts scanned text into a text file that a word processor can edit
Web browser	HyperText Markup Language (HTML) codes on other computers	Converts the HTML codes into text and graphics	Displays Web pages on-screen

Programming is problem-solving

Essentially, a program tells the computer how to solve a specific problem. Because the world is full of problems, the number and variety of programs that people can write for computers is practically endless.

But to tell a computer how to solve one big problem, you usually must tell the computer how to solve a bunch of little problems that make up the bigger problem. If you want to make your own video game, for example, you need to solve some of the following problems:

- Determine how far to move a cartoon figure (such as a car, a spaceship, or a man) on-screen as the user moves a joystick.

- Detect whether the cartoon figure bumps into a wall, falls off a cliff, or runs into another cartoon figure on-screen.

- Make sure that the cartoon figure doesn't make any illegal moves, such as walking through a wall.

- Draw the terrain surrounding the cartoon figure and make sure that if the cartoon figure walks behind an object such as a tree, the tree realistically blocks the figure from sight.

- Determine whether bullets that another cartoon figure fires are hitting the player's cartoon figure. If so, determine the amount of damage, how it affects the movement of the damaged cartoon figure, and how the damage appears on-screen.

The simpler that the problem is that you need to solve, the more easily you can write a program that tells the computer how to work. A program that displays a simple Ping-Pong game with two stick paddles and a ball is much easier to write than a program that displays World War II fighter airplanes firing machine guns and dropping bombs on moving tanks, while dodging anti-aircraft fire.

Programming isn't difficult; it's just time-consuming

Programming really isn't that difficult or mysterious. If you can write step-by-step instructions directing someone to your house, you can write a program.

The hardest part about programming is identifying all the little problems that make up the big problem that you're trying to solve. Because computers are completely stupid, you need to tell them how to do everything.

If you're giving a friend instructions to get to your house, for example, you may write down the following information:

1. Go south on Highway I-5.
2. Get off at the Sweetwater Road exit.
3. Turn right at the light.
4. Turn into the second driveway on the left.

Of course, if you try giving these instructions to a computer, the computer gets confused and wants to know the following additional information:

1. Where do I start and exactly how far south do I drive down Highway I-5?
2. How do I recognize the Sweetwater Road exit, and how do I get off at this exit?
3. After I turn right at the light, how far to the right do I turn, and do you mean the traffic light or the street light on the corner?
4. After I turn into the second driveway on the left, what do I do next? Park the car? Honk the horn? Gun the engine and accelerate through your garage door?

You need to tell computers how to do everything, which can make giving them instructions as aggravating and frustrating as telling children what to do. Unless you specify everything that you want the computer to do and exactly how to do it, the computer just plain doesn't do what you want it to do.

Sometimes programs never work

After spending years writing a program, people sometimes find that throwing away the whole thing and starting over is easier (and cheaper) than trying to figure out why the current program isn't working and how to make it work.

Back in the mid-1980s, for example, the United States government had the bright idea to develop a self-propelled, anti-aircraft weapon nicknamed the *Sergeant York*. The purpose of the Sergeant York weapon was simple: Find an enemy aircraft and shoot it down.

Unfortunately, the program controlling the Sergeant York never quite worked correctly. After spending millions of dollars and countless hours rewriting the program, testing it, and rewriting it again, the programmers thought that they'd finally gotten the program to work right.

To celebrate their achievement, the company that made the Sergeant York weapon staged a demonstration for the top Pentagon generals and officials. They put the Sergeant York in a field, sat all the people from the Pentagon in a nearby grandstand, and flew a remote-controlled drone overhead to demonstrate the Sergeant York's capability to track and shoot down an enemy airplane.

But instead of aiming at the overhead target, rumor has it that the Sergeant York leveled its twin 40mm cannons toward the ground and swiveled its guns until they pointed directly at the grandstand where all the Pentagon officials were sitting.

Needless to say, the Pentagon officials created quite a commotion as they scrambled to get out of the line of fire. Fortunately, the Sergeant York didn't fire its cannons into the grandstand, but after this disastrous demonstration, the Pentagon cancelled further development and scrapped the entire Sergeant York project.

So if you ever start writing a program and feel like giving up before it ever works, you're in good company, along with the Pentagon, military contractors, Fortune 500 corporations, and practically everyone else in the world.

What Do I Need to Know to Program a Computer?

If you're the type who finds the idea of making a program (such as a video game) more exciting than actually using it, you already have everything you need to program a computer. If you want to learn computer programming, you need a healthy dose of the following three qualities:

✔ **Desire:** If you want something badly enough, you tend to get it (although you may serve time in prison afterward if you do something illegal to get it). If you have the desire to learn how to program a computer, your desire helps you learn programming, no matter what obstacles may get in your way.

✔ **Curiosity:** A healthy dose of curiosity can encourage you to experiment and continue learning about programming long after you finish reading this book. With curiosity behind you, learning to program seems less a chore and more fun. And as long as you're having fun, you tend to learn and retain more information than does someone without any curiosity whatsoever (such as your boss).

✔ **Imagination:** Computer programming is a skill, but imagination can give your skill direction and guidance. A mediocre programmer with lots of imagination always creates more interesting and useful programs than a great programmer with no imagination. If you don't know what to do with your programming skill, your talent goes to waste without imagination prodding you onward.

Desire, curiosity, and imagination are three crucial ingredients that every programmer needs. If you possess these qualities, you can worry about trivial details such as learning a specific programming language (such as C++), studying advanced math, or attending a university where you can buy a college degree that you can just as easily make with your computer and a desktop-publishing program instead.

Learning to program a computer may (initially) seem an impossible task, but don't worry. Computer programming is relatively simple to understand; everything just tends to fall apart after you try to put a program into actual use.

Chapter 2

All about Programming Languages

....

....

*P*rogramming is nothing more than writing step-by-step instructions telling the computer exactly what you want it to do. Because computers are stupid, they require exact instructions, and this limitation is what makes programming so time consuming.

Computers don't understand English (or French, Chinese, Arabic, Spanish, or any other language that human beings use). Because computers are functionally brain-dead, people must write instructions for a computer by using a special language, hence, the term *programming language*.

A collection of instructions that tell the computer what to do is known as a *program*. The instructions, written in a specific programming language, is known as the *source code*.

Why So Many Different Programming Languages?

You have many programming languages to choose among because each language serves a specific purpose, and people are always creating new languages to solve different types of problems.

Essentially, computers really understand only one language, which consists of zeroes and ones, also known as *machine language*. A typical program that you could write in machine language might look something like the following example:

```
0010 1010 0001 1101
0011 1100 1010 1111
0101 0110 1101 0101
1101 1111 0010 1001
```

Machine language has the following two major drawbacks:

- ✔ You can easily type a 0 or 1 by mistake, thereby preventing you from giving the computer the correct instructions.

- ✔ Machine language takes a long time to write (and an even longer time to understand what the language is actually telling the computer to do).

Because of these two huge problems, few people write programs in machine language. To make writing a program easier, programmers quickly invented a simpler programming language known as *assembly language*.

The joy of assembly language

The whole purpose of assembly language is to enable you to write programs faster and easier than using machine language. So rather than force programmers to write cryptic programs using 0s and 1s, assembly language uses short, easy-to-remember (to programmers, that is) phrases such as JMP, MOV, and ADD, which represent specific machine-language instructions.

Not only does this convention make assembly language source code shorter and easier to write, but it also makes the code easier to read and modify later. A typical assembly language program looks like the following example:

```
title Nap Program
; This program displays "Take a nap!" on the screen
dosseg
.model small
.stack 100h
.data
my_message db 'Take a nap!',0dh,0ah,'$'
.code
main    proc
        mov ax,@data
        mov ds,ax
        mov ah,9
        mov dx,offset my_message
```

```
        int 21h
        mov ax,4C00h
        int 21h
        main endp
end main
```

Making programs easy to read and modify is crucial because most programs never work right the first time you use them. And if you want to add new features to a program later, you need to understand how the current program works so that you know how to modify it.

Programmers created assembly language for their convenience only. The computer itself has no idea how to read or use any instructions written in assembly language.

Because computers can't read assembly language instructions, programmers created special programs that translate assembly language into machine language. These special programs are known as *assemblers*. If you give your computer a program written in assembly language without an assembler, your computer won't have the slightest idea how to read assembly language.

So after you write a program in assembly language, you have to feed it to an assembler, which translates your assembly language program into machine code, which your computer can understand.

Assembly language offers the following two distinct advantages over machine language:

- ✔ Assembly language programs are easier to read than machine language programs.

- ✔ Assembly language programs are easier to write (and modify) than machine language programs.

Of course, assembly language has the following disadvantages:

- ✔ Programs that you create by using assembly language run slower and gobble up more space (both physical disk space and memory) than equivalent programs that you may create with machine language.

- ✔ You can't easily transfer (or, to use programming lingo, port) a program that you write in assembly language for one computer to another computer.

- ✔ Writing a program in assembly language can prove extremely tedious, time-consuming, and complicated. That's why few people bother to write large programs in assembly language.

In general, the easier the programming language is to read and write, the slower and larger are the programs it creates. The Holy Grail of computer programming is to create programs that are easy to write, run as fast as possible, and take up as little space as possible.

C: The portable assembler

To combat the drawbacks of assembly language, programmers created a wide variety of different programming languages with names such as COBOL and FORTRAN. (See the following section, "High-level programming languages," to find out more about the advantages and disadvantages of these types of programming languages.)

But some programmers felt that they needed a language that offers the power to access hardware (as does assembly language) but is easier to read, write, and modify (as are COBOL and FORTRAN). Eventually, they invented a programming language known simply as *C*.

Programmers based the C programming language on an early programming language by the name of *B* (although no programming language known as A ever existed).

Programmers wanted to make programming as easy as possible for themselves, so they made the C programming language look more like actual words that people can understand, as the following example demonstrates:

```
main()
{
    printf ("Take a nap!\n");
}
```

This C program is equivalent to the assembly language program found in the preceding section of this chapter that displays "Take a nap!" on-screen. Comparing the two, you can see that the C language source code is smaller and easier to read than the equivalent assembly language source code.

By using assembly language, programmers sacrifice readability for speed and size. A program that you write in C runs slower and creates larger program files than does an equivalent assembly language program. That's because assembly language is closer to the native language of computers (which is machine code) than C. So C programs need to first get translated into assembly language code before finally being converted into machine language code. This two-step process tends to be less efficient than writing an equivalent assembly language program. C source code, however, is much easier to read, write, and modify than assembly language source code (and far easier to read, write, and modify than an equivalent machine-language source code).

The programmers who created the C programming language had the following three main goals:

- ✔ To create a language that's easier to read and write than assembly language.

- ✔ To offer programmers the capability to access all the parts of the computer just as they can by using assembly language.

- ✔ To provide a small, simple language that you can easily port from one computer to another. Programs that you write in C can run on different computers without massive rewriting, which is the main drawback with assembly- and machine-language programs.

This third goal may look strange, so here's the rationale behind it: Computers don't understand C any better than they understand assembly language. (Computers are notorious for not understanding much of anything, which is why programming must be so precise.) If you write an entire program using C, your computer doesn't have the slightest clue how to read your instructions.

To make a computer read and understand instructions written in C, you must convert your C program into equivalent machine-language instructions. Programmers created special programs, known as *compilers*, to do this conversion for them. A compiler takes your C program and converts it into machine language, which is like translating a Jules Verne novel from French into English.

As is true of translations between human languages, the simpler the language, the easier is the translation. Translating a children's book from French into Japanese is much easier than translating a mathematics dissertation from French into Japanese, mainly because a children's book uses simple words, while a mathematics dissertation uses more complicated words. Similarly, translating C into machine language code is more difficult than translating assembly language into machine language code.

So the only way that you can run a C program on another computer is if someone's already written a C compiler for that other computer. Because C is a simple language, writing C compilers for different computers is relatively easy, especially if you compare it with the same task for other programming languages, such as Ada or LISP.

Because C compilers are fairly easy to write, you can find C compilers for almost every computer in the world. Theoretically, you can write a C program for the Macintosh, copy it to a computer running Windows XP, recompile it, and run the program with little or no modification.

Although, in theory, C programs can run on different computers without modification, the reality is that you almost always must modify a C program slightly or drastically to get it to run on a different computer. Modifying a C program, however, is still much easier than modifying an assembly or machine-language program.

Given its power and portability, C has quickly become one of the most popular programming languages in the world. The majority of all programs are written in C although most newer programs are now written in a C derivative language called C++. Some of the more famous (or infamous) programs that have been written in C or C++ include operating systems such as Windows 95/98/Me/NT/2000/XP, Unix, and Linux, as well as major commercial programs such as Quicken, Netscape Navigator, and Microsoft Word.

Although C is popular, it has its share of flaws:

- C creates larger and slower programs than equivalent assembly or machine-language programs.

- The C language gives programmers access to all parts of a computer, including the capability to manipulate the computer's memory. Unfortunately, all this power can prove as dangerous as giving a hyperactive monkey a chainsaw and a hand grenade. If you don't write your C programs carefully, they can accidentally wreck your computer's memory, causing your program to crash your computer.

In a desperate attempt to make C programming more reliable, programmers developed languages similar to C, such as *C++, Java, Perl, Python,* and *C#.* All of these C-derived languages add a special feature known as *object-orientation,* which encourages programmers to write small programs that they can easily reuse and modify. In addition, these other languages try to protect programmers from writing programs that can mess up the computer's memory, as C programs can do, which decreases the chance of writing a program that crashes an entire computer.

High-level programming languages

Because writing machine- or assembly-language programs was so difficult and confusing, people developed additional languages that look more like human languages, with names such as FORTRAN, COBOL, BASIC, Pascal, and Ada. By making programming languages look more like ordinary human languages, the creators of these high-level languages hoped to make programs easier to write and modify later on.

One of the first high-level languages was *FORTRAN* (which stands for *FOR*mula *TRAN*slator). FORTRAN was designed specifically for mathematical calculations. Another early high-level language was *COBOL* (*CO*mmon *B*usiness-*O*riented *L*anguage), which was designed for business data processing.

Because each language has a specialized purpose, most people aren't going to use FORTRAN or COBOL to write video games, operating systems, or word processors (although you can still do so if you really want).

Because programming was still too difficult for many people, computer scientists soon created both Pascal and BASIC to teach people programming. BASIC — *Beginner's All-purpose Symbolic Instruction Code* — was designed to teach complete novices how to program. Beginners could start learning to program by using C, but the complexities of C can discourage people too soon — sort of like trying to teach a three-year-old how to ride a bicycle by putting him on a motorcycle in the middle of rush-hour traffic.

The main advantage of BASIC is its simplicity. To print the words "Take a nap!" on-screen, you need only the one following command:

```
PRINT "Take a nap!"
```

If you compare it with the equivalent C or assembly language source code, BASIC source code enables you to focus on the task that you want to accomplish instead of worrying about the cryptic commands of a specific programming language.

Pascal (named after the French philosopher, Blaise Pascal) is another language designed to help beginners learn how to program. The main difference between BASIC and Pascal is that Pascal encourages you to write well-structured programs that you can easily read, understand, and modify at a later date. The following is a Pascal program that displays "Take a nap!" on-screen:

```
Program Message (Input, Output);
Begin
  Writeln ('Take a nap!');
End.0
```

Compared with Pascal, BASIC is much less structured, which makes writing a BASIC program easy but makes reading and understanding large BASIC programs much more difficult. Pascal is more structured and forces you to plan your program before you write, as you do if you first plan a trip before leaving home. This planning may take longer, but your program and your trip will be more organized than if you rush into writing the program right away, which can be as disorganized as showing up in Paris in the middle of the night with no hotel reservations. On the other hand, BASIC enables you to start writing your program right away, which is more likely to lead to a more disorganized program.

BASIC is such a popular language that programmers tried to combine the structured features of Pascal with the simplicity of BASIC to create various dialects of BASIC. Liberty BASIC (see Chapter 5) is one example of a structured version of BASIC.

As usual, high-level programming languages such as Pascal, BASIC, FORTRAN, Ada, and COBOL have their own share of problems:

- High-level programming languages create larger and slower programs than equivalent C, assembly language, or machine-language programs.

- High-level programming languages shield you from accessing all the parts of the computer, preventing you from using the power available in C, assembly language, or machine-language programs. As a result, writing certain types of programs, such as operating systems or disk utility programs (such as the Norton Utilities), is more difficult (but not impossible) in high-level languages.

- High-level programming languages more closely resemble human languages, so writing a compiler for a high-level language is more difficult. If your computer doesn't have a compiler for your favorite high-level language (such as Ada), you can't write a program for your computer in that particular programming language.

Of course, nobody would use high-level programming languages such as Pascal, BASIC, FORTRAN, Ada, and COBOL unless they offered some advantages over C, assembly language, or machine language. Following are several reasons for using a high-level programming language:

- You can write programs much faster in a high-level programming language than you can in assembly language or machine language. (You can write a program in C in roughly the same amount of time as in a high-level language such as Pascal.)

- Learning and mastering a high-level programming language takes less time than learning and mastering machine language, assembly language, or C programming.

- Because high-level programming languages shield you from accessing all parts of a computer, they protect you from writing programs that accidentally mess up the computer, causing it to crash.

- Reading and modifying a program written in a high-level language is much easier than reading and modifying an equivalent program written in C, assembly language, or machine language.

- Programs written in high-level languages can run on a variety of computers. If you write a program in a high-level language, you can (theoretically) port that program to run on a different computer.

Naturally, high-level languages have their own share of problems, which include the following:

- Programs written in high-level languages are more complicated to translate into machine code, which means that a program written in Ada or COBOL will likely run much slower and require more memory and disk space than a similar program written in C, assembly, or machine language

> ✔ Creating a compiler for a high-level language is much harder than creating one for C. As a result, not all computers have compilers available for every high-level language. So if you write a program in Modula-2 or LISP, you may find it nearly impossible to port to another computer or operating system.

Rapid Application Development (RAD) programming languages

Most programming languages were designed back in the days when computer screens displayed nothing but text. The screen didn't show graphics, mouse pointers, buttons, or windows.

Because computer screens could display only text, languages such as C++, BASIC, and Pascal just had simple commands to display information, such as the following BASIC command:

```
PRINT "This sentence appears on-screen."
```

After computers developed fancy graphical user interfaces with windows, scroll bars, and toolbars, people began demanding programs that included all these fancy graphical features as well. To help programmers create programs with fancy user interfaces, many companies developed special dialects of existing languages, which they dubbed *rapid application development* (*RAD*) languages.

RAD languages enable programmers to design the way that they want their program to look (the user interface) and then write source code to make that user interface actually do something useful, such as display information in a window. Figure 2-1 shows such an interface in Real Basic.

Some popular RAD languages are *Visual Basic* and *Real Basic* (based on BASIC), *Delphi* and *Kylix* (based on Pascal), *Visual C#* (based on C++), and *JBuilder* (based on Java).

RAD languages offer the following benefits:

> ✔ You can write programs with graphical user interfaces much faster by using RAD than you can by using ordinary C++, BASIC, or Pascal. Figure 2-2 shows StoryCraft, a story-creating program that two professional fiction writers developed to help people create original stories for novels, short stories, plays, or screenplays.

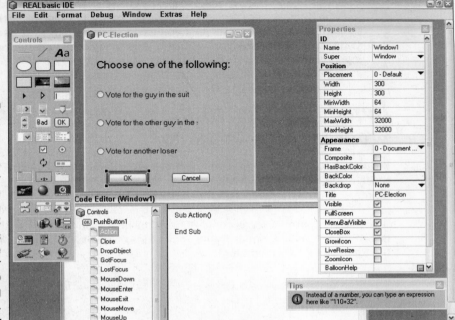

Figure 2-1:
Real Basic
enables you
to create
a user
interface
and then
write BASIC
commands
to make
that user
interface do
something
useful.

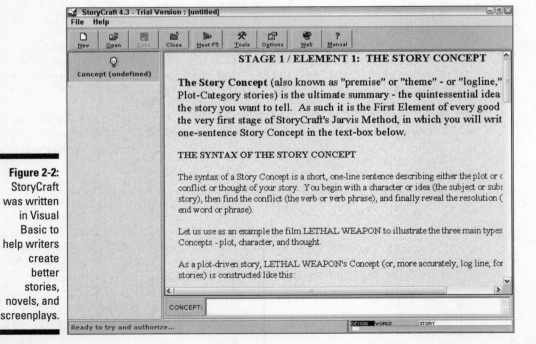

Figure 2-2:
StoryCraft
was written
in Visual
Basic to
help writers
create
better
stories,
novels, and
screenplays.

✔ RAD languages simplify the process of creating user interfaces so that you can focus on getting the rest of your program to work. Without a RAD language, you'd need to write instructions to make the user interface work and then write additional instructions to make the rest of the program work as well, essentially doubling your work and the chance of making a mistake.

✔ Because RAD languages derive from existing high-level languages (C++, BASIC, and Pascal), you can learn and start programming in a RAD language right away if you already know C++, BASIC, or Pascal.

Not surprisingly, RAD languages have a few major drawbacks, which shouldn't surprise you because nothing involving computers is ever perfect. The following list describes these drawbacks:

✔ Programs that you write in RAD languages are rarely portable between different computers. Visual Basic runs only on Microsoft Windows 98/Me/NT/2000/XP, for example, so if you write a program in Visual Basic, you can never run it on a Macintosh, Linux, or other computer operating system without extensive modification.

✔ RAD languages create larger and slower programs than the equivalent programs written in pure C++, BASIC, or Pascal. A RAD language may help you create programs faster, but you sacrifice speed and program size.

Database programming languages

Programming languages such as C++, BASIC, and Pascal were designed as general-purpose languages, which means that you can use them to write a flight simulator, an accounting program, a voice-recognition program, or a word processor.

One of the most popular uses for computers, however, is storing and retrieving information, such as names, addresses, phone numbers, prison records, credit history, and past job experience. Computers store such information in a database.

Almost every business relies on databases to store information about customers, inventories, and employees, so nearly every company uses a database program.

Unfortunately, most people don't want to know the strange and often bizarre commands necessary to store, retrieve, or print information from a database. To make databases easier to use, most databases include a programming language.

If you write programs using a database's programming language, you can create custom databases for different companies. Best of all, database programming languages enable you to create custom databases much faster than using a general-purpose language such as C++ or BASIC. If you use a database programming language, you write instructions only to manipulate the database information. If you use a general-purpose language such as C++, you must write instructions to store information and then write additional instructions to manipulate that information, essentially doubling the amount of work to accomplish the same task.

Most popular database programs, such as *FileMaker* and *Microsoft Access,* offer their own special programming language. For manipulating large amounts of data such as on big mainframe computers, database programs tend to use a language known as *SQL* (which stands for *S*tructured *Q*uery *L*anguage). The following SQL code displays the message "Take a nap!"

```
select 'Take a nap!' from dual;
```

Database programming languages can fill the following specific needs:

- If you're writing a program that stores huge chunks of information, you can write a program much faster by using a database programming language than by using a general-purpose language such as C++ or Pascal.

- Database programming is a lucrative field. If you know how to create customized databases, you almost never need to worry about being unemployed or not making enough money.

Of course, database programming languages aren't for everybody. They have several crucial limitations, as the following list describes:

- Database programs are often tied to a specific computer. If you write a custom database using FileMaker, for example, you can run your program only on a computer that can also run the FileMaker program. Because FileMaker is currently limited to the Macintosh and Windows operating systems, you can't run a FileMaker program on a computer that uses Linux.

- Database programming languages are great at making custom databases but lousy at making anything else, such as video games, word processors, or utility programs (such as anti-virus utilities). If you need to create a variety of programs, you can't rely on a database programming language by itself.

Scripting programming languages

Writing a program from scratch gives you the most flexibility but can take a really long time and drive you nuts in the process. Suppose, for example, that you want to write a word processor specifically for creating screenplays.

If you decide to use a general-purpose language such as C++ or Pascal, you first need to write instructions that create a simple word processor; you then need to write additional instructions to give the word processor the features necessary to create and format screenplays.

As an alternative to going mad by writing everything yourself, many programs offer their own scripting languages. Rather than write an entire word processor from scratch, you can buy an existing word processor (such as WordPerfect or Microsoft Word) and then use that word processor's scripting language to make the word processor do what you want it to do (such as create and format screenplays). A scripting language enables you to focus on the task that you want to accomplish without worrying about irrelevant details.

Most Microsoft programs, such as Word, Excel, PowerPoint, and Access, offer a scripting language known as *Visual Basic for Applications* (*VBA*), which is nearly identical to Visual Basic. The Macintosh operating system also includes a scripting language, known as *AppleScript,* so you can write programs to automate your Mac (to a limited extent). The following code shows how to use AppleScript to display the message, "Take a nap!" on-screen:

```
on DisplayMessage()
 display dialog "Take a nap!" buttons {"OK"}
end DisplayMessage
DisplayMessage()
```

Scripting programming languages can come in handy in many of the following ways:

- ✔ A scripting language enables you to modify an existing program, such as a word processor or spreadsheet. That way, you can create sophisticated programs quickly with very little programming.

- ✔ Scripting languages are generally easier to learn than more powerful programming languages, such as C++. As a result, you can learn and start writing programs faster.

But before you jump wholeheartedly into learning and using a scripting language, beware of the following problems:

- ✔ Scripting languages are tied to a specific program. If you customize a word processor by using a scripting language, your program runs only on computers that run that particular word processor. If you customize Microsoft Word, your program works only on computers that can run Microsoft Word, such as Windows and Macintosh computers.

- ✔ Selling and distributing your programs is much more difficult. To use your program, people must buy or already own the program (word processor, spreadsheet, and so on) that you customize. So if you create a custom program for WordPerfect, Microsoft Word users can't use it.

- A scripting language provides much less flexibility than does a general-purpose programming language such as C++. Make sure that the tradeoff of convenience and ease of programming is worth the limitations of using a scripting language.

Web-page programming languages

In the early days of the Internet, people communicated through plain old text without fancy graphics, animation, or forms that make up today's Web pages. Although people have been reading text for years, it can get boring and difficult to read if you view it on a computer screen that requires constant scrolling to view an entire document.

To remedy this problem and spruce up the appearance of text, programmers created *HyperText Markup Language* (*HTML*), which defines the graphical appearance of Web pages. Figure 2-3 shows a typical Web page as its HTML code defines it.

HTML codes tell a browser how to display a page. So whenever you use a browser to view a Web page (such as `www.dummies.com`), your browser automatically converts the HTML code into the fancy graphics, as shown in Figure 2-4.

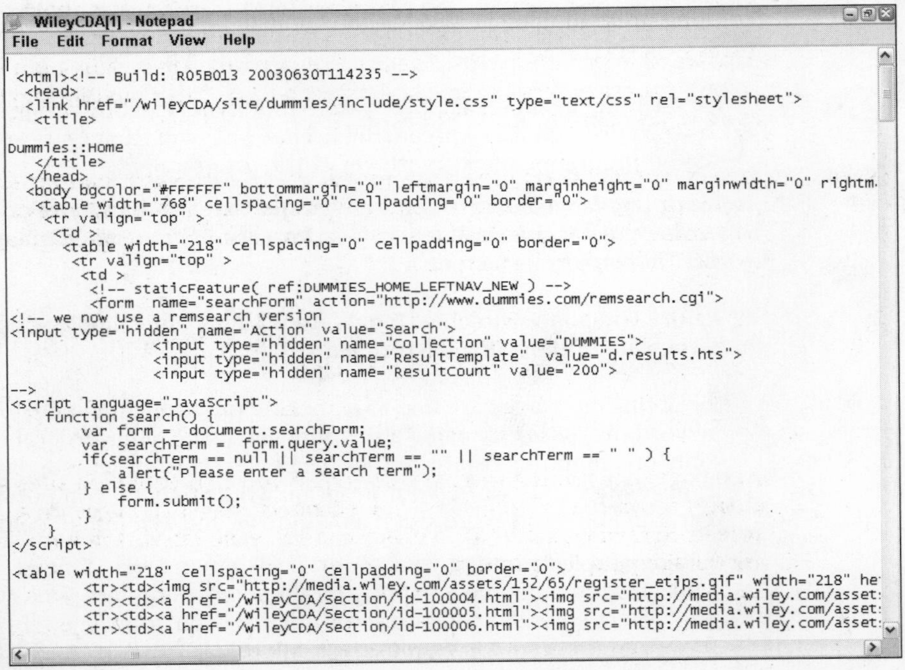


```
<html><!-- Build: R05B013 20030630T114235 -->
 <head>
 <link href="/wileyCDA/site/dummies/include/style.css" type="text/css" rel="stylesheet">
  <title>

Dummies::Home
  </title>
 </head>
 <body bgcolor="#FFFFFF" bottommargin="0" leftmargin="0" marginheight="0" marginwidth="0" rightm.
  <table width="768" cellspacing="0" cellpadding="0" border="0">
   <tr valign="top" >
    <td >
     <table width="218" cellspacing="0" cellpadding="0" border="0">
      <tr valign="top" >
       <td >
        <!-- staticFeature( ref:DUMMIES_HOME_LEFTNAV_NEW ) -->
        <form  name="searchForm" action="http://www.dummies.com/remsearch.cgi">
<!-- we now use a remsearch version
<input type="hidden" name="Action" value="Search">
                <input type="hidden" name="Collection" value="DUMMIES">
                <input type="hidden" name="ResultTemplate"  value="d.results.hts">
                <input type="hidden" name="ResultCount" value="200">
-->
<script language="JavaScript">
    function search() {
        var form =  document.searchForm;
        var searchTerm =  form.query.value;
        if(searchTerm == null || searchTerm == "" || searchTerm == " " ) {
            alert("Please enter a search term");
        } else {
            form.submit();
        }
    }
</script>

<table width="218" cellspacing="0" cellpadding="0" border="0">
        <tr><td><img src="http://media.wiley.com/assets/152/65/register_etips.gif" width="218" he
        <tr><td><a href="/WileyCDA/Section/id-100004.html"><img src="http://media.wiley.com/asset:
        <tr><td><a href="/WileyCDA/Section/id-100005.html"><img src="http://media.wiley.com/asset:
        <tr><td><a href="/WileyCDA/Section/id-100006.html"><img src="http://media.wiley.com/asset:
```

Figure 2-3: HTML code can look messy and unreadable.

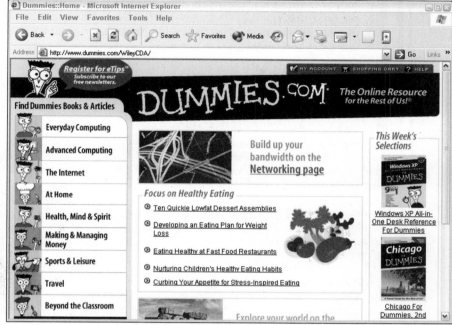

Figure 2-4:
The cryptic HTML code from Figure 2-3 actually defines the appearance of the For Dummies Web site.

After a while, people got tired of plain ol' HTML Web pages that resemble billboards that you view through your computer screen. To make Web pages capable of interacting with the user (for playing games, filling out forms, and so on), programmers created special Web-page programming languages such as *Java, JavaScript,* and *VBScript.*

Java can create two types of programs: stand-alone applications (such as games or word processors) and smaller applets, which can run off a Web page. The following code shows how a Java application can display the words, "Take a nap!" on-screen:

```
public class DisplayMessage {
   public static void main (String args[]) {
system.out.println ("Take a nap!");
   }
}
```

Web-page programming languages enable you to create Web sites that more closely resemble video games than scanned images of paper on a computer screen. Such interactive Web pages can increase interest in your Web site and encourage people to return.

Web-page programming languages offer the following advantages:

- ✔ You can create interactive Web pages to make your site more interesting to look at and to encourage viewers to stay on your site longer.

- ✔ The language is easy to learn and enables you to create programs that anyone around the world with Internet access can use.

Then again, Web page programming languages are very limited in their capabilities, as the following list describes:

- ✔ Not all browsers support all features of Web page languages such as JavaScript or VBScript. As a result, users of older browsers can't run programs that you create by using Web-page languages.

- ✔ For Internet users saddled with slow access (such as through a 28.8 baud modem), programs that you create in a Web-page language (such as VBScript) can run slowly, discouraging visitors from visiting your Web site.

- ✔ Only people with Internet access can run programs that you create with a Web-page language (except for Java). If you want to sell a program to others, you don't want to use a Web-page language.

So What's the Best Programming Language to Learn?

No single "best" programming language exists. If you want to write programs professionally, you want to learn at least one high-level language (most likely C++ because it's currently the most popular of the high-level languages) and one database programming language (such as SQL). You can't go wrong learning C++. With so many companies writing programs in C++, people with C++ programming experience can get a job almost anywhere.

But the immense popularity of C++ programming means that competition is often high. Because thousands of older computers still run COBOL programs that need constant updating, many programmers are finding a lucrative career learning to write and modify COBOL programs. With fewer COBOL programmers available, companies often must pay COBOL programmers a higher salary.

For those planning to work for themselves, one of the most lucrative markets is writing custom databases for other companies. To get into this field, you obviously must know a database programming language, such as SQL or VBA, which Microsoft Access uses. If you plan to create Web pages, you need to know HTML and gain some familiarity with Java, JavaScript, VBScript, and the other Internet programming languages. Ultimately, the best programming language to know is the one that enables you to accomplish the task that you want as quickly and easily as possible, whether that language is C++, BASIC, Java, SQL, or assembly language.

For a quick introduction to the way different programming languages solve the same problem, visit the Hello World! Web site at www.latech.edu/~acm/ HelloWorld.shtml. This Web site provides sample programs, written in a variety of programming languages, which tell the computer to display the words "Hello World!" on-screen.

Chapter 3

How to Write a Program

*A*lthough you can sit down at your computer and start writing a program right now without any planning whatsoever, the result would likely to prove as messy as trying to bake a cake by throwing all the ingredients together without following a recipe.

You can write a simple program that displays your cat's name on-screen without much planning, but for anything more complex, you want to take time to design your program on paper before you even touch a computer. After you're sure that you know what you want your program to do and how you want it to look on-screen, you can worry about writing a program that actually accomplishes this task.

Before You Write Your Program

If you design your program before writing it, you don't waste time writing a program that doesn't work or that solves the wrong problem and isn't worth trying to salvage afterward. By planning ahead of time, you increase the odds that your program actually works and performs the task that you want.

The following three items are crucial to consider in designing a program:

✔ **The user:** Who's going to use your program?

✔ **The target computer:** Which computer do people need to run your program? Is it a Windows 98/Me/NT/2000/XP computer, a Macintosh, a mainframe, a computer running Linux, a handheld Palm or PocketPC, or a supercomputer?

> ✔ **You:** Are you going to write the entire thing yourself or get help from others? If you're going to get others to help you, which parts of the program are they going to write?

When you're designing a program, you don't need to worry about which programming language you're going to use. Once you know exactly what you want your program to do, then you can choose which programming language might be easiest to use.

The program's users

If you're the only person who's going to use your program, you can pretty much make your program look and act any way you want, just as long as you know how to make it work. But if you plan to give or sell your program to others, you need to know who's going to use your program.

Knowing your program's typical user is critical. If users don't like your program for any reason, they're unlikely to use it. Whether the program actually works is often irrelevant.

By designing your program with the user in mind, you increase the odds that people use your program and (you hope) buy a copy for themselves.

Even if you write a program that works perfectly, users still may ignore it because they don't like the way it looks, they don't understand how to give it commands, it doesn't work the same way as the old program they currently use, the colors don't look right to them, and so on. The goal is to make your program meet your users' needs, no matter how weird, bizarre, or illogical they may seem. (The needs — not the users.)

The target computer

After you identify the user, you need to know what type of computer the user intends to run the program on. The type of computer that your program runs on can determine which computer languages you can use, the hardware that your program can expect to find, and even the maximum size of your program.

If you're writing a program to run on a Macintosh, for example, your program can take advantage of sound, color graphics, a large hard disk, and plenty of memory. You need to rewrite that same program drastically, however, to run it on a Palm handheld computer, with its limited sound capability, much simpler color graphics, and limited amount of memory and storage space.

Portability and cross-platform issues

Rather than pick a single computer, many programmers try to write programs that can run on a variety of computers, such as the Macintosh and Windows 98/Me/NT/2000/XP. Any program that can run on two or more different types of computers is *cross-platform*. Microsoft Word is a cross-platform program because you can buy separate versions that run in the Macintosh and Windows environments.

A program that can run on multiple computers increases your number of potential customers, but also increases the number of potential problems that you must face. Some of the problems include offering customer support for each version of your program and trying to make each program version work the same although they may run on completely different operating systems and computers with totally different capabilities.

At one time, WordPerfect offered versions of its word processor that ran on MS-DOS, Windows, the Macintosh, the Amiga, and the Atari ST. So besides hiring enough programmers to work on

each word-processor version, the makers of WordPerfect also needed to hire technical support people who knew how to answer questions for each computer type. Needless to say, this situation cost the company a bundle every month. Developing and supporting so many different versions of WordPerfect cut into the company's profits, so WordPerfect dropped support for the Amiga, Macintosh, and Atari ST because keeping them wasn't worth the cost.

Currently, two of the most popular cross-platform compilers include Real Basic and Delphi/Kylix. Real Basic lets you write programs that can run on Macintosh, Linux, and Windows with minor modifications, while Delphi and Kylix let you write programs that can run on both Windows and Linux. If you want your program to run on different operating systems, you'll need to use a cross-platform compiler. As another alternative, you can always write your program in C/C++ and then compile it on different operating systems and tweak each version to make it run under specific operating systems.

If you can copy and run your program on another computer with little or no modification, your program is considered *portable*. The computer language that you use to write your program can affect its portability. That's why so many people use C/C++ — C and C++ programs tend to be more portable than other programming languages.

Your own programming skill

When designing any program, consider your own programming skill. You may get a great idea for a program, but if you're a beginner with little experience, writing your program may take a long time — if you don't give up out of frustration first.

Beware of the golden handcuffs

Rather than learn programming themselves, many people hire someone to write programs for them. But take care! Freelance programmers sometimes live by a rule known as the "golden handcuffs," which means that they get the gold and you get the handcuffs.

Here's how the golden handcuffs work: You hire someone to write your program, and the programmer takes your money. Then that person writes a program that doesn't work quite the way that you want. Rather than lose the money you already invested in developing the program, you pay the programmer more money, and then this programmer develops a new version of your program that doesn't quite work either.

At this point, you're handcuffed. Do you keep paying money to a programmer who never completely finishes the job, or do you give up altogether? What's worse, you can't hire a new programmer to work on the same program because the original programmer owns your program's source code, so nobody else can modify it. Thus the only way that you can modify the program is to hire the original programmer again and again and again and. . . .

Your programming skill and experience also determine the programming language that you choose. Experienced programmers may think nothing about writing entire programs in C or C++. But novices may need to spend a long time studying C and C++ before writing their programs, or they may choose an easier programming language, such as BASIC.

Some novices take the time to learn difficult languages, such as C/C++, and then go off and write their program. Others take an easier approach and choose a simpler language such as Visual Basic so they can create (and market) their programs right away. Don't be afraid to tackle a heavy-duty language such as C/C++, but don't be afraid to use a simpler language such as Visual Basic either. The important goal is to finish your program so you can start using it and (possibly) start selling it to others.

Many programmers create their program by using a language such as Visual Basic and then later hire more experienced programmers to rewrite their programs in a more complex language such as C/C++, which can make the program faster and more efficient.

The Technical Details of Writing a Program

Few people create a program overnight. Instead, most programs evolve over time. Because the process of actually typing programming commands can prove so tedious, time-consuming, and error-prone, programmers try to avoid actually writing their programs until they're absolutely sure that they know what they're doing.

Prototyping

To make sure that they don't spend months (or years) writing a program that doesn't work right or that solves the wrong problem, programmers often *prototype* their programs first. Just as architects often build cardboard or plastic models of skyscrapers before a construction crew starts welding I-beams together, programmers create mock-ups (prototypes) of their programs first.

A prototype usually shows the user interface of the program, such as windows, pull-down menus, and dialog boxes. The prototype may look like an actual program, but clicking menus doesn't do anything. The whole idea of the prototype is to show what the program looks like and how it acts, without taking the time to write commands to make the program actually work.

After the programmer is happy with the way the prototype looks, she can proceed, using the prototype as a guideline toward completing the final program.

General purpose versus specialized programming languages

General purpose programming languages, such as C/C++, BASIC, Pascal, assembly language, and so on, give you the ability to create practically anything you want, but it may take a long time to do so. To make programming faster and easier, many people have developed specialized programming languages for solving specific types of problems.

For example, SNOBOL is a little known language specifically designed for manipulating text. If that's what you need, then writing a program in SNOBOL can be much quicker than using C/C++. Of course, if you want to do something else besides text manipulation, programming in SNOBOL will likely be a horrible choice.

Similarly, programmers often use LISP and Prolog to create artificially intelligent programs as both LISP and Prolog include commands for decision-making. While you could create an artificially intelligent program using COBOL or BASIC, you would have to write at least twice as many instructions in either FORTRAN, C/C++, or COBOL to accomplish what a single LISP or Prolog command could accomplish.

So the moral of the story is that you can make programming a lot easier if you just choose the right programming language to help you solve the right problem.

Using multiple programming languages

Instead of writing an entire program using one programming language (such as C++), some compilers can convert source code into a special file known as an *object file*. The purpose of object files is that one programmer can write a program in C++, another in assembly language, and still a third in Pascal. Each programmer writes his portion of the program in his favorite language and stores it in a separate object file. Then the programmers connect (or link) all these object files together to create one big program. The program that converts multiple object files into an executable program is known as a *linker*.

In the world of Microsoft Windows, another way to write a program using multiple languages is to use *dynamic link libraries* (*DLLs*), which are special programs that don't have a user interface. One programmer can use C, another can use Java, and a third can use COBOL to create three separate DLL files. Then a fourth programmer can write a program using another language such as Visual Basic, which creates the user interface and uses the commands that each separate DLL file stores.

A third way to write a program is to use your favorite language (such as Pascal) and then write assembly language instructions directly in parts of your program. (Just be aware that not all compilers enable you to switch between different languages within the same program.)

Finally, Microsoft offers a programming framework dubbed *.NET*. By using the .NET framework, one programmer can program in C#, another can program in FORTRAN, and still another can program in BASIC. Then their different programs can share data and communicate with other programs through the .NET framework and create a single user interface that unifies these separate programs. The whole point to all of these different methods is that by using different programming languages, you can take advantage of each language's strengths, while minimizing its weaknesses.

Many programmers use Visual Basic because it's easy for creating prototypes quickly. After you use Visual Basic to create a prototype that shows how your user interface works, you can start adding actual commands to later turn your prototype into an honest-to-goodness working program.

Choosing a programming language

After you refine your prototype until it shows you exactly how your program is to look and act, the next step is choosing a programming language to use.

You can write any program by using any programming language. The trick is that some languages make writing certain types of programs easier.

The choice of a programming language to use can pit people against one another in much the same way that religion and politics do. Although you can't find a single "perfect" programming language to use for all occasions, you may want to consider a variety of programming languages. Ultimately, no one cares what language you use as long as your program works.

Defining how the program should work

After choosing a specific programming language, don't start typing commands into your computer just yet. Just as programmers create mock-ups (prototypes) of their program's user interface, they often create mock-up instructions that describe exactly how a program works. These mock-up instructions are known as *pseudocode*.

If you need to write a program that guides a nuclear missile to another city to wipe out all signs of life within a 100-mile radius, your pseudocode may look as follows:

```
1. Get the target's coordinates.
2. Get the missile's current coordinates.
3. Calculate a trajectory so the missile hits the target.
4. Detonate the nuclear warhead.
```

By using pseudocode, you can detect flaws in your logic before you start writing your program — places where the logic behind your program gets buried beneath the complexity of a specific programming language's syntax.

In the preceding example, you can see that each pseudocode instruction needs further refining before you can start writing your program. You can't just tell a computer, "Get the target's coordinates" because the computer wants to know, "Exactly how do I get the target's coordinates?" So rewriting the preceding pseudocode may look as follows:

```
1. Get the target's coordinates.
        a. Have a missile technician type the target
        coordinates.
        b. Make sure that the target coordinates are
        valid.
        c. Store the target coordinates in memory.
2. Get the missile's current coordinates.
3. Calculate a trajectory so the missile hits the target.
4. Detonate the nuclear warhead.
```

You can refine the instructions even further to specify how the computer works in more detail, as follows:

```
1. Get the target's coordinates.
        a. Have a missile technician type the target
        coordinates.
        b. Make sure that the target coordinates are
        valid.
            1) Make sure that the target coordinates are
        complete.
```

(continued)

```
              2) Check to make sure that the target
      coordinates are within the missile's range.
              3) Make sure that the target coordinates
      don't accidentally aim the missile at friendly
      territories.
          c. Store the target coordinates in memory.
2. Get the missile's current coordinates.
3. Calculate a trajectory so the missile hits the target.
4. Detonate the nuclear warhead.
```

When programmers define the general tasks that a program needs to accomplish and then refine each step in greater detail, they say that they're doing a *top-down design*. In other words, they start at the top (with the general tasks that the program needs to do) and then work their way down, defining each task in greater detail until the pseudocode describes every possible step that the computer must go through.

Writing pseudocode can prove time-consuming. But the alternative is to start writing a program with no planning whatsoever, which is like hopping in your car and driving north and then wondering why you never seem to wind up in Florida.

Pseudocode is a tool that you can use to outline the structure of your program so that you can see all the possible data that the computer needs to accomplish a given task. The idea is to use English (or whatever language you understand best) to describe the computer's step-by-step actions so that you can use the pseudocode as a map for writing the actual program in whatever language (C/C++, FORTRAN, Pascal, Java, and so on) that you choose.

The Life Cycle of a Typical Program

Few programs are written, released, and left alone. Instead, programs tend to go through various cycles where they get updated continuously until they're no longer useful. (That's why many people buy a new word processor every few years even though the alphabet hasn't changed in centuries.)

Generally, a typical program goes through a development cycle (where you first create and release it), a maintenance cycle (where you eliminate any glaring bugs as quickly as possible), and an upgrade cycle (where you give the program new features to justify selling the same thing all over again).

The development cycle

Every program begins as a blank screen on somebody's computer. During the development cycle, you nurture a program from an idea to an actual working program. The following steps make up the development cycle:

1. **Come up with an idea for a program.**

2. **Decide the probable identity of the typical user of the program.**

3. **Decide which computer the program is to run on.**

4. **Pick one or more computer languages to use.**

5. **Design the program by using pseudocode or any other tool to outline the structure of the program.**

6. **Write the program.**

7. **Test the program.**

   This step is known as *alpha testing*.

8. **Fix any problems that you discover during alpha testing.**

   Repeat Steps 7 and 8 as often as necessary.

9. **Give out copies of the program to other people to test.**

   This step is known as *beta testing*.

10. **Fix any problems that people discover during beta testing.**

    Repeat Steps 9 and 10 as often as necessary.

11. **Release the program to the unsuspecting public and pray that it works as advertised.**

The maintenance cycle

Most programmers prefer to create new programs than maintain and modify existing ones, which can prove as unappealing as cleaning up somebody else's mess in an apartment. But the number of new programs that programmers create every year is far less than the number of existing programs, so at some point in your life, you're likely to maintain and update a program that either you or somebody else wrote.

The following list describes typical steps that you may need to follow to maintain an existing program:

1. **Verify all reports of problems (or *bugs*) and determine what part of the program may be causing the bug to appear.**

2. **Fix the bug.**

3. **Test the program to make sure that the bug is really gone and that any changes you make to the program don't introduce any new bugs.**

4. **Fix any problems that may occur during testing.**

5. **Repeat Steps 1 through 4 for each bug that someone reports in the program.**

   Given the buggy nature of software, these steps may go on continuously for years.

6. **Release a software *patch*, which users can add to an existing version of the program to incorporate corrections that you make to "patch up" the problems.**

The upgrade cycle

Companies don't make money fixing software and making it more stable, reliable, and dependable. Instead, companies make money by selling new versions of their programs that offer additional features and options that most people probably don't use or need in the first place.

Still, because so many programs undergo modification to take advantage of new hardware or software, you may find yourself occasionally upgrading a program by adding new features to it. The following steps make up the upgrade cycle:

1. **Determine what new feature you want to add to the program.**

2. **Plan how this new feature is to work (by using pseudocode or another tool to help structure your ideas).**

3. **Modify the program to add this new feature.**

4. **Test this new feature (by using alpha testing) to make sure that it works and doesn't introduce new bugs into the program.**

5. **Fix any problems that may occur during alpha testing.**

6. **Give out copies of the program to other people to beta test.**

7. **Fix any problems that the beta testers report.**

8. **Repeat Steps 1 through 7 for each new feature that you need to add to the program.**

9. **Release the program as a new version and wait for the public to start reporting bugs that keep the program from working correctly so that you can start the maintenance cycle all over again.**

Despite all the university courses and such important-sounding titles as "software engineer," programming is still less of a science and more of an art. Writing, modifying, and updating software doesn't require a high IQ or an advanced mathematics degree as much as it requires creativity, determination, and plenty of imagination. You can write a program any way that you want, but the best way to prevent possible problems later on is to be organized and methodical in your approach.

Chapter 4

The Tools of a Computer Programmer

· ·

In This Chapter

▶ Writing programs in an editor

▶ Using a compiler or an interpreter

▶ Squashing bugs with a debugger

▶ Writing a Help file

▶ Creating an installation program

· ·

*T*o help make computer programming easier, programmers use a variety of tools that perform a specific purpose. After you know what each tool does and how to use it, you can start writing your own programs in no time.

You need the following two crucial tools to write a program:

✔ An *editor* (so that you can write your instructions to the computer).

✔ A *compiler* which converts your instructions into machine language so that the computer knows what you want it to do. Instead of using a compiler, many programming languages use an *interpreter*. The main difference between the two is that an interpreter converts your instructions into machine language and stores them in memory each time you run the program, whereas a compiler converts your instructions into machine language once and saves those instructions in a file often called an EXE or executable file.

Linux and the open source movement

In the early days of computers, programmers freely created and shared the source code for their programs. The idea was that, if enough people voluntarily worked together on a single program, the chances were good that the program would actually work.

Then programmers decided that they should get paid for their hard work, so they started keeping the source code for their programs to themselves, which helped to spawn the software industry as we know it today (with all its missed deadlines, unreliable programs, and horribly written software manuals).

But now the idea of sharing the source code (often known as the *open source movement*)

has resurfaced with the emergence of the Linux operating system. Users can again peek at the source code without paying for it.

Having access to the source code gives you the option of modifying the program if you want or (more likely) hiring someone else to modify it for you. In any event, access to the source code prevents you from being at the mercy of companies that refuse to reveal their source code so that they can force you to pay for program upgrades that still may not fix or add the features that you want.

You may want to use the following additional tools in writing a program:

- ✔ A *debugger* (which helps identify problems or bugs in your program).

- ✔ A *Help file* authoring program (so that your program can provide Help on-screen instead of needing to supply the user with a decent manual).

- ✔ An *installation program* (to copy your program to the user's computer).

If you buy a specific programming language, such as Visual Basic, Delphi, or Real Basic, you usually get an editor, compiler, and a debugger, which means you just need to buy a separate Help file authoring program and an installation program.

Writing Programs in an Editor

As you write a program, you must type your instructions in a *text* (or *ASCII*) file. Although you can use a word processor to create a text file, a word processor offers fancy formatting features (such as changing fonts or underlining text), which you don't need to write a program.

An ASCII file consists of nothing but characters that you can type from a keyboard. ASCII stands for American Standard Code for Information Interchange, which is simply a universal file format that any computer can use.

A program consists of one or more instructions that tell the computer what to do. The instructions that make up a program are known as the program's *source code*.

Rather than struggle with a word processor, programmers created special programs for writing, editing, and printing the source code of a program. Almost no one writes a program correctly the first time, so the majority of a programmer's time is spent editing the source code. As a result, the program that enables you to write, edit, and print a program is known as an *editor*.

An editor looks like a word processor but may offer special features to make programming easier, such as automatically formatting your source code, offering shortcuts for editing your source code, or providing pop-up Help as you're typing program commands. An example of an editor's pop-up Help is shown in Figure 4-1. Anytime that you need to write or modify the source code of a program, you must use an editor.

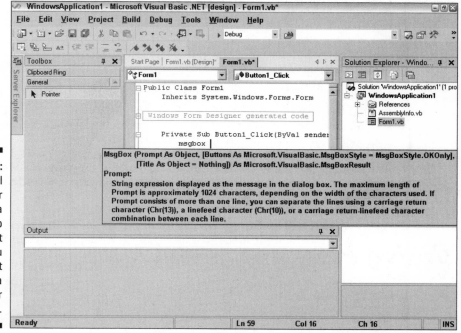

Figure 4-1:
The Visual
Basic editor
displays a
pop-up
window that
shows you
the correct
syntax for a
particular
command.

Using a Compiler or an Interpreter

After you type your instructions in an editor by using a programming language such as C++ or Java, guess what? The computer doesn't have the slightest idea what you just created. Computers understand only machine language, so you need to use another special program to convert your source code (the instructions that you write in C++ or Java) into machine language.

You can use either of the following two types of programs to convert source code into machine language:

- A compiler
- An interpreter

Compilers

A *compiler* takes your source code, converts the entire thing into machine language, and then stores these equivalent machine language instructions in a separate file, often known as an *executable file*. The process is like having a translator study an entire novel written in Spanish and then translate it into Arabic.

Whenever a compiler converts source code into machine language, it's *compiling* a program.

After you compile a program, you can just give away copies of the executable (machine-language) version of your program without giving away your source code version. As a result, most commercial programs (such as Microsoft PowerPoint and Quicken) are compiled.

After you use a compiler to convert source code into machine language, you never need to use the compiler again (unless you make changes to your source code).

A compiler creates machine language for a specific microprocessor, such as the PowerPC (which the Macintosh uses) or the Intel Pentium family of microprocessors (including clone microprocessors, such as the AMD Athlon). If you write a program in BASIC and want to run it on a Macintosh and a Windows computer, you need to compile your program twice: once for the Macintosh and once for the Windows environment.

Not all compilers are equal, although two different compilers may convert the same language into machine language. Given identical C++ source code, for example, one C++ compiler may create a program that runs quickly, whereas a second C++ compiler may create a smaller file that runs much slower.

Interpreters

A second, but less popular, way to convert source code into machine language is to use an *interpreter*. An interpreter converts each line of your source code into machine language, one line at a time. The process is like giving a speech in English and having someone translate your sentences, one at a time, into another language (such as French).

Unlike what a compiler does, an interpreter converts source code into machine language but stores the machine-language instructions in the computer's memory. Every time that you turn off the computer, you lose the machine-language version of your program. To run the program again, you must feed the source code into the interpreter again.

If anyone wants to run your program, that person needs both an interpreter and the source code for your program. Because your source code enables everyone to see how you wrote your program (and gives others a chance to copy or modify your program without your permission), very few commercial programs use an interpreter.

Most Web-page programming languages use interpreters, such as JavaScript and VBScript. Because different computers can view Web pages, you can't compile programs that you write in JavaScript or VBScript into machine language. Instead, your computer's browser uses an interpreter to run a JavaScript or VBScript program.

In the old days, when computers were slow and lacking in sufficient memory and storage space, interpreters were popular because they gave you instant feedback. The moment you typed an instruction into the computer, the interpreter told you whether that instruction would work and even showed you the results. With an interpreter, you could write and test your program at the same time. Now, computers are so fast that programmers find using a compiler easier than using an interpreter.

P-code: A combination compiler and interpreter

Getting a program to run on different types of computers is often a big pain in the neck. Both Macintosh and Windows programs, for example, use pull-down menus and dialog boxes. You need to write one set of commands to create pull-down menus on the Macintosh, however, and a second set of commands to create the identical menus in Windows.

Because one program almost never runs on multiple computers without extensive modification, programmers combined the features of a compiler with an interpreter to create something called *p-code*.

Instead of compiling source code directly into machine language, p-code compiles source code into a special intermediate file format. To run a program compiled into p-code, you use an interpreter. This two-step process means that after you compile your program into p-code, you can run your p-code interpreted program on any computer that has the right p-code interpreter.

Java is the most popular programming language that uses p-code. After you compile a Java program into p-code, you can copy that p-code to a Macintosh, a Windows computer, or a Linux computer. As long as that computer uses a Java p-code interpreter, you can run the Java program on that computer without modification.

Best of all, programs that you compile into p-code can run without the original source code, which means that you can protect your source code and still give your program away to others.

Just in case you're wondering, Liberty BASIC, which comes with this book, takes BASIC instructions and saves them in a separate file that uses p-code. If you distribute any compiled programs that you create using Liberty BASIC, you need to also distribute a special run-time file that can translate your Liberty BASIC p-code on another computer.

Naturally, p-code has its own disadvantages. Programs that you create by using p-code tend to run much slower than programs that you compile directly into machine language. Although p-code programs can run without a copy of the original source code that you use to create them, you can also *decompile* p-code programs.

Decompiling a p-code program can reveal the original source code that the programmer used to create the program. So if you write a program in Java and compile it into p-code, a rival can decompile your p-code program and see your original Java source code. Your rival then ends up with a nearly identical copy of your source code, essentially stealing your program.

You can actually decompile any program, including programs that you compile into machine language. But unlike with decompiling p-code programs, decompiling a machine-language version of a program never gets you the original high-level language source code that the programmer used to write the program. If you compile a program into machine language, the original source code can be written in C++, COBOL, FORTRAN, BASIC, Ada, LISP, Pascal, or any other programming language in the world. Because the decompiler has no idea what language the original source code was written in, it can only decompile a machine-language version of a program into equivalent assembly language. After you decompile a program into assembly language source code, you can rewrite or modify that source code. Decompiling effectively allows you to steal the ideas of others.

So what do I use?

If you want to write programs to sell, use a compiler, which protects your original source code. If you want to write a program to run on your Web page, you can use either an interpreter or p-code. If you want to write a program that can run on different types of computers, p-code may prove your only choice. As a safer but more cumbersome alternative, you can also use multiple compilers and modify your program to run on each different computer.

The language that you choose can determine whether you can use a compiler, an interpreter, or p-code. You often convert Java programs into p-code, for example, although you can compile them directly into machine language. On the other hand, you usually compile C++ and rarely interpret or convert it into p-code.

Squashing Bugs with a Debugger

Few computer programs work 100 percent correctly, which explains why computers crash, lose airline reservations, or just act erratically at times. Mathematically, writing a program that works 100 percent correctly every time is impossible because testing a program for all possible types of computers, hardware, and additional software that may interfere with the way your program runs is impossible.

A problem that keeps a program from working correctly is known as a *bug*.

In the early days, computers used mechanical relays and vacuum tubes instead of circuit boards and microprocessors. One day, the computer failed to work correctly. The scientists examined their program; it should have worked. So they next examined the computer itself and found that a moth had gotten smashed in a mechanical relay, preventing it from closing and thus keeping the computer from working correctly. From that point on, problems in computers have been known as *bugs*, even though real bugs are much less annoying and dangerous than computer bugs.

Because writing a program that works 100 percent correctly all the time is virtually impossible, operating systems (such as Windows XP) unavoidably contain bugs that keep them from working correctly. When you convert your source code into machine language, you must use a compiler or interpreter, which is another program that contains its share of bugs. Finally, your own program may contain bugs of its own. With so many places for bugs to creep in, you shouldn't be surprised that bugs infest computers like cockroaches infest a cheap apartment complex.

Although you can do little about bugs in other people's programs (except not buy the programs), you can reduce (but not completely eliminate) bugs in your own program by using a *debugger*. A debugger is a special program (which may also contain bugs) that can help you track down and wipe out bugs in programs that you write.

A debugger provides several ways to track down bugs in your program:

- ✔ **Stepping:** The debugger runs your program, line-by-line, so that you can see exactly which line may contain the bug. This process is like reread-ing written instructions to get to another person's house if you're lost. By going over these instructions, one by one, you can find out where you made a wrong turn.

- ✔ **Breakpoints:** Rather than force you to step through an entire program, line-by-line, *breakpoints* enable you to specify where you want to start examining your program line-by-line. So if you were lost, instead of rereading the instructions to get to another person's house from start to finish, you skip those instructions that you know you followed correctly and examine only the remaining instructions that you aren't sure that you followed correctly. Similarly, by using breakpoints, you can selec-tively examine only parts of your program, line-by-line, and skip over the parts that you know already work.

- ✔ **Watching:** Watching enables you to see your program storing data in memory and to determine what that data may be. If your program stores incorrect data (such as saving a name instead of a telephone number), you know exactly where in your program the bug is occurring. Figure 4-2 shows a sample debugger at work that highlights a specific instruction in your program and displays a window that shows the value of specific data. Each time you examine a line in your program, the debugger shows you how that particular line affects the value you're watching. As soon as you see the value change, the debugger shows you exactly which line in your program caused that change. This process is like having some-one to tell you to drive 10 miles south down a certain road after turning right. The moment that you exceed 10 miles, a *watchpoint* alerts you so that you know exactly where you almost made a mistake and got lost.

A debugger essentially shows you exactly how a computer is going to interpret the instructions in your program. Of course, if you fix one bug, you may intro-duce several new ones. That's why writing bug-free programs is impossible.

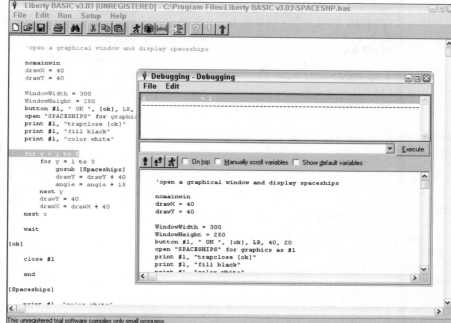

Figure 4-2:
One window
displays the
source
code, and a
second
window
shows all
the values
you're
watching.

Writing a Help File

Nobody has trouble using a doorknob, a toaster, or a microwave oven, but people still complain that computers and VCRs are too hard to use.

The problem with VCRs lies in the cryptic controls that aren't easy to figure out just by looking at them. Similarly, the problem with computer programs is that programs are too complex to use at first glance. If you can make a program that's actually easy to use, people can actually use it.

Because computer programs are still being designed for programmers by other programmers, computers still mystify the average user. To help the poor befuddled user, most programs now offer Help files.

A *Help file* provides instructions and explanations on-screen. Theoretically, if the user experiences trouble with the program, he can browse through the Help file, find an explanation or step-by-step instructions, and continue using the program. Figure 4-3 shows Microsoft PowerPoint , which desperately tries to guide users through its complicated maze of commands by providing a Help file and a cartoon Office Assistant.

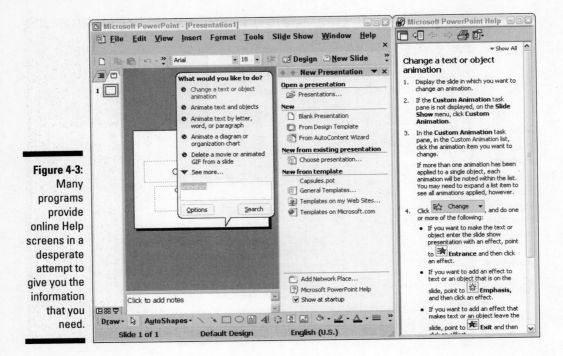

Figure 4-3:
Many programs provide online Help screens in a desperate attempt to give you the information that you need.

Although Help files still can't substitute for designing a program that's easy to use in the first place, most programs offer Help files anyway. To keep your program modern and up-to-date, include a Help file with your program.

To create a Help file, you can use a special Help file-authoring program, which simplifies the process of creating and organizing topics for your Help file, as shown in Figure 4-4.

Creating an Installation Program

After you write your program, test it, debug it, and write a Help file for it, the final step is to give or sell copies of your program to others. Although you can copy your program onto a floppy disk or CD and force buyers to manually copy your program to their hard drive, doing so can cause problems. Users may not copy all the files correctly, for example. And forcing users to manually copy your program to their hard drive may prove such a nuisance that most people don't bother even trying to use your program.

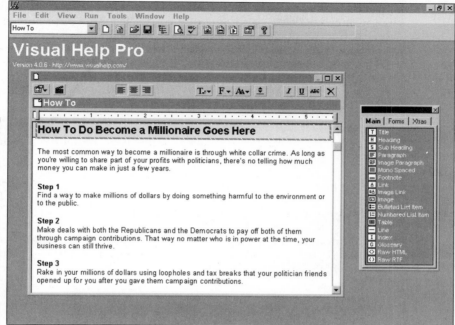

Figure 4-4:
Help file-
creation
programs,
such as
Visual Help
Pro, simplify
the process
of making
an online
Help file for
your
program.

To make copying a program to a user's hard drive as easy as possible, most commercial programs include a special installation program. Users run this installation program, which automatically copies a program and all necessary files to the appropriate location on the user's hard drive. By making the installation of a program practically foolproof, software publishers make sure that users install the programs correctly.

So the final step to distributing your program to others is to use a special installation program, which can smash all your program files into a single file that can automatically install itself on another computer.

Installation programs offer the following features for distributing programs to others:

✔ **File compression:** Most programs are fairly large, which means that they can't fit on a single floppy disk. Rather than force users to insert a series of floppy disks or compact discs (CDs) into their computer to install your program, an installation program smashes your files so that they can fit on as few floppy disks or compact discs as possible.

✔ **Display graphics and play sounds:** Installing a program usually takes a few minutes while the computer copies files from the floppy or CD to its hard drive. Rather than force the user to stare into space, an installation program can display advertisements or messages to make the installation process mildly interesting. Other uses for graphics include displaying an hourglass icon or a status bar that shows how far the installation is complete, such as 54 percent complete. That way, users know how much longer they need to wait.

✔ **Simplify the copying process:** Most important, an installation program simplifies copying your program to the user's hard drive, making the entire process accurate, fast, and foolproof.

The first impression that people get from your program is through its installation process, so an installation program helps give your program a professional appearance.

Of course, you need to make sure that your installation program installs your program correctly or the first impression that users get from your program will be a highly negative one.

Part II

Learning
Programming with
Liberty BASIC

The 5th Wave   By Rich Tennant

"Can't I just give you riches or something?"

In this part . . .

No matter what programming language you use (C/C++, BASIC, Prolog, COBOL, C#, Perl, Ada, Pascal, Java, and so on), all computer programs tend to follow the same general principles. If you understand how to write a program by using one language (such as BASIC), you find that understanding a second or third programming language (such as C/C++ and Java) is much easier.

To give you a chance for hands-on programming, this book explains how to use Liberty BASIC, which is a real Windows compiler that enables you to write and create real Windows programs that you can sell or give away. Just load the Liberty BASIC compiler, type the sample Liberty BASIC programs into your computer, and run them to see how they work.

Occasionally in this part, you see a Liberty BASIC program along with an equivalent program in another language (such as C/C++, Pascal, or Java), so you can understand how other programming languages may work. You can look at these programs to see how other programming languages accomplish the same tasks while looking entirely different from an equivalent Liberty BASIC program.

Chapter 5

Getting Your Hands on a Real Language: Liberty BASIC

*T*he best way to learn anything is to start practicing it. If you want to learn computer programming, you should start writing programs on your computer as soon as possible.

You can learn to program by starting out with one of hundreds of programming languages designed for novices, such as Pascal, LOGO, and SmallTalk. But the most popular beginner's programming language is still BASIC. BASIC is simple enough to help you understand the concepts behind programming yet powerful enough to enable you to create commercial-quality programs.

To help you in your quest to learn programming, this book comes with a shareware copy of Liberty BASIC. As long as you're running Windows 95/98/ Me/NT/2000/XP, you can run and use Liberty BASIC on your computer. Most of this book provides examples in Liberty BASIC that you can type yourself.

If you have a Macintosh, you can't run Liberty BASIC unless you buy a special Windows emulation program such as VirtualPC from Microsoft (at www.microsoft.com). As an alternative, you can use either True Basic (www.truebasic.com) or Future Basic (www.stazsoftware.com). True Basic, Future Basic, and Liberty BASIC all use BASIC language, so the sample programs in this book designed for Liberty BASIC should run under both True Basic and Future Basic with only minor modifications.

If for some odd reason you're both technically knowledgeable enough to use Linux, yet still want to learn how to program, you can download a free BASIC interpreter, YABASIC (which stands for Yet Another BASIC), by visiting www.yabasic.de.

Why Learn Liberty BASIC?

If you're interested in learning to program, you may wonder, "Why not jump right in and start learning C++ or Java?" (Then again, if you want to learn how to swim, why not jump right into the ocean and start swimming with the sharks?) Although you can start learning to program by using any language, Liberty BASIC offers several advantages that you won't find in other language compilers.

Liberty BASIC is (almost) free

Liberty BASIC is a shareware program that you can evaluate for free until you decide whether it's worth paying for. That way, you can experiment with computer programming without spending any money buying programs, such as Visual C++ or JBuilder only to realize they may be too complicated and confusing for you.

Liberty BASIC is easy

Liberty BASIC can teach you the fundamentals of programming so that you can get real-life experience programming your own computer. Other programming languages, such as C++ or Java, can force you to master needlessly complicated topics, such as pointers, object-orientation, and memory allocation. Rather than let these other programming languages bury you under an additional layer of complexity that only gets in your way, learn Liberty BASIC.

Best of all, the BASIC programming language was specially designed to teach novices how to program, so learning BASIC can teach you how programming works. Once you learn the fundamentals of programming with Liberty BASIC, you can apply your programming knowledge to help you better learn another programming language, such as C++ or Java.

Liberty BASIC runs on Windows

When computers used to run the ancient operating system of MS-DOS, Microsoft tossed in a free BASIC interpreter called QBASIC. Although you can still run QBASIC in most versions of Windows (such as Windows 98 but not Windows 2000), people have been screaming for a Windows-based version of BASIC that they can use to teach themselves programming.

Because Microsoft has no intention of creating a Windows-based version of QBASIC, the next alternative is to use Liberty BASIC. You can not only write BASIC programs in Liberty BASIC on any computer that runs Microsoft Windows, but you can also create real, honest-to-goodness Windows applications using Liberty BASIC that you can sell or give away as well.

If you pay for the full version of Liberty BASIC, you can create real Windows programs that you can sell to others. The shareware version of Liberty BASIC (which comes with this book) allows you to write programs, but won't allow you to compile and distribute them to others.

You can start using Liberty BASIC today

Liberty BASIC comes with this book, so everyone reading this book can start using it right away (unless, of course, you're not using Windows). That makes Liberty BASIC a natural learning tool to complement this book.

If trying to understand certain programming concepts confuses you, you can quickly type a sample Liberty BASIC program and see for yourself exactly how certain programming features work. By combining theory with hands-on experience, this book and Liberty BASIC can help you pick up computer programming in no time.

Installing Liberty BASIC

To install Liberty BASIC by using the CD that comes with this book, refer to the installation instructions in the Appendix.

Because software changes so rapidly, a newer version of Liberty BASIC may be available by the time you read this book. If you download a newer version from the Liberty BASIC Web site (at www.libertybasic.com), you may need to go through some extra steps to install Liberty BASIC on your computer.

If you download Liberty BASIC from the Liberty BASIC Web site, the file is compressed in a self-extracting EXE file. To decompress this file, you need to download and save this file somewhere on your hard disk, and then double-click on the Liberty Basic EXE file (which has a cryptic name such as lb400win. exe). When you double-click on the Liberty Basic EXE file, the Liberty Basic installation program guides you, step-by-step, into installing Liberty Basic on your computer.

Loading Liberty BASIC

As you install Liberty BASIC, the program creates its own directory and adds Liberty BASIC to your Program menu. To load Liberty BASIC, follow these steps:

1. **Click the Start button on the Windows taskbar.**

   The Start menu opens.

2. **Choose Programs⇨Liberty BASIC⇨Liberty BASIC.**

   The Liberty BASIC program appears.

To make loading Liberty BASIC easier and faster, you can place a Liberty BASIC icon on the Windows desktop.

To place a Liberty BASIC icon on your Windows desktop, follow these steps:

1. **Right-click the Windows desktop.**

   A pop-up menu appears.

2. **Choose New⇨Shortcut.**

   A Create Shortcut dialog box appears.

3. **Click Browse.**

   A Browse dialog box appears.

4. **Find and click the Liberty BASIC program and then click Open.**

   You may need to change directories or drives to find the Liberty BASIC program if it isn't stored in the C:\Program Files\Liberty Basic directory. After you click Open, the Create Shortcut dialog box appears again.

5. **Click Next.**

   The Select a Title for the Program dialog box appears.

6. **Type a name, such as Liberty BASIC, in the Select a Name for the Shortcut text box and click Finish.**

   The Liberty BASIC icon appears on your desktop. The next time that you want to load Liberty BASIC, just double-click this icon.

Your First Liberty BASIC Program

The Liberty BASIC editor is where you write, edit, and run your BASIC program. To see the power of Liberty BASIC, type the following into the Liberty BASIC editor:

```
PRINT "This BASIC program mimics a really bad boss."
PRINT
PRINT "What is your name?"
INPUT Name$
PRINT "Hello " + Name$ + ". You're fired! Have a nice day."
END
```

Liberty BASIC, like most versions of BASIC, doesn't care whether you type commands in uppercase, lowercase, or a mixture of both. Most programmers, however, like to use all uppercase to identify all the BASIC commands that they use in a program.

Unlike a word processor, the Liberty BASIC editor doesn't wrap words from one line to the other, which means that you can keep typing all the way to the far right until your text scrolls out of view.

This program tells the computer to perform the following tasks:

1. The first line prints the message This BASIC program mimics a really bad boss. on-screen.

2. The second line prints (adds) a blank line directly underneath the message.

3. The third line prints What is your name? on-screen.

4. The fourth line displays a question mark (?) as a prompt and waits for the user to type a name. As soon as the user presses the Enter key, the BASIC program stores whatever the user types into a temporary memory location that it identifies as Name$.

5. The fifth line prints the message "Hello (following it by the name that the user types in the fourth line). You're fired! Have a nice day." The plus sign (+) tells Liberty BASIC to add the word "Hello" with the words that it stores in Name$.

6. The sixth line tells the computer that this is the end of the program.

Running a Liberty BASIC program

After you finish typing a BASIC program, press Shift+F5 or choose Run⇨Run from the Liberty BASIC menu bar to run the program. Figure 5-1 shows what the BASIC program from the preceding section looks like when run on Liberty BASIC.

As you run this program, Liberty BASIC displays the text in a window that it calls the *main window*. You can use the menu bar in the main window to print or save any text that appears in the main window.

Main window

Figure 5-1:
Running
your first
Liberty
BASIC
program.

Saving a Liberty BASIC program

Although you can type your Liberty BASIC programs over and over whenever you want to run them, saving your program to a hard drive or floppy disk is much easier. Then you can load and edit the program later.

To save a program, follow these steps:

1. **Choose File⇨Save from the Liberty BASIC menu bar, or click the Save File icon on the Liberty Basic toolbar as shown in Figure 5-2.**

   The Save As dialog box appears.

2. **Type a name for your file in the Filename text box.**

   You may want to change folders or drives to store your Liberty BASIC file.

3. **Click OK.**

Liberty BASIC automatically adds a BAS file extension to Liberty BASIC programs that you save. Unless you have a good reason to change this file extension, use the BAS extension to help you identify your Liberty BASIC programs from any other files stored on your computer.

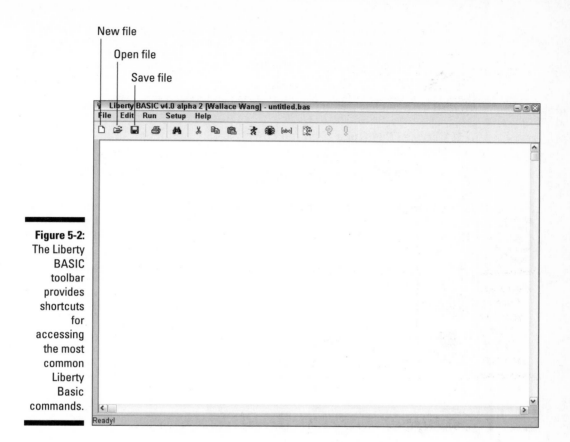

New file

Open file

Save file

Figure 5-2:
The Liberty
BASIC
toolbar
provides
shortcuts
for
accessing
the most
common
Liberty
Basic
commands.

Loading or starting a Liberty BASIC program

Liberty BASIC can display only one BASIC program on-screen at a time. Any time that you want to view another BASIC program, you must get rid of the BASIC program that you currently have on-screen.

To create a brand new program, follow these steps:

1. **Choose File⇨New File from the Liberty BASIC menu bar, or click the New File icon on the Liberty BASIC toolbar.**

   If you haven't saved the BASIC program you're currently displaying, a Please Confirm dialog box appears.

2. **Click Yes to save the current file or click No if you don't want to save your changes.**

   Liberty BASIC displays a blank screen, ready for you to type a new BASIC program.

To load a previously saved program, follow these steps:

1. **Choose File⇨Open from the Liberty BASIC menu bar, or click the Open File icon on the Liberty BASIC toolbar.**

   If you haven't saved the BASIC program you're currently displaying, a Please Confirm dialog box appears.

   Liberty BASIC automatically remembers the last seven files you opened, so for a quick way to load a recently opened file, just click the File menu followed by the name of the file you want to open, which appears at the bottom of the File menu.

2. **Click Yes to save the current file or click No if you don't want to save your changes.**

   The Open a BAS File dialog box appears. You may need to change directories or drives to find where you saved the file.

3. **Click the file that you want to open and then click OK.**

   Your chosen program appears.

Using Keystroke Commands in Liberty BASIC

The Liberty BASIC editor works like a simple word processor. You can use the mouse or the keyboard to navigate a BASIC program. Table 5-1 shows the different keys that you can press and what they do.

Table 5-1	Commands for the Liberty BASIC Editor
Keystroke Command	*What It Does*
Home	Moves the cursor to the front of the line
End	Moves the cursor to the end of the line
Shift+Arrow key	Highlights text in the direction of the arrow
Delete	Deletes the character directly above the cursor or deletes an entire highlighted block of text

Keystroke Command	What It Does
Backspace	Deletes the character to the left of the cursor
Ctrl+F	Finds and replaces text in your program
Ctrl+A	Selects your entire program
Ctrl+Z	Takes back the effects of the last command you chose (the Undo command)

Getting Help Using Liberty BASIC

As do most programs, Liberty BASIC provides an online Help system. To access Help, follow these steps:

1. **Choose Help⇨Liberty BASIC Help.**

   The Help Contents window appears, listing various Help topics, as shown in Figure 5-3.

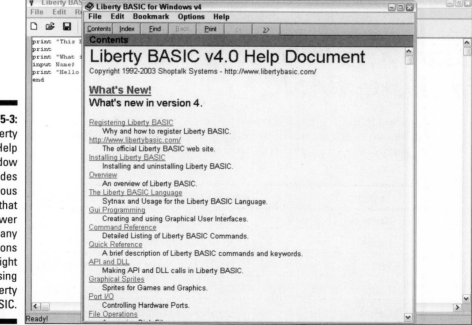

Figure 5-3: The Liberty BASIC Help window provides lists various topics that can answer any questions you might have using Liberty BASIC.

2. **Click a Help topic that you want to read.**

    Depending on the topic you choose, the Help window displays different information about using Liberty BASIC.

3. **Click the Close box of the Help window after you finish.**

Exiting Liberty BASIC

Eventually, you may need to exit Liberty BASIC so that you can do something else with your computer. To exit Liberty BASIC, follow these steps:

1. **Choose File➪Exit from the menu bar, or click the close box (which appears in the upper right-hand corner) of the Liberty Basic window.**

    If you haven't saved the Liberty BASIC program you're currently displaying, a dialog box asks whether or not you want to save the file.

2. **Click Yes to save the current file or click No if you don't want to save your changes.**

    Another dialog box appears, asking whether you're sure you want to exit Liberty BASIC.

3. **Click Yes to exit (or No to return to Liberty BASIC).**

    Liberty BASIC gracefully exits.

Chapter 6

Handling Input and Output

● ●

In This Chapter

▶ Getting input and output the primitive way

▶ Getting input and output the modern way

▶ Printing stuff out

● ●

*E*very program takes in data (*input*), manipulates that data in some way, and spits the data back out in some form (*output*).

In the old days, programmers gave input to the computer by using a variety of methods, ranging from physically rearranging switches on the computer to using paper tape, punch cards, teletype machines (which resembled typewriters), and finally keyboards and touch-screen monitors. As computers spit back some form of output, it usually appears on paper or on-screen on a monitor.

Despite the fact that today's computers include pop-up windows, dialog boxes, command buttons, and scroll bars, most of today's programming languages are still rooted in the past, when programs waited for the user to type a name or a number. Then the program shoved that information up a line and printed the resulting output directly below it.

That's why most programming languages such as BASIC (and even C/C++) contain built-in commands for reading and displaying data one line at a time on-screen. Naturally, such programs look fairly primitive, especially if you compare them with today's modern programs, but be patient. As you're learning programming for the first time, understanding how programs can accept input and spit data back out is much more important (at this time) than worrying about how a program actually looks on-screen.

Inputting and Outputting Data: The Old-Fashioned Way

Input occurs whenever a program accepts data from an outside source. Some examples of where a program can get input include the following:

✔ Anything the user types from the keyboard

✔ The movement of the computer mouse

✔ Data that someone previously stores in a file (such as a word processor document or the high score of a video game)

✔ Data that feeds into the computer from an outside source (such as a Web page sent through a modem or an image captured through a scanner)

Output occurs whenever a program displays data back, usually after it manipulates the data in some way. Some common examples of output include the following:

✔ Data that appears on-screen (such as text, pictures, or video images)

✔ Data that prints on paper through a printer

✔ Sound that plays through a computer's speakers (such as audio files previously downloaded off the Internet)

In BASIC, the simplest way to output data is to use the PRINT command, which simply displays whatever appears inside double quotes. In the following example, the BASIC command does nothing but display the text What are you looking at? on-screen, as shown in Figure 6-1.

```
PRINT "What are you looking at?"
END
```

The PRINT command in Liberty BASIC displays text in a window known as the *main window*. If you don't want the main window to appear, just use the command NOMAINWIN. Later when you start writing programs that use a graphical user interface (as explained in Chapter 14), you won't need to display the main window to display data on-screen.

As the PRINT command gives your program the capability to output data, the INPUT command gives your program the capability to accept data from the keyboard. To use the INPUT command, you simply type the word INPUT, following it with a character or phrase that you want to represent whatever the user types at the keyboard, as in the following example:

```
PRINT "What is the name of your boss?"
INPUT Myboss$
PRINT Myboss$ + "? That sounds like the name of a moron!"
END
```

If you type the preceding example into Liberty BASIC, the program displays the text What is the name of your boss? If you type a name and press Enter, the program responds by displaying the name that you typed, following it with a question mark and the text That sounds like the name of a moron!, as shown in Figure 6-2.

An equivalent C program

Unlike BASIC, other programming languages force you to enclose instructions inside special words or symbols that act as parentheses (so to speak) that wrap around the beginning and ending of your program. In the C/C++ language, for example, the smallest program you can write consists of the word `main`, which you follow with parentheses and curly brackets, as in the following example:

```
main ()
{
}
```

If you write instructions by using C/C++, you must enclose them inside these strange curly brackets. Just to show you how drastically different identical programs can look if you write them in different programming languages, here's an equivalent C program that enables the user to type a name (as input) and displays on-screen whatever name the user types, following it with the words, `That sounds like the name of a moron!`:

```
main ()
{
  char myboss[15];
  printf ("What is the name of
    your boss.\n");
  scanf ("%s", &myboss);
  printf ("%s", myboss);
  printf ("? That sounds like
    the name of a moron!");
}
```

Figure 6-1: The main window is a special window for displaying text from the PRINT command.

Don't worry too much about the technical details in using the PRINT and INPUT commands because they represent the old way of getting input and displaying output on-screen. In Windows and other modern operating systems, including the Mac OS, programs offer fancier ways of accepting input and displaying output through the use of a *graphical user interface* (*GUI*), often pronounced as *goo-ey*.

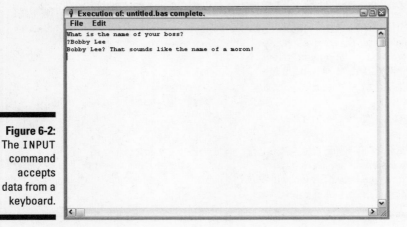

Figure 6-2:
The INPUT command accepts data from a keyboard.

Inputting and Outputting Data: The Modern Way

Most computers now use a graphical user interface to display data. Because commands such as PRINT and INPUT were geared for ancient computers that few people use any more, most programming languages now include special commands for creating and displaying data by using windows and dialog boxes.

Every programming language provides different types of commands to create and display data in windows, dialog boxes, and menus. The commands in this chapter are unique to Liberty BASIC and probably won't work in other versions of BASIC.

Getting input

One of the simplest ways to ask for input from the user is to use a special Prompt dialog box. To create a Prompt dialog box, you need to use the

PROMPT command, following it with the text that you want to display (such as asking the user to type a name or number) and a character or word that represents whatever the user types in, as in the following example:

```
NOMAINWIN
PROMPT "What is the name of your boss?"; name$
```

The first command (NOMAINWIN) turns off the main window, as described earlier in the chapter. The next command (PROMPT) displays the Prompter dialog box, as shown in Figure 6-3.

Figure 6-3:
The
PROMPT
command
displays a
dialog box
so that
people can
type data
into your
program.

What is the name of your boss?

OK   Cancel

Displaying output

The simplest way to display output to the user is to use a Notice dialog box. To create a Notice dialog box, you need to use the NOTICE command, following it with any text that you want to display. The following program uses the NOTICE command to display text along with the name that the user types into the Prompt dialog box. In this case, the NOTICE command displays a Notice dialog box, as shown in Figure 6-4.

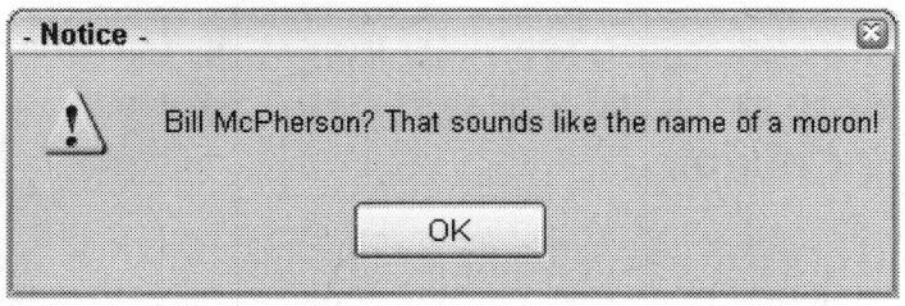

Figure 6-4:
The
NOTICE
command
creates a
dialog box
that displays
information
to the user.

- Notice -

Bill McPherson? That sounds like the name of a moron!

OK

```
NOMAINWIN
PROMPT "What is the name of your boss?"; name$
NOTICE name$ + "? That sounds like the name of a moron!"
END
```

Sending Data to the Printer

One of the most popular ways to output data is to print it out on paper, also known as a *hard copy*. In Liberty BASIC, the commands for sending data to a printer are LPRINT and DUMP, as shown in the following example:

```
LPRINT "Save the dolphins! Kill the tuna!"
DUMP
END
```

The LPRINT command sends data to your default printer. The DUMP command simply tells your printer to start printing right away.

You can skip the DUMP command if you want, but then the LPRINT command may not start printing immediately.

The LPRINT command starts printing in the upper-left corner of the page. If you want to start printing your data in a different location on a page, you may need to add extra lines or spaces to change the vertical and horizontal position where your text starts printing.

To change the vertical position, just use the LPRINT command by itself, as follows:

```
LPRINT
LPRINT "Save the dolphins! Kill the tuna!"
DUMP
END
```

In the preceding example, the first LPRINT command prints a blank line, and the second LPRINT command prints the text Save the dolphins! Kill the tuna!

To change the horizontal position, use the SPACE$(*x*) command where the letter *x* represents how many spaces you want to insert. If, for example, you want to insert five spaces before printing any text, you use the SPACE$(5) command, as in the following example:

```
LPRINT "Save the dolphins! Kill the tuna!"
LPRINT SPACE$(5); "Save the dolphins! Kill the tuna!"
DUMP
END
```

The preceding program would make your printer print the following message:

```
Save the dolphins! Kill the tuna!
     Save the dolphins! Kill the tuna!
```

When using the SPACE$(*x*) command, you need to use the semicolon (;), following it with the data that you want to print, which you surround with double quotation marks.

This chapter provides a brief explanation for getting input and displaying output, just so you can understand the way a computer program gets data and spits it back out again for the user to see. For more details about creating a more modern user interface that offers windows, dialog boxes, and menus, skip to Chapter 14.

Chapter 7

Variables, Constants, and Comments

. . . .

In This Chapter

▶ Using variables

▶ Creating and using constants

▶ Adding comments to your code

. . . .

*W*hen a program accepts input, the first thing the computer needs to do is find a place to store any data that it gets from the user. Because computers are like one giant brain, they simply store data in memory.

Of course, if you stuff enough data into a computer, it's likely to lose track of all the data in its memory (much like a person might do). So to help the computer find data that it already stored, computer programs use something called *variables*.

A variable simply acts like a storage bin. You can stuff any type of data into a variable, such as numbers or words, and then retrieve them back out again so you can stuff different data into that variable all over again. Although variables can only store one chunk of data at a time, they can be reused over and over again to store different data. The contents of a variable may vary at any given time, hence the name *variable*.

Besides storing data in variables, programs also use things known as *constants* and *comments*. Constants represent a fixed value that a program may need, and comments are explanations that programmers use to explain how a program works.

Although the idea of using variables, constants, and comments may seem mysterious to you, relax. You'll see their purpose as soon as you start writing your own programs.

Storing Data in Variables

If you know your program will need to temporarily store data that it gets from the user, you must first create enough variables to hold that data. If you don't create enough variables to hold all the data that your program needs, your program will simply lose any data you give it, which effectively makes your program utterly useless.

So before you write a program, you need to identify the following:

- How many variables do I need to store all the data my program needs?
- What names should I give each variable?
- What type of data does each variable need to hold (numbers, text, and so on)?

Each variable must have a distinct name to keep your computer from getting confused. The names can be anything from the name of your dog to variations of four-letter words. However, it's a good idea to give variables names that describe the type of data that the variable holds, such as FirstName or FakeIDNumber.

Variables have the following two uses:

- For storing inputted data
- For storing calculations that use inputted data or previous calculations

Although you always want to give your variables descriptive names, keep in mind that every programming language uses slightly different rules for what's an acceptable name for a variable. In Liberty BASIC, for example, the rules for naming variables are as follows:

- The first character of a variable name must be a letter, such as *A* or *S*. You can't create a variable in which the first character is a number, as in 7me.
- Variables can contain a period, such as in My.Boss. You can't, however, use spaces in a variable's name, as in My Boss.
- Upper and lowercase letters are significant in variable names, which means that Liberty BASIC considers the variable Phonenumber completely different from the variable PHONENUMBER.
- The name of a variable can't be identical to a Liberty BASIC keyword, such as END or PRINT.

If a programming language treats upper and lowercase variable names differently, programmers say that the language is *case-sensitive*. C/C++, Java, and C# are case-sensitive, but Pascal and most versions of BASIC aren't. (Liberty BASIC is one of those rare exceptions that is case-sensitive.)

Case-sensitive programs, such as C/C++, Java, and Liberty BASIC, make it really easy to make a mistake in your program by typing a variable name differently, such as MyAge and Myage. When you name your variables, be consistent, such as always using lowercase or always using uppercase. If you mix and match upper- and lowercase, you greatly increase the odds that you'll mistype a variable name. If you mistype a variable name, your program may not work correctly, and you may have a hard time figuring out why.

Creating a variable

In most programming languages such as C/C++ or Java, you have to go through three steps to create a variable:

1. **Name all your variables and list your variables near the beginning of the program.**
2. **Define what type of data you want each variable to hold.**
3. **Assign data (numbers or a string) to your variable.**

In most versions of BASIC (including Liberty BASIC), you can name a variable and assign data to that variable all at the same time. In Liberty BASIC, the two types of data a variable can hold are limited to numbers and string. A string is just any text such as "Bob" or "I hate copycat book publishers." A number can be an integer (such as 54) or a real number (such as 54.903). Is this an advantage? Yes and no.

The advantage of BASIC's simple way to create a variable is that you can create new variables any time you need them. However, if you write a large program, it can be really easy to lose track of all the variables that your program uses.

So that's why more modern languages like C/C++ and many dialects of BASIC (including Visual BASIC and RealBASIC) have adopted the three-step method for creating variables. This three-step process offers the following advantages:

✔ By naming all of your variables and listing them near the beginning of your program, anyone can see quickly, at a glance, all the variables that your program uses.

✔ By defining the type of data a variable can hold, you can prevent a variable from holding the wrong type of data (such as a string instead of a number), which can prevent your program from trying to manipulate the wrong type of data. In the world of computer programming, defining what type of data your variable can hold is called *declaring your variables*.

✔ When you finally assign data to a variable after you have declared what type of data your variable can hold, your compiler won't compile your program until it checks that the data you stuff into each variable matches each variable's declaration. So if you try to stuff a number into a variable that expects a string, your compiler won't compile your program, thus preventing you from releasing a program that doesn't work properly. (Of course, it's possible for a program to still run incorrectly, but at least it won't be because you stuffed the wrong type of data into a variable.)

To show you how to create variables in Liberty BASIC, the following example uses two variables. One variable (Salary) stores data that represents a user's salary, and the second variable (TaxOwed) stores a calculation.

```
NOMAINWIN
Salary = 25000
TaxOwed = Salary * .95
NOTICE "This is how much tax you owe = $"; TaxOwed
END
```

This Liberty BASIC program tells the computer to do the following:

1. The first line tells Liberty BASIC not to display the main window.

2. The second line tells the computer to store the number 25000 in the variable Salary.

3. The third line tells the computer, "Multiply the number that the variable Salary stores by the number .95. Then store the value of this calculation in another variable, TaxOwed."

4. The fourth line tells the computer, "Display a NOTICE dialog box with the text, This is how much tax you owe = $" and follow it by the number that the variable TaxOwed represents.

5. The fifth line tells the computer that the program is at an end.

In a more modern dialect of BASIC that allows you to declare your variables ahead of time, such as Visual BASIC, the previous example might look like this:

```
Dim Salary As Integer
    Dim TaxesOwed As Single
    Salary = 25000
    TaxesOwed = Salary * 0.95
    TextBox1.Text() = CStr(TaxesOwed)
```

This fragment of a Visual BASIC program tells the computer to do the following:

1. The first line tells Visual BASIC to create a variable called Salary and makes sure that it stores only integer data types.

2. The second line tells Visual BASIC to create a variable called TaxesOwed and make sure it stores only single data types, which are numbers such as 3.402 or –193.8.

3. The third line tells Visual BASIC to stuff the value of 25000 into the Salary variable.

4. The fourth line tells Visual BASIC, "Multiply the number that the variable `Salary` contains by the number `.95`. Then store the value of this calculation in another variable, `TaxOwed`."

5. The fifth line tells Visual BASIC, "Take the value stored in the `TaxesOwed` variable and display them on the screen."

Don't worry too much about understanding the Visual BASIC example. Just get the idea that Visual BASIC uses a dialect of BASIC, and that declaring your variables near the top of your program can help you identify the number of variables used and the type of data each variable can hold.

Assigning a value to a variable

In Liberty BASIC, variables contain nothing until you assign values to them. Because the whole purpose of a variable is to store data, you can assign a value to a variable in the following three ways:

- Assign a fixed value to a variable.
- Assign the result of a calculation to a variable.
- Use the `PROMPT` command to get data from the user and make that data the variable.

Putting a fixed value in a variable

The simplest way to assign a value to a variable is to use the equal sign. This method enables you to assign a number or a string to a variable, as in the following example:

```
CEOSalary = 9000000
Message2Workers$ = "So I make more than I'm worth. So what?"
```

In the first line, you assign the number `9000000` to a variable by the name of `CEOSalary`. In the second line, you assign the string `So I make more than I'm worth. So what?` to the variable `Message2Workers$`.

If you assign a string to a variable, the variable name must include the dollar sign ($) at the end. If you assign a number to a variable, don't include a dollar sign in the variable name.

Until you assign a value to a variable, its value is either zero (0) or a blank string (" ").

Assigning a calculated value to a variable

Because variables can represent numbers or strings that may change, you can assign calculations to a variable. If you want to store a numerical value in a variable, just assign it a mathematical calculation, as follows:

```
DumbestPersonIQ = 6
BossIQ = DumbestPersonIQ / 3
```

In this example, Liberty BASIC creates a variable called `BossIQ`. Then it takes the value stored in the variable `DumbestPersonIQ` and divides it by three. It then assigns the result to the `BossIQ` variable. In this case, the value that it assigns to `BossIQ` is 2.

You can also assign a string calculation to a variable, as follows:

```
Cry$ = "I want to eat"
NewCry$ = Cry$ + " food that is really bad for me!"
```

In this example, the first line stores the string `I want to eat` in the variable `Cry$`. The second line creates a new variable, `NewCry$`. Then it combines the value of the `Cry$` variable (`I want to eat`) with the string `" food that is really bad for me!"`

Thus the `NewCry$` variable now represents the string, `"I want to eat food that is really bad for me!"`

To see how Liberty BASIC can assign numbers and strings to variables, type the following program:

```
NOMAINWIN
Parents = 2
Whacks = 20
MotherAxWhacks = Parents * Whacks
FatherAxWhacks = MotherAxWhacks + 1
FirstName$ = "Lizzie"
LastName$ = " Borden"
FullName$ = FirstName$ + LastName$
NOTICE FullName$ + " had an ax, gave her mother " _
+ chr$(13) + str$(MotherAxWhacks) + " whacks. When she saw
            what" _
+ chr$(13) + "she had done, gave her father " _
+ str$(FatherAxWhacks) + "."
END
```

This Liberty BASIC program tells the computer to do the following:

1. The first line tells Liberty BASIC not to display the main window.

2. The second line creates the variable `Parents` and assigns it a value of 2.

3. The third line creates the variable `Whacks` and assigns it a value of 20.

4. The fourth line creates the variable `MotherAxWhacks`. Then it multiplies the value of the `Parents` variable (which is 2) by the value of the `Whacks` variable (which is 20). Thus it assigns the value of the `MotherAxWhacks` variable the value of 2 * 20, or 40.

5. The fifth line creates the variable `FatherAxWhacks`. Then it adds 1 to the value of the `MotherAxWhacks` variable (which is 40). Thus it assigns the value of the `FatherAxWhacks` variable the value 40 + 1, or 41.

6. The sixth line creates the variable `FirstName$` and assigns it the value of `Lizzie`. (Notice that the `FirstName$` variable includes a dollar sign to tell the computer that you want this variable to hold only strings.)

7. The seventh line creates the variable `LastName$` and assigns it the value of `Borden`. (Notice the leading space, so that the first character in LastName$ will be a space.)

8. The eighth line creates the variable `FullName$` and assigns it the combination of the `FirstName$` variable and the `LastName$` variable. Thus the value of the `FullName$` variable is `Lizzie` plus `" Borden"`, or `Lizzie Borden`.

9. The ninth line creates a Notice dialog box that displays the value that you assign to the variable `FullName$` (which is `Lizzie Borden`) along with the string `" had an ax, gave her mother "`. Notice that the end of this line ends with an underscore, which tells Liberty BASIC that the rest of the commands continue on the next line.

10. The tenth line inserts a Return character (which you represent by using the ASCII number 13), followed by the value of `MotherAxWhacks` (which is 40) and the string `" whacks. When she saw what"`.

11. The eleventh line inserts a Return character (which you represent by using the ASCII number 13), followed it by the string `" she had done, gave her father "` and the value you assign to the `FatherAxWhacks` variable (which is 41). The output of the program appears in Figure 7-1.

12. The twelfth line tells Liberty BASIC to add the number represented by the `FatherAxWhacks` variable (41), convert it to a string (using the `str$` command), and add a period at the end of the string.

13. The thirteenth line tells Liberty BASIC that the program is at an end.

Figure 7-1:
A Liberty
BASIC
program
displaying
its output in
a Notice
dialog box.

If you mistype a variable name, such as typing `FatherWhacks` instead of `FatherAxWhacks`, Liberty BASIC assumes that you want to create a new variable and gives it a value of zero (0) or a blank (""). If your program doesn't work right, make sure that you typed all variable names correctly.

Stuffing a value into a variable with the PROMPT command

The `PROMPT` command displays a dialog box for the user to type some data — either a string or a value. The following example uses the `PROMPT` command to ask the user for a value. As soon as the user types a value (such as the number **49**) into the Prompt dialog box, the computer stores that value into the variable `Salary`. Then the program uses a second variable (`TaxOwed`) to store a calculation.

```
NOMAINWIN
PROMPT "How much money did you make last year?"; Salary
TaxOwed = Salary * .95
NOTICE "This is how much tax you owe = $"; TaxOwed
END
```

This Liberty BASIC program tells the computer to do the following:

1. The first line tells Liberty BASIC not to display the main window.

2. The second line displays a Prompt dialog box that asks, "`How much money did you make last year?`" After the user types a number, Liberty BASIC stores that number in the variable `Salary`.

3. The third line multiplies the value of Salary by `.95`. Whatever this value is, Liberty BASIC stores it in the variable `TaxOwed`.

4. The fourth line creates a Notice dialog box that reads, `This is how much tax you owe = $`, following it with the value that the `TaxOwed` variable represents.

5. The fifth line tells Liberty BASIC that the program is at an end.

An equivalent C program

Just so that you don't start thinking that all programs look like Liberty BASIC, here's how a C program looks that's equivalent to the one in the previous section, "Stuffing a value into a variable with the `PROMPT` command":

```
main ()
{
  float salary, taxowed;
```
```
  printf ("How much money did
    you make last year? ");
  scanf ("%f", &salary);
  taxowed = salary * .95;
  printf ("This is how much tax
    you owe = %8.2f", taxowed);
}
```

If you want the user to type a string (such as a name) into the Prompt dialog box, you need to add a dollar sign at the end of the variable to hold the string, such as YourName$. The dollar sign just tells Liberty BASIC that this particular variable holds only a string, which can consist of a name, a ZIP Code, or a street address.

In the following example, the Prompt dialog box stores a string:

```
NOMAINWIN
PROMPT "What is your name?"; YourName$
Message$ = YourName$ + ", you deserve a raise!"
NOTICE Message$
END
```

This Liberty BASIC program tells the computer to do the following:

1. The first line tells Liberty BASIC not to display the main window.

2. The second line displays a Prompt dialog box that asks, What is your name? Liberty BASIC stores whatever you type in the variable YourName$.

3. The third line adds the string , you deserve a raise! to the string that Libery BASIC stores in the YourName$ variable. This combination of ", you deserve a raise!" and the YourName variable Liberty BASIC stores in the variable Message$.

4. The fourth line creates a Notice dialog box that displays the string that Liberty BASIC stores in the Message$ variable.

5. The fifth line tells Liberty BASIC that the program is at an end.

If the user types a number in the Prompt dialog box in Step 2, such as 45, Liberty BASIC treats that number as just a string of symbols, such as 45.

Declaring your variables

Variables enable a program to store and manipulate data. As a result, identifying all the variables that a program uses and what type of data it stores in them can help you understand how a specific program works.

Unlike most programming languages, the BASIC programming language enables you to create and use variables anywhere in a program. Although this capability can prove convenient while you're writing a program, you may find it difficult to understand later while you're trying to modify that same program.

Study, for example, the earlier Lizzie Borden program. Quick: How many variables does this program use? If you can't tell right away, you must waste time going through the entire program, line by line, to find the answer. (The answer is seven variables: `Parents`, `Whacks`, `MotherAxWhacks`, `FatherAxWhacks`, `FirstName$`, `LastName$`, and `FullName$`.)

To enable you (or anyone else) to more easily identify all the variables that a program uses, most programming languages, such as C/C++ and Pascal, force you to declare your variables at the beginning of your program. Declaring your variables at the beginning has the following two purposes:

- ✔ To identify the *names* of all variables that a program uses
- ✔ To identify the total number of *variables* that a program uses

Knowing the total number of variables that a program uses can help you better understand how a program works because you can determine all the places where the program may store data.

Liberty BASIC supports the original (and some may claim a purer) dialect of the BASIC programming language, which lacks modern programming language constructs that have been added in later versions of the BASIC programming dialect, such as variable declarations and constants.

To declare a variable ahead of time in some versions of BASIC, such as Visual Basic (but not Liberty BASIC), you use the `DIM` command, as follows:

```
DIM Eyeballs
```

The preceding command tells your computer to create a variable by the name of `Eyeballs`. You can define multiple variables at once, just by separating them with a comma, as the following example shows:

```
DIM Eyeballs, Bullets, Logs
```

The preceding command tells your computer to create three variables by the names of `Eyeballs`, `Bullets`, and `Logs`.

Now if you rewrite the preceding Lizzie Borden program and declare all variables at the start of the program, you can easily identify and count all variables that the program uses. As you can see in the following revised version, written in QBASIC (another BASIC dialect similar to Liberty BASIC), this program declares variables ahead of time so that you can easily count and identify all the variables that the program uses:

```
DIM Parents, Whacks, MotherAxWhacks, FatherAxWhacks
DIM FirstName$, LastName$, FullName$
Parents = 2
Whacks = 20
MotherAxWhacks = Parents * Whacks
FatherAxWhacks = MotherAxWhacks + 1
FirstName$ = "Lizzie"
LastName$ = " Borden"
FullName$ = FirstName$ + LastName$
PRINT FullName$ + " had an ax, gave her mother ";
          MotherAxWhacks;
PRINT " whacks. When she saw what she had done, gave her";
PRINT " father "; FatherAxWhacks
END
```

In this example, you can quickly see that this program uses three variables to hold strings (`FirstName$`, `LastName$`, and `FullName$`) in addition to four variables to hold values (`Parents`, `Whacks`, `MotherAxWhacks`, `FatherAxWhacks`).

TECHNICAL STUFF

An equivalent Java program

Java closely resembles C/C++, so if you know C/C++, you should little trouble learning Java. Just to give you some exposure to what a Java program looks like, study the following program to get a better idea how another programming language accomplishes the same task as the QBASIC program in the accompanying text:

```
public class TrivialApplication
   {
 public static void main(String
   args[]) {
 int parents, whacks, mother-
   axwhacks, fatheraxwhacks;
 String firstname, lastname,
   fullname;
 parents = 2;
 whacks = 20;
 motheraxwhacks = parents *
   whacks;
 fatheraxwhacks = mother-
   axwhacks + 1;
 firstname = "Lizzie";
 lastname = " Borden";
 fullname = firstname + last-
   name;
 System.out.println(fullname +
   " had an ax, gave her
   mother " + motheraxwhacks);
 System.out.println("whacks.
   When she saw what she had
   done, gave her");
 System.out.println(" father "
   + fatheraxwhacks);
 }
}
```

If you run this Java program, it behaves just as the QBASIC version does.

Defining the type of data that variables can hold

In addition to enabling you to create and name your variables at the beginning of a program, most programming languages (but not Liberty BASIC) also force you to define the type of data that each variable can hold. Defining your data types serves the following two purposes:

✔ It identifies the type of data that each variable can hold. If you clearly identify what type of data a variable can hold, you (or another programmer) can better understand where a program may store data and what type of data it can store in each specific variable.

✔ It prevents bugs by keeping variables from storing the wrong types of data by mistake.

Just so that you can see how other programming languages declare variables and the data types that they can hold, the following example shows how the C programming language declares a variable by the name of IQ to hold an integer value:

```
main ()
{
   int IQ
}
```

In the Pascal programming language, that same variable declaration may look as follows:

```
Program Main;
Var
   IQ : integer;
End.
```

And in certain BASIC dialects, such as Visual Basic, that same variable declaration looks like the following example:

```
DIM IQ AS INTEGER
```

Declaring variables isn't just for the convenience of the computer; it's for the convenience of the programmer who must read, understand, and modify a program later.

Using Constants

The value stored in a variable can be changed while the program's running; that's why they're called *variables* (because their values can vary). Sometimes, however, you may want to use a fixed value throughout your program. Look, for example, at the following program. Can you figure out what the number .1975 stands for?

```
Balance = 43090
OurProfit = Balance * .1975
Balance = Balance + OurProfit
PRINT "Pay this amount, or we'll get you = "; Balance
PRINT "Today's current loan sharking interest rate = "; .1975
END
```

A quick glance at the preceding program shows that the meaning of the number .1975 isn't obvious. Because the meaning of numbers isn't always clear without additional explanation, programmers use *constants*. By using a constant, you can use a descriptive name to represent a fixed value.

Liberty BASIC supports an older version of the BASIC programming language that doesn't support constants. However, other versions of BASIC (such as Visual Basic and most other programming languages) do support constants.

To see how constants work, study the following program written in the Pascal programming language:

```
Program UnderstandingConstants;
Const
   InterestRate = 0.1975;
Var
   OurProfit : real;
   Balance : real;
Begin
   Balance := 43090;
   OurProfit := Balance * InterestRate;
   Balance := Balance + OurProfit;
   Writeln ('Pay this amount or we'll get you! = ',
            Balance:6:2);
   Writeln ('Today's current loan sharking interest rate = ',
            InterestRate:1:4);
End.
```

If you run this program, you'll see the following output:

```
Pay this amount or we'll get you = 51600.28
Today's current loan sharking rate = 0.1975
```

As you can see in the above program, the value of 0.1975 is used twice in the program (on lines 9 and 12). If the interest rate changed from 0.1975 to 0.2486 and your program did not use constants, you would have to exhaustively search through your entire program and change every line that uses the value of 0.1975 to 0.2486. For short programs like the above program, this is tolerable. In huge programs, however, this would be time-consuming and error-prone.

So to save time and ensure accuracy, programmers use constants. By using constants in the above Pascal programming example, you only need to change the value of the constant InterestRate (in line 3) from 0.1975 to 0.2486. The computer automatically inserts this new value in lines 9 and 12, which also contain the constant InterestRate.

Constants have the following two key advantages:

✔ They identify numeric or string values with a descriptive name.

✔ Changing the value of a constant automatically modifies your entire program quickly and accurately.

Commenting Your Code

If you write a small program, anyone can readily understand how it works by following it line-by-line. But if you write a large program, understanding what the program does can prove difficult for others (and even for you) without spending a long time studying each line.

To make understanding (and ultimately maintaining) a program easier (because programmers are a notoriously lazy bunch), every programming language enables you to insert comments into your source code. Comments enable you to store directly in your source code explanations to identify the following information:

✔ Who wrote the program

✔ The creation and last modification dates of the program

✔ What the program does

✔ How the program works

✔ Where the program gets, saves, and outputs data

✔ Any known problems with the program

In Liberty BASIC, you can add comments in one of the following two ways:

✔ By using the REM (short for *REMark*) statement.

✔ By using the apostrophe (').

The following program shows how to use both the REM statement and the apostrophe to insert comments into a program. Although you can use both types of comments in a single program, you want to use only one or the other for consistency's sake.

```
' Created on March 29, 2005
' Written by John Doe
' This program displays a not-so-subtle
' message to potential copycats to
```

```
' come up with their own ideas rather
' than steal mine.
REM This program does nothing more than
REM print a message on-screen to
REM insult any potential authors browsing
REM through this book in hopes of stealing
REM ideas to use in a competing book.
NOMAINWIN ' Keeps the main window from appearing
NOTICE "Don't steal ideas from this book!"
END ' This last line ends the program
```

Because comments are for the benefit of humans only, the computer looks at the preceding Liberty BASIC program as follows:

```
NOMAINWIN
NOTICE "Don't steal ideas from this book!"
END
```

The apostrophe is more versatile than the REM statement for making a comment because the apostrophe can create a comment that appears as a separate line or as part of an existing line. The REM statement can create only a comment that appears on a separate line.

Comments exist solely for your benefit. The computer completely ignores any comments that you insert in a program. So make your comments useful but not too wordy; otherwise, they become more of a nuisance than an aid.

Comments can prove valuable for telling Liberty BASIC to temporarily ignore one or more lines of code. Rather than delete an entire line, test to see whether the program works, and then retype the previously deleted line; for example, you can just comment out the line, as follows:

```
NOMAINWIN
' A = SQR((B * B) + (C + C))
END
```

If you run this program, Liberty BASIC sees only the following:

```
NOMAINWIN
END
```

To restore the commented line, just remove the apostrophe so that Liberty BASIC sees the program as follows:

```
NOMAINWIN
A = SQR((B * B) + (C + C))
END
```

Chapter 8

Crunching Numbers and Playing with Strings

. . . .

In This Chapter

▶ Performing mathematical operations

▶ Using Liberty BASIC's built-in math functions

▶ Pulling strings with your data

▶ Converting strings into numbers

. . . .

*O*ne of the most important parts of a computer program is its capability to manipulate any data that it receives and to spit out a useful answer that people are willing to pay for (so that you can make money). The two types of data that your program must manipulate are *numbers* and *words* (known as *strings* by the programming community).

Some common number-manipulating programs include spreadsheets, accounting programs, and even video games (because they need to calculate the correct way to display jet fighters or dragons popping on-screen to enable you to mow them down with a machine gun). Common string-manipulating programs include databases (which store, sort, and rearrange such data as names), word processors, and foreign-language translation programs.

Adding, Subtracting, Dividing, and Multiplying

The four basic ways to manipulate numbers are adding, subtracting, dividing, and multiplying. By using these four mathematical operations, you can create any type of complicated mathematical formula.

To add, subtract, divide, or multiply two numbers (or two variables that represent numbers), you use the symbols shown in Table 8-1.

Table 8-1	Mathematical Operators		
Mathematical Operation	*Symbol to Use*	*Example*	*Result*
Addition	+	2 + 5	7
Subtraction	–	77 – 43	34
Division	/ (forward slash)	20 / 4	5
Multiplication	*	4 * 7	28
Exponentiation	^	2 ^ 3	8

The division symbol (/) usually appears in two places on your keyboard: on the same key as the question mark (?) and on the numeric keypad. The exponentiation symbol (^) appears on the 6 key. You can also use the subtraction symbol (–) to indicate negative numbers, such as –34.5 or –90.

Although you already understand how addition, subtraction, division, and multiplication work, you may be less familiar with exponentiation.

Exponentiation simply multiplies one number by itself several times. The formula 4 ^ 3, for example, tells Liberty BASIC take the number 4 and multiply it by itself three times. So 4 ^ 3 really means 4 * 4 * 4, or 64.

Using variables

Any mathematical calculation (addition, subtraction, division, or multiplication) creates a single value, which you can store in a variable as follows:

```
TaxYouOwe = 12500 * 1.01
```

Rather than use specific numbers to create mathematical formulas (such as 12,500 * 1.01), however, you can substitute variables in the following way:

```
PROMPT "How much money did you make last year"; NetIncome
TaxYouOwe = NetIncome * 1.01
NOTICE "You owe this much in taxes = "; TaxYouOwe
END
```

To make your mathematical calculations easier to understand, always use variables or constants rather than actual numbers. In the preceding example, you can't tell what the number 1.01 represents. Rather than use an actual number, substitute a descriptive constant in the formula, as follows:

```
TaxRate = 1.01
PROMPT "How much money did you make last year"; NetIncome
TaxYouOwe = NetIncome * TaxRate
NOTICE "You owe this much in taxes = "; TaxYouOwe
END
```

If you use a constant (in this case, making `TaxRate` represent the number 1.01), you can quickly understand what the number 1.01 means and why to use it in the mathematical formula.

You can use variables in the following two ways in mathematical formulas:

✔ To represent numbers that the mathematical formula uses

✔ To store the value that the mathematical formula calculates

Be careful when naming variables. If you mistype a variable name or mix uppercase with lowercase letters, Liberty BASIC assumes that you're creating a new variable, and it assigns a value of zero or a blank to the "new" variable. If your program isn't working right, check to make sure that you spelled the variables correctly and used exactly the same upper- and lowercase letters.

Working with precedence

Simple formulas such as `NetIncome * TaxRate` are easy to understand; you just multiply the values that both variables represent. You can create more powerful mathematical formulas, however, by combining addition, subtraction, division, or multiplication, as in the following example:

```
TaxYouOwe = PastTaxes + NetIncome * TaxRate
```

If the value of `NetIncome` is 50,000, the value of `TaxRate` is 1.01, and the value of `PastTaxes` is 2,500, the computer looks at the formula as follows:

```
TaxYouOwe = 2500 + 50000 * 1.01
```

So now the question is whether Liberty BASIC adds 2,500 to 50,000 and then multiplies the whole thing by 1.01 (in which case the answer is 53,025) or multiplies 50,000 by 1.01 first and then adds 2,500 (in which case the answer is 53,000).

Because the result of combining addition, subtraction, division, and multiplication in a single formula can confuse the living daylights out of people, programming languages create something mysterious known as *precedence* that tells the computer which mathematical operations to calculate first. Liberty BASIC calculates mathematical operators in the following order, from top (first) to bottom (last):

- Exponentiation (^)
- Multiplication (*) and (^); division (/)
- Addition (+) and subtraction (−)

Before running the following Liberty BASIC program, try to figure out how the computer calculates a result:

```
MyMoney = 3 + 4 ^ 5 - 8 / 5 * 7
PRINT MyMoney
END
```

This Liberty BASIC program tells the computer to do the following:

1. The first line tells the computer to create the variable `MyMoney`.

   Because the computer calculates exponential values first, Liberty BASIC calculates the value of 4 ^ 5, which is 1,024. The formula now looks as follows:

   ```
   MyMoney = 3 + 1024 - 8 / 5 * 7
   ```

   Next, the computer calculates all multiplication and division (/). Because multiplication and division have equal precedence, the computer starts calculating with the first multiplication or division (/) operator that it finds, moving from left to right. The computer calculates the value of 8 / 5 first (1.6) and then multiplies it by 7. So the formula now looks as follows:

   ```
   MyMoney = 3 + 1024 - 11.2
   ```

   Finally, the computer calculates all addition and subtraction, moving from left to right. First it calculates the value of 3 + 1,024 (which is 1,027); it then subtracts 11.2 from it. Thus the final answer looks as follows:

   ```
   MyMoney = 1015.8
   ```

2. The second line tells the computer to print the value that the `MyMoney` variable stores, which is `1015.8`.

3. The third line tells the computer that the program is at an end.

The computer always calculates operators from left to right if operators are equal in precedence, such as multiplication and division or addition and subtraction.

Using parentheses

Trying to remember the precedence of different mathematical operators can prove confusing. Even worse is that the ordinary precedence of mathematical operators can mess up the way that you want the computer to calculate a result. Suppose, for example, that you type the following:

```
BigValue = 3 + 4 ^ 5
PRINT BigValue
END
```

With this program, the computer first calculates the exponential value of 4 ^ 5 (which is 1,024), and then it adds 3 to it, for a total of 1,027.

But what if you really want the computer to add 3 to 4 and then perform the exponential? In this case, you must use parentheses to tell the computer, "Hey, add 3 to 4 first and then calculate the exponential," as in the following example:

```
BigValue = (3 + 4) ^ 5
PRINT BigValue
END
```

This program adds 3 and 4 to get 7, so the formula becomes BigValue = 7 ^ 5, or 16,807.

Anytime that the computer sees something trapped within parentheses, it calculates those values first. Then it uses its normal rules of precedence to figure out how to calculate the rest of the formula.

Use parentheses to enclose only one mathematical operator at a time, such as (3 + 4). Although you can use parentheses to enclose multiple mathematical operators, such as (3 + 4 ^ 5), doing so essentially defeats the purpose of using parentheses to make clear what the computer is to calculate first. You can, of course, use multiple parentheses to create fairly complex formulas, such as in the following formula:

```
EasyTaxCode = ((3 + 4) ^ 5 / 3 - 8) / 5 * -7
```

(Without the parentheses in the preceding formula, Liberty BASIC calculates an entirely different result.)

Using Liberty BASIC's Built-In Math Functions

By combining mathematical operators, you can create practically any type of mathematical formula. But creating some mathematical formulas may prove too cumbersome, so as a shortcut, Liberty BASIC (and many other programming languages) provides built-in mathematical functions that you can use, as shown in Table 8-2.

Table 8-2	Liberty BASIC's Built-in Mathematical Functions
Function	*What It Does*
ABS (x)	Returns the absolute value of x
ACS (x)	Returns the arccosine of x
ASN (x)	Returns the arcsine of x
ATN (x)	Returns the arctangent of x
COS (x)	Returns the cosine of x
EXP (x)	Returns a number raised to a specified power (x)
INT (x)	Returns the largest integer less than or equal to a specific number or expression
LOG (x)	Returns the natural logarithm of x (Note: The value of x must be a positive, nonzero number.)
SIN (x)	Returns the sine of x
SQR (x)	Returns the square root of x
TAN (x)	Returns the tangent of x

If you don't understand terms like arcsine or logarithm, you probably don't need to use them anyway. The important point to remember is that all programming languages, such as Liberty BASIC, include built-in mathematical functions that you can use if you need them.

The preceding equation calculates the square root of nine (9), which is three (3).

To see how the Liberty BASIC mathematical functions work, run the following program and type different numbers (negative, positive, decimal, and so on) between 0 and 1.0 to see how the program works:

```
PROMPT "Type in a number"; AnyNumber
PRINT "The ABS value = "; ABS(AnyNumber)
PRINT "The ACS value = "; ACS(AnyNumber)
PRINT "The ASN value = "; ASN(AnyNumber)
PRINT "The ATN value = "; ATN(AnyNumber)
PRINT "The COS value = "; COS(AnyNumber)
PRINT "The EXP value = "; EXP(AnyNumber)
PRINT "The INT value = "; INT(AnyNumber)
PRINT "The LOG value = "; LOG(ABS(AnyNumber))
PRINT "The SIN value = "; SIN(AnyNumber)
PRINT "The SQR value = "; SQR(AnyNumber)
PRINT "The TAN value = "; TAN(AnyNumber)
PRINT
END
```

You can use only positive numbers with the LOG function or in calculating a square root.

The arcsine and arccosine functions can accept only a number between 0 and 1.0. If you choose a higher or lower number, neither function works, and Liberty BASIC displays an error message.

Manipulating Strings

Besides manipulating numbers, computers can also manipulate strings. A string is anything that you can type from the keyboard, including letters, symbols (such as #, &, and +), and numbers.

In Liberty BASIC, a string is anything that appears inside quotation marks, as in the following example:

```
PRINT "Everything enclosed in quotation marks"
PRINT "is a string, including the numbers below:"
PRINT "72 = 9 * 8"
PRINT "You can even mix letters and numbers like this:"
PRINT "I made $4,500 last month and still feel broke."
END
```

In the preceding program, the formula 72 = 9 * 8 is actually a string, even though it consists of numbers. That's because Liberty BASIC treats anything inside quotation marks as a string, including any numbers inside of quotation marks.

TECHNICAL STUFF

How C/C++ handles strings

Unlike BASIC (and many other languages such as Pascal and Java), the C/C++ language doesn't use a string data type. Instead, C/C++ programs use a more primitive data type known as a *character* (abbreviated `char`).

A character data type can hold only one character (such as a letter, symbol, or number), so to manipulate strings, C/C++ programs must use an *array* of characters. (Don't worry. Read more about arrays in Chapter 16. The important thing right now is to realize that C/C++ programs must handle strings differently from BASIC.)

Just to give you an idea of how C/C++ programs handle strings, look at the following program. In this example, this C program defines the variable `myrelative` and defines it as an array that can hold 10 characters:

```
main ()
{
 char myrelative[10];
 printf ("Type the name of a
    male relative you
    hate.\n");
 scanf ("%s", &myrelative);
 printf ("%s", myrelative);
 printf (" says he doesn't like
    you either!");
}
```

Declaring variables as strings

As with numbers, you can use strings directly in your program, as follows:

```
PRINT "Print me."
PRINT 54
END
```

Just as with numbers, you may want to store strings in variables so you can reuse that particular string over and over again by typing just the variable rather than the entire string. That way, your program can receive a string, store the string in a variable, and then manipulate the string to create a useful result, such as displaying a message to the user on-screen.

As you create a variable, you must tell Liberty BASIC, "Hey, I want this variable to hold only strings!" In technical terms, you're declaring a string as a *string data type*. To create a variable to hold a string, Liberty BASIC enables you to create a variable and add the dollar sign ($) to the end of the variable name, as in the following example:

```
StringVariable$ = "This variable can hold only strings."
```

If you fail to declare a variable as a string data type, but you still try to stuff a string into the variable, Liberty BASIC displays an error message and prevents your program from running. By ensuring that you store the correct data in variables, compilers such as Liberty BASIC try to make sure that you write programs that won't have any unexpected bugs.

Smashing strings together

Unlike with numbers, you can't subtract, divide, or multiply strings. But you can add strings (which is technically known as *concatenating strings*). To concatenate two strings, you use the plus sign (+) to essentially smash two strings into a single string, as the following example shows:

```
PROMPT "What is your name?"; MyName$
PRINT "Hello, " + MyName$ + ". Isn't it time to take"
PRINT "an early lunch from your job now?"
END
```

This Liberty BASIC program tells the computer to do the following:

1. The first line tells the computer to print the message `What is your name?` on-screen and then wait for the user to type something. Liberty BASIC stuffs whatever the user types into the string variable `MyName$`.

2. The second line tells the computer to create one big string that uses the string it's storing in the `MyName$` variable. If it's storing the name "Tasha" in the `MyName$` variable, the third line prints, `Hello, Tasha. Isn't it time to take`.

3. The third line prints, `an early lunch from your job now?`.

4. The fourth line tells the computer that the program is at an end.

If you concatenate strings, make sure that you leave a space between the two strings so that they don't appear smashed together (`likethis`). In the previous example, notice the space in the second line following the word `Hello` and the comma.

Playing with Liberty BASIC's String Functions

If just storing and concatenating strings were all that you could do, Liberty BASIC may seem pretty boring to you. That's why Liberty BASIC includes a bunch of built-in functions to give you all sorts of fun ways to manipulate strings.

Playing with UPPERCASE and lowercase

If strings consist of letters, they can appear in the following three ways:

- ✔ in all lowercase, like this
- ✔ IN ALL UPPERCASE, LIKE THIS (WHICH CAN LOOK ANNOYING AFTER A WHILE)
- ✔ As a mix of UPPERCASE and lowercase letters, Like This

To convert every character in a string to lowercase, you can use the special function LOWER$. To convert every character in a string to uppercase, you can use another function — UPPER$.

Both functions take a string and convert it to either uppercase or lowercase, as in the following example:

```
UPPER$("hello") ' HELLO
LOWER$("GOOD-BYE") ' good-bye
```

Run the following program to see how these two functions work:

```
PROMPT "What would you like to convert"; ThisString$
PRINT "This is what happens when you use LOWER$:"
PRINT LOWER$(ThisString$)
PRINT
PRINT "This is what happens when you use UPPER$:"
PRINT UPPER$(ThisString$)
END
```

If you run this program and type in the string I Don't Like Anyone Who Copies My Work, the program displays the following:

```
This is what happens when you use LOWER$:
i don't like anyone who copies my work

This is what happens when you use UPPER$:
I DON'T LIKE ANYONE WHO COPIES MY WORK
```

Both the LOWER$ and UPPER$ functions work only with letters. They don't do anything with symbols (such as $, %, or @) or numbers.

Counting the length of a string

If you need to manipulate strings, you may want to know the actual length of a string. To count the number of characters in a string, you can use the LEN function, which looks as follows:

```
LEN("Greetings from Mars!")
```

In this example, the length of the string is 20 characters, including spaces and the exclamation point. Run the following program to see how the LEN function works:

```
PROMPT "Type a string:"; CountMe$
TotalLength = LEN(CountMe$)
PRINT "The total number of characters in your string is:"
PRINT TotalLength
END
```

So if you run this program and type in the string Beware of copycat publishers, you'll see the following:

```
The total number of characters in your string is:
28
```

In calculating the total length of a string, the LEN function removes any spaces before or after any visible characters, as shown in Table 8-3.

Table 8-3	How the LEN Function Counts Spaces in a String
String	*String Length*
" Hello!"	6 characters (eliminates the five spaces in front of the string)
"What are you looking at? "	24 characters (eliminates the five spaces at the end of the string)
"Boo! Go away!"	13 characters (counts the spaces between the words)

Trimming the front and back of a string

Because strings can have spaces before (known as *leading spaces*) or after (known as *trailing spaces*) any visible character, you may want to eliminate these leading or trailing spaces before counting the length of a string.

Fortunately, Liberty BASIC includes a special function to do just that, as the following example shows:

```
TRIM$(" Hello, there!") ' "Hello, there!"
TRIM$("Good-bye! ") ' "Good-bye"
```

To see how the TRIM$ function can strip away leading and trailing spaces, try the following program:

```
AString$ = " Hello, there!"
PRINT "The original length of the string = "; LEN(AString$)
TempString$ = TRIM$(AString$)
PRINT TempString$
PRINT "The new length is now = "; LEN (TempString$)
END
```

If you run this program, this is what you see:

```
The original length of the string = 14
Hello, there!
The new length is now = 13
```

Inserting spaces

Sometimes you may want to create spaces without pressing the spacebar multiple times to do so. For an easy way to create spaces, Liberty BASIC provides the SPACE$ function, which looks as follows:

```
SPACE$(X)
```

In this example, X represents the number of spaces that you want to insert. The SPACE$ function in the following program simply inserts five spaces between the string Hello and the string Bo the Cat.:

```
AString$ = "Bo the Cat."
PRINT "Hello" + SPACE$(5) + AString$
END
```

Yanking characters out of a string

If you have a long string, you may want only part of that string. You may have a string consisting of somebody's first and last name, for example, but you want only the last name. You can use one of the following Liberty BASIC functions to rip away one or more characters from a string:

- ✔ LEFT$ (string, X) rips away X number of characters starting from the left of the string.

- ✔ RIGHT$ (string, X) rips away X number of characters starting from the right of the string.

- ✔ MID$ (string, X, Y) rips away Y number of characters, starting at the Xth character from the left.

To see how these three functions work, run the following program and see what happens:

```
FakeName$ = "John Barkley Doe"
FirstName$ = LEFT$(FakeName$, 4)
PRINT "This is the first name = "; FirstName$
LastName$ = RIGHT$(FakeName$, 3)
PRINT "This is the last name = "; LastName$
MiddleName$ = MID$(FakeName$, 6, 7)
PRINT "This is the middle name = "; MiddleName$
END
```

This program does nothing more than strip out the first, last, and middle names from the longer string `John Barkley Doe`.

Looking for a string inside another string

If you have a long string, you may want to know the location of another word or phrase inside the longer string. Suppose, for example, that you had a string containing a list of names, as in the following example:

```
"John, Julia, Matt, Mike, Sam, Chris, Karen"
```

If you want to know in what position the name "Matt" appears in the preceding string, you can use the magical `INSTR` command, as follows:

```
Names$ = "John, Julia, Matt, Mike, Sam, Chris, Karen"
Position = INSTR(Names$, "Matt", 1)
PRINT "The name Matt is located in position = "; Position
END
```

This Liberty BASIC program tells the computer to do the following:

1. The first line creates the string variable `Names$` that stores the string `John, Julia, Matt, Mike, Sam, Chris, Karen`.

2. The second line tells the computer to set the value of the `Position` variable to the value that the `INSTR` function returns.

    The `INSTR` function tells the computer, "Starting at position 1, look at the string that the variable `Names$` represents and look for the string `Matt`." In this case, the string `Matt` appears in position 14 in the `Names$` string.

3. The third line prints `The name Matt is located in position = 14`.

4. The fourth line tells the computer that the program is at an end.

To use the INSTR function, you need to specify the following three items:

✔ The position where you want to start searching.

  In the preceding example, the position is 1, which represents the start of the string. You can, however, tell the computer to start looking from any position. If you tell the computer to start looking from position 20, it can never find the name "Matt" in the Names$ variable.

✔ The string that you want to search.

✔ The string that you want to locate.

Strings are case-sensitive, which means that, to the computer, the strings "MATT" and "Matt" are two completely different strings. In the following program, INSTR can't find the string "MATT" because it thinks the strings "MATT" and "Matt" aren't the same:

```
Names$ = "John, Julia, Matt, Mike, Sam, Chris, Karen"
Position = INSTR(Names$, "MATT", 1)
PRINT "The name Matt is located in position = "; Position
END
```

If the INSTR function can't find the string that you're looking for, the value of the INSTR function is zero.

Converting strings into numbers (and vice versa)

A string can consist of letters, symbols, and numbers. The most common use for storing numbers as a string is if the numbers represent something special, such as a telephone number or address. If you want the computer to print a telephone number, you must store that number as a string, as follows:

```
PRINT "555-1212"
```

This command prints the string 555-1212 on-screen. The quotation marks tell the computer, "Anything inside the quotation marks is a string." What happens if you try the following command?

```
PRINT 555-1212
```

Liberty BASIC interprets this command to mean, "Subtract the number 1,212 from the number 555 and print the result (which is –657) on-screen."

If you have a number but you want to treat it as a string, you can use Liberty BASIC's STR$ function, which works as follows:

```
STR$(Number)
```

The STR$ function tells Liberty BASIC, "Take a number (such as 45) and turn it into a string." If you have a number 34 and use the STR$ function, Liberty BASIC converts that number 34 into a string "34".

To print both a string and a number, for example, you normally need to use the PRINT command with a semicolon, as in the following example:

```
BossIQ = 12
PRINT "This is the IQ of your boss ="; BossIQ
END
```

You can, however, use the STR$ function to convert the BossIQ variable into a string, as follows:

```
BossIQ = 12
NewString$ = "This is the IQ of your boss = " + STR$(BossIQ)
PRINT NewString$
END
```

The main difference between the first example and the second example is that the number BossIQ is now part of the string NewString$.

Naturally, Liberty BASIC enables you to convert strings into numbers as well. If you have a string (such as "46"), you can't perform any mathematical operations on it. You can, however, convert that string into a number by using Liberty BASIC's VAL function, which works as follows:

```
VAL("String")
```

The VAL function tells Liberty BASIC, "Take a string (such as "45") and turn it into a number." If you have a string "45" and use the VAL function, Liberty BASIC converts that string "45" into the number 45.

If you use the VAL function on a string that doesn't represent a number, such as the string "Hello!", the VAL function returns a zero value.

To see how the VAL function works, run the following program:

```
YearBorn$ = "1964"
PROMPT "You were born in "; YearBorn$
Year = 2005 - VAL(YearBorn$)
NOTICE "In 2005, you were this old = "; Year
END
```

If you run this program, the program displays a Prompt dialog box that says, You were born in 1964. Then it displays a Notice dialog box that says, In 2005, you were this old = 35.

Chapter 9

Making Decisions with Control Statements

*T*he whole purpose of a program is to make the computer behave in a certain way. The most primitive programs act exactly the same way each time that you run them, such as displaying, "Hello, world!" or the name of your cat on-screen.

Such primitive programs may work fine for learning to program, but they're relatively useless otherwise, because most programs need to accept data and modify their behavior based on any data that they receive.

Many banks, for example, use a computer to analyze risks before they loan money. If you have an income over a certain amount and don't have a history of declaring bankruptcy every two years, the bank's computer may approve your loan before it approves a loan for someone who has no income or assets. In this case, the bank's computer program must accept data and decide what to do based on that data.

Each time that you feed the program different data, the program may spit out a different answer. To find out how to give your program the capability to make decisions, you must use something mysterious known as *control statements*.

Using Boolean Expressions

Whenever you make a decision, such as what to eat for dinner, you ask yourself a question such as, "Do I feel like eating a hamburger?" If the answer is yes, you go to a restaurant that serves hamburgers.

Computers work in a similar way. Although people can ask questions, computers check a *Boolean expression*. A Boolean expression is anything that represents one of two values, such as true/false or zero/nonzero.

Boolean expressions are part of Boolean algebra, which was named after a man by the name of George Boole. (If you study hard and create your own branch of mathematics, someone may name it after you, too.) The simplest Boolean expression is one that compares two values, as shown in Table 9-1.

Table 9-1	Evaluating Boolean Expressions	
Boolean Expression	*What It Means*	*Boolean Value*
4 < 54	4 is less than 54	True
4 > 54	4 is greater than 54	False
4 = 54	4 is equal to 54	False
4 <= 54	4 is less than or equal to 54	True
4 >= 54	4 is greater than or equal to 54	False
4 <> 54	4 is not equal to 54	True

Symbols such as <, >, =, <=, >=, and <> are known as *relational operators*.

Try running the following program to guess which sentence the program prints out:

```
IF (4 < 54) THEN
 PRINT "This prints out on-screen."
ELSE
 PRINT "Why did you pick this sentence?"
END IF
END
```

This BASIC program tells the computer to do the following:

1. The first line tells the computer to evaluate the Boolean expression (4 < 54). Because this is true, the computer can proceed to the second line.

2. The second line tells the computer to print the message, This prints out on-screen. Then the computer skips over the third and fourth lines to the fifth line of the program.

3. The third line tells the computer, "In case the Boolean expression (4 < 54) happens to prove false, proceed to the fourth line of the program."

4. The fourth line tells the computer to print the message, Why did you pick this sentence? Because the Boolean expression (4 < 54) is never false, the third and fourth lines never run.

5. The fifth line simply identifies the end of the IF THEN ELSE statement (which you find out more about in the section "IF THEN ELSE statements," later in this chapter).

6. The sixth line tells the computer that the program is at an end.

You can assign a variable to a Boolean expression in the following way:

```
Guilty = (4 < 54)
```

This example assigns the value of true to the variable Guilty. The preceding statement tells the computer, "The Boolean expression of (4 < 54) is true. Thus the value of the Guilty variable is true."

Liberty BASIC doesn't really know the difference between true and false. Because Liberty BASIC can't assign a true value to a Boolean expression, Liberty BASIC just assigns the number -1 to the Boolean expression, which represents the value true. If Liberty BASIC wants to assign a false value to a Boolean expression, it assigns the number 0 to the Boolean expression.

Try running the following program:

```
Guilty = (4 < 54)
IF Guilty THEN
  PRINT "Slap him on the wrist and let him go."
ELSE
  PRINT "This sentence never prints out."
END IF
END
```

Each time that you run the preceding program, it prints only the message, "Slap him on the wrist and let him go."

Using variables in Boolean expressions

The sample program in the preceding section uses a Boolean expression (4 < 54) that's fairly useless because it's always true. Every time that you run the program, it just prints out the message, "Slap him on the wrist and let him go."

For greater flexibility, Boolean expressions usually compare two variables or one variable to a fixed value, as in the following examples:

```
(MyIQ < AnotherIQ)
(Taxes < 100000)
```

The value of the first Boolean expression (MyIQ < AnotherIQ) depends on the value of the two variables MyIQ and AnotherIQ. Run the following program to see how it follows a different set of instructions, depending on the value of the MyIQ and AnotherIQ variables:

```
PROMPT "What is your IQ"; MyIQ
PROMPT "What is the IQ of another person"; AnotherIQ
IF (MyIQ > AnotherIQ) THEN
 PRINT "I'm smarter than you are."
ELSE
 PRINT "You have a higher IQ to make up for your lack of
          common sense."
END IF
END
```

If you run this program and type different values for MyIQ and AnotherIQ, the program behaves in two possible ways, printing on-screen either I'm smarter than you are. or You have a higher IQ to make up for your lack of common sense.

If you use variables in Boolean expressions, you give the computer more flexibility in making decisions on its own.

Using Boolean operators

Examining a single Boolean expression at a time can prove a bit cumbersome, as the following example shows:

```
PROMPT "How much money did you make"; Salary
PROMPT "How much money did you donate to political
          candidates"; Bribes
IF (Salary > 500) THEN
 IF (Bribes > 700) THEN
   PRINT "You don't need to pay any taxes."
 END IF
END IF
END
```

The only time that this program prints the message, You don't need to pay any taxes on-screen is if both Boolean expressions (Salary > 500) and (Bribes > 700) are true.

Rather than force the computer to evaluate Boolean expressions one at a time, you can get the computer to evaluate multiple Boolean expressions by using *Boolean operators*. A Boolean operator does nothing more than connect two or more Boolean expressions to represent a true or a false value.

Every programming language uses the following four Boolean operators:

✔ AND

✔ OR

✔ XOR

✔ NOT

The AND operator

The AND operator links two Boolean expressions. You can, for example, rewrite the program in the preceding section as follows by using the Boolean operator AND:

```
PROMPT "How much money did you make"; Salary
PROMPT "How much money did you donate to political
        candidates"; Bribes
IF (Salary > 500) AND (Bribes > 700) THEN
 PRINT "You don't need to pay any taxes."
END IF
END
```

In this case, the program prints out the message, You don't need to pay any taxes only if both (Salary > 500) is true and (Bribes > 700) is true. If either Boolean expression is false, this program doesn't print anything.

Run the preceding program and use the values in Table 9-2 to see what happens.

Table 9-2   Different Values Determine How the AND Operator Works

Value of Salary	Value of Bribes	What the Program Does
100	100	Nothing
900	100	Nothing
100	900	Nothing
900	900	Prints the message

The AND operator can represent a true value only if both Boolean expressions that it connects also are true.

To show how the AND operator works, programmers like to draw something known as a *truth table,* which tells you whether two Boolean expressions that the AND operator connects represent a true or a false value. Table 9-3 is a truth table listing the values for the following two Boolean expressions:

```
(Boolean expression 1) AND (Boolean expression 2)
```

Table 9-3	**The Truth Table for the AND Operator**	
Value of *(Boolean Expression 1)*	*Value of* *(Boolean Expression 2)*	*Value of the Entire* *(Boolean Expression 1)* *AND (Boolean Expression 2)*
False	False	False
True	False	False
False	True	False
True	True	True

The OR operator

The OR operator links two Boolean expressions but produces a true value if either Boolean expression represents a true value. For an example of how this operator works, run the following program:

```
PROMPT "How far can you throw a football"; Football
PROMPT "What is your IQ"; IQ
IF (Football > 50) OR (IQ <= 45) THEN
  PRINT "You have what it takes to become a professional
           athlete!"
END IF
END
```

In this case, the program prints the message, You have what it takes to become a professional athlete! if either (Football > 50) is true or (IQ <= 45) is true. Only if both Boolean expressions are false does the program refuse to print anything.

Run the preceding program and use the values in Table 9-4 to see what happens.

Table 9-4 Different Values Determine How the OR Operator Works

Value of Football	Value of IQ	What the Program Does
5	70	Nothing
70	70	Prints the message
5	5	Prints the message
70	5	Prints the message

The OR operator can represent a false value only if both Boolean expressions that it connects are also false.

Table 9-5 is a truth table to show how the OR operator works for Boolean expressions such as the following examples:

```
(Boolean expression 1) OR (Boolean expression 2)
```

Table 9-5   The Truth Table for the OR Operator

Value of (Boolean Expression 1)	Value of (Boolean Expression 2)	Value of the Entire (Boolean Expression 1) OR (Boolean Expression 2)
False	False	False
True	False	True
False	True	True
True	True	True

The XOR operator

The XOR operator links two Boolean expressions but produces a true value only if one Boolean expression represents a true value and the other Boolean expression represents a false value. For an example of how this operator works, run the following program:

```
PROMPT "Is your spouse around (Type 1 for Yes or 0 for No)";
        SpouseHere
PROMPT "Is your best friend around (Type 1 for Yes or 0 for
        No)"; BestfriendHere
IF (SpouseHere = 0) XOR (BestfriendHere = 0) THEN
 PRINT "You won't be lonely tonight!"
END IF
END
```

The only two times that this program prints the message, You won't be lonely tonight! is if your spouse is around (SpouseHere = 1) but your best friend isn't (BestfriendHere = 0) or if your best friend is around (Bestfriendhere = 1) but your spouse isn't (SpouseHere = 0).

If your spouse is around (SpouseHere = 1) and your best friend is around (BestfriendHere = 1), nothing happens. Similarly, if your spouse is gone (SpouseHere = 0) and your best friend is gone (BestfriendHere = 0), nothing happens.

Run the preceding program and use the values in Table 9-6 to see what happens:

Table 9-6 Different Values Determine How the XOR Operator Works

Value of SpouseHere	Value of BestfriendHere	What the Program Does
0	0	Nothing
1	0	Prints the message
0	1	Prints the message
1	1	Nothing

The XOR operator can represent a false value only if both Boolean expressions that it connects are false or if both Boolean expressions are true.

Table 9-7 is the truth table to show how the XOR operator works for the following Boolean expressions:

```
(Boolean expression 1) XOR (Boolean expression 2)
```

Table 9-7 The Truth Table for the XOR Operator

Value of (Boolean Expression 1)	Value of (Boolean Expression 2)	Value of the Entire (Boolean Expression 1) XOR (Boolean Expression 2)
False	False	False
True	False	True
False	True	True
True	True	False

The NOT operator

The NOT operator affects a single Boolean expression. If the Boolean expression is true, the NOT operator makes it false. If the Boolean expression is false, the NOT operator makes it true. Essentially, the NOT operator converts a Boolean expression to its opposite value.

The following Boolean expression, for example, is true:

```
(4 < 54)
```

But this Boolean expression is false:

```
NOT(4 < 54)
```

If you want to assign a value of false to the Guilty variable, use the NOT operator as follows:

```
Guilty = NOT(4 < 54)
```

This statement tells the computer, "The Boolean expression of (4 < 54) is true. But the NOT operator turns a true value to false, so the value of the Guilty variable is false." To get a better idea how this works, run the following program:

```
Guilty = NOT(4 < 54) ' The value of Guilty is false
IF Guilty THEN
  PRINT "This sentence never prints out."
ELSE
  PRINT "The defendant is not guilty because he's rich."
END IF
END
```

Each time that you run the preceding program, it prints the message, The defendant is not guilty because he's rich.

Exploring IF THEN Statements

The most common way to control which instruction the computer follows next is to use the IF THEN statement. This statement checks whether or not a certain condition is true. If so, it tells the computer to follow one or more instructions.

The IF THEN statement looks as follows:

```
IF (Boolean expression) THEN
' Follow one or more instructions listed here
END IF
```

For an example of how this statement works, type and run the following program:

```
PROMPT "Do you eat cow lips? (Type Y for Yes or N for No)";
        Answer$
IF (Answer$ = "Y") THEN
  PRINT "I have a nice hot dog you might like then."
END IF
END
```

Only if you type **Y** (using uppercase) does the program print the message, I have a nice hot dog you might like then.

If you want the computer to follow exactly one instruction following an IF THEN statement (such as the PRINT instruction in the preceding example), you can shorten the IF THEN statement to the following:

```
PROMPT "Do you eat cow lips? (Type Y for Yes or N for No)";
        Answer$
IF (Answer$ = "Y") THEN PRINT "I have a nice hot dog you
        might like then."
END
```

If you want the computer to follow two or more instructions following an IF THEN statement, you must enclose them with the END IF line, as follows:

```
PROMPT "How many cats do you own"; Answer
IF (Answer >= 1) THEN
  PRINT "You have my sympathies."
  PRINT "Have you ever thought of getting"
  PRINT "your head examined real soon?"
END IF
END
```

IF THEN ELSE statements

The IF THEN statement tells the computer to follow one or more instructions only if a certain condition is true. If that condition is not true, the computer ignores all the instructions trapped inside the IF THEN statement.

The IF THEN ELSE statement is slightly different because it tells the computer to follow one set of instructions in case a condition is true and a different set of instructions if the condition is false. The IF THEN ELSE statement looks as follows:

```
IF (Boolean expression) THEN
  ' Follow one or more instructions listed here
ELSE
  ' If the condition is false, then follow these
  ' instructions instead
END IF
```

For an example of how this statement works, run the following program and see what happens:

```
PROMPT "How long were you in medical school"; Answer
IF (Answer > 4) THEN
  PRINT "Congratulations! You should be able to"
  PRINT "play a good game of golf in no time."
ELSE
  PRINT "You may not have been in medical school for"
  PRINT "very long, but at least you should know"
  PRINT "how to put on a white lab coat."
END IF
END
```

Unlike the IF THEN statement, the IF THEN ELSE statement always forces the computer to follow one set of instructions no matter what. In this program, if the answer is greater than four, the computer prints out, Congratulations! You should be able to play a good game of golf in no time.

If the answer isn't greater than four, the computer prints out, You may not have been in medical school for very long, but at least you should know how to put on a white lab coat.

The IF THEN ELSE statement always makes the computer follow one set of instructions. If you use the ordinary IF THEN statement, the computer may or may not follow one set of instructions.

Working with SELECT CASE Statements

Listing multiple conditions in an IF THEN ELSE statements can prove tedious and messy, as the following example shows:

```
PROMPT "How old are you"; Answer
IF (Answer = 21) THEN
 PRINT "Congratulations! You may be able to rent a"
 PRINT "car in some states."
END IF

IF (Answer = 20) THEN
 PRINT "You can't rent a car, but you're pre-approved"
 PRINT "for 20 different credit cards."
END IF

IF (Answer = 19) THEN
 PRINT "You're still officially a teenager."
END IF

IF (Answer = 18) THEN
 PRINT "You're old enough to join the military and"
 PRINT "fire an automatic rifle, but you still can't"
 PRINT "buy beer legally. Figure that one out."
END IF

IF (Answer = 17) THEN
 PRINT "You can see R-rated movies on"
 PRINT "your own (but you've probably done that for years)."
END IF
END
```

As an alternative to multiple `IF THEN ELSE` statements, many programming languages offer a `SELECT CASE` statement, which looks as follows:

```
SELECT CASE Variable
CASE Value1
 ' Follow these instructions if the Variable = Value1
CASE Value2
 ' Follow these instructions if the Variable = Value2
END SELECT
```

The `SELECT CASE` statement provides different instructions depending on the value of a particular variable. If you rewrite the preceding `IF THEN ELSE` statement, the program looks as follows:

```
PROMPT "How old are you"; Answer
SELECT CASE Answer
CASE 21
 PRINT "Congratulations! You may be able to rent a"
 PRINT "car in some states."
CASE 20
 PRINT "You can't rent a car, but you're pre-approved
 PRINT "for 20 different credit cards."
```

```
CASE 19
  PRINT "You're still officially a teenager."
CASE 18
  PRINT "You're old enough to join the military and"
  PRINT "fire an automatic rifle, but you still can't"
  PRINT "buy beer legally. Figure that one out."
CASE 17
  PRINT "You can see R-rated movies on"
  PRINT "your own (but you've probably done that for years)."
END SELECT
END
```

If the user types **21**, the program prints, `Congratulations! You may be able to rent a car in some states.` If the user types **19**, the program prints, `You're still officially a teenager.` If the user types **17**, the program prints, `You can see R-rated movies on your own (but you've probably done that for years).`

Of course, if the user types any value that the `SELECT CASE` statement doesn't list, such as **22** or **16**, the `SELECT CASE` statement doesn't run any of the instructions within its structure.

To make sure that the computer follows at least one set of instructions in a `SELECT CASE` statement, just add a `CASE ELSE` command at the very end, as follows:

```
PROMPT "How old are you"; Answer
SELECT CASE Answer
CASE 21
  PRINT "Congratulations! You may be able to rent a"
  PRINT "car in some states."
CASE 20
  PRINT "You can't rent a car, but you're pre-approved"
  PRINT "for 20 different credit cards."
CASE 19
  PRINT "You're still officially a teenager."
CASE 18
  PRINT "You're old enough to join the military and"
  PRINT "fire an automatic rifle, but you still can't"
  PRINT "buy beer legally. Figure that one out."
CASE 17
  PRINT "You can see R-rated movies on"
  PRINT "your own (but you've probably done that for years)."
CASE ELSE
  PRINT "This sentence prints out if the user does NOT"
  PRINT "type numbers 17, 18, 19, 20, or 21."
END SELECT
END
```

If you run this program and type **21**, the program prints out `Congratulations!` `You may be able to rent a car in some states.` If the user types **20**, the program prints out, `You can't rent a car, but you're pre-` `approved for 20 different credit cards.` If the user types **19**, the program prints out, `You're still officially a teenager.` If the user types **18**, the program prints out, `You're old enough to join the military and fire an automatic rifle, but you still can't buy beer legally. Figure that one out.` If the user types **17**, the program prints out, `You can see R-rated movies on your own (but you've probably done that for years).` If the user types any other number (such as **54** or **97**, the program prints out, `This sentence prints out if the user does NOT type numbers 17, 18, 19, 20, or 21.`

Checking a range of values

You often use the `SELECT CASE` statement to check whether a variable happens to exactly match a specific value, such as the number 21 or the string `"yes"`. But sometimes you may want to run a set of instructions if a variable falls within a range of values, such as any number between 3 and 18. In that case, you must list all the possible values on a single CASE statement, as in the following example:

```
CASE 1, 2, 3, , 4
```

This checks whether a variable represents the number 1, 2, 3, or 4 as shown in the following program:

```
PROMPT "How many water balloons do you have? "; Answer
SELECT CASE Answer
CASE 1, 2, 3, 4
  NOTICE "You need more water balloons."
CASE 5, 6, 7, 8
  NOTICE "Now you need a target."
CASE ELSE
  NOTICE "What are you? A peace-loving hippie freak?"
END SELECT
END
```

In this example, if the user types a number from 1 to 4, the program prints, `You need more water balloons.` If the user types a number from 5 to 8, the program prints, `Now you need a target.` If the user types any number les than 1 or greater than 8, the program prints, `What are you? A peace-loving hippie freak?`

Make sure that you don't use the same value on two separate CASE statements, as happens in the following example:

```
PROMPT Type a number. "; Answer
SELECT CASE Answer
CASE 1, 2
  NOTICE "This always prints if you type a 2."
CASE 2, 3
  NOTICE "This never prints if you type a 2."
END SELECT
```

In the preceding SELECT CASE statement, the program prints This always prints if you type a 2 if the user types 2, but the program never prints the instructions under the second CASE statement (CASE 2, 3). That's because the first CASE statement runs first, preventing the second CASE statement from getting a chance to run at all.

Checking a relational operator

Sometimes, checking for an exact value or a range of values may still prove too limiting. You may, for example, compare a variable to another value by using one of those friendly symbols known as *relational operators*. A relational operator enables the SELECT CASE statement to determine whether a variable is greater than (>), less than (<), greater than or equal to (>=), less than or equal to (<=), or not equal to (<>) a specific value.

To use a relational operator, you must use a slightly different version of the CASE statement as shown in the following example:

```
INPUT "How many cats do you own"; Answer
SELECT CASE
CASE (Answer <= 5)
  PRINT "You need more cats."
CASE (Answer > 5)
  PRINT "Are you out of your mind?"
END SELECT
END
```

If the user types any number equal to or less than 5, the program prints, You need more cats. If the user types any number greater than 5, the program prints, Are you out of your mind?

TECHNICAL STUFF

Beware of the SELECT CASE statement in C/C++ and Java

In BASIC and many other programming languages such as Pascal, the SELECT CASE statement runs only one set of instructions the moment that it finds a match, such as printing You're still officially a teenager. in the Liberty BASIC example in the section, "Working with SELECT CASE Statements," earlier in this chapter, if the user types the number **19**.

C/C++ and Java programs, however, behave much differently. If you use these languages, you must specifically tell the computer to stop following instructions in a SELECT CASE statement (technically known as a switch statement in C/C++ and Java) by using the command break.

Consider, for example, the following C program:

```
#include <stdio.h>
main ()
{
  char akey;
  printf ("Type a lower case
    letter ");
  scanf(" ");
  scanf ("%c", &akey);
  switch (akey) {
  case 'a': printf ("You pressed
    the A key.\n");
  case 'b': printf ("You pressed
    the B key.\n");
  }
}
```

If you run this program and press the A key, this C program prints the following:

```
You pressed the A key.
You pressed the B key.
```

In C/C++ and Java, the computer follows every set of instructions in the switch statement from the first match that it finds to the end. To make sure that a C/C++ or Java program stops following any instructions in a switch statement, you must insert the break command as follows:

```
#include <stdio.h>
main ()
{
  char akey;
  printf ("Type a lower case
    letter ");
  scanf(" ");
  scanf ("%c", &akey);
  switch (akey) {
  case 'a': printf ("You pressed
    the A key.\n");
  break;
  case 'b': printf ("You pressed
    the B key.\n");
  }
}
```

If you eventually plan to program in C/C++ or Java, you need to remember this subtle difference or you may find your C/C++ or Java programs acting different from similar BASIC programs.

The two crucial differences when using relational operators in a SELECT-CASE statement is:

✔ The SELECT CASE variable (which is "Answer" in the above example), does not appear directly after the SELECT CASE command.

✔ The relational expression (such as "Answer <= 5") appears directly after each CASE statement.

Make sure that your relational operators don't overlap another part of the SELECT CASE statement, as happens in the following example:

```
SELECT CASE
CASE (Answer < 10)
 PRINT "This always prints."
CASE (Answer < 12)
 PRINT "This prints only if the user types 11."
END SELECT
```

In this SELECT CASE statement, the program prints This always prints if the user types any number less than 10, but the program prints the instructions under the second CASE statement (CASE IS < 12) only if the user types **11**. *or 10*

Chapter 10

Repeating Yourself with Loops

In This Chapter

▶ Looping with the `WHILE-WEND` commands

▶ Looping a fixed number of times with the `FOR-NEXT` loop

In general, programmers try to get the computer to do as much as possible so that they can do as little as possible. Ideally, you want to write the smallest programs possible, not only because small programs are easier to debug and modify, but also because smaller programs require less typing.

One way that programmers write as little as possible is by using programming structures known as *loops*. The idea behind a loop is to make the computer repeat one or more instructions. Consider, for example, the following program that prints the numbers 1 through 5 on-screen:

```
PRINT 1
PRINT 2
PRINT 3
PRINT 4
PRINT 5
END
```

If you want to expand this program to print out five million numbers, guess what? You must type five million instructions. Because you really don't want to type that many instructions, you can use loops to make the computer repeat the same instructions multiple times. The computer does the hard work. Consider the following, which in programming lingo is called a `FOR-NEXT` loop:

```
FOR I = 1 TO 5
   PRINT I
NEXT I
END
```

This program just prints out the following:

```
1
2
3
4
5
```

As you can see, when you use a loop, you can write shorter programs.

If you run this program, it does exactly the same thing as the first BASIC program. The loop version of this program, however, can print out five numbers or five million numbers (by changing the number 5 in the program to 5000000). Loops make the computer do more without forcing you to type additional instructions.

Although loops can help create shorter programs, the tradeoff is that loops are also harder to read and understand than a straightforward list of instructions. If you create a loop, make sure that you write a comment in the program to explain exactly what you expect the loop to do. (See Chapter 7 for more information about comments.)

A loop forces the computer to run the same instructions over and over, but eventually the computer needs to know when to stop. To tell the computer when to stop looping, you use a *condition* that represents either true or false.

In the world of mathematics and programming, anything that represents a true or false value is known as a *Boolean expression;* see Chapter 9. Some examples of Boolean expressions are 4 > 9.48 (which in Boolean arithmetic represents as a false value).

Using the WHILE-WEND Loop

Loops are handy for repeating one or more instructions. Of course, whenever you create a loop, you need to make the loop stop eventually.

One of the most common problems with loops is something known as an *endless loop*, which means that the computer follows a set of instructions but never stops. If a program gets caught in an endless loop, the program may appear to freeze on-screen. Usually, the only way to get out of an endless loop is to turn the computer off and then on again.

One way to make a loop eventually stop is to check if a certain condition is true. To do this in Liberty BASIC, you can create a special loop called a WHILE-WEND loop that looks as follows:

```
WHILE (Boolean expression is true)
 ' One or more instructions
WEND
```

To repeat one or more instructions, you just sandwich them between the
WHILE and WEND commands, as shown in the following example:

```
I = 1
WHILE I < 5
 PRINT "The square of "; I; " is "; I * I
 I = I + 1
WEND
END
```

This program does the following:

1. The first line creates the variable I and sets its value to 1.

2. The second line tells the computer that a loop is starting and that the
   computer is to run the instructions between the WHILE and WEND commands as long as the Boolean expression I < 5 is true.

3. The third line tells the computer to print The square of 1 is 1 the
   first time that the WHILE-WEND loops runs and The square of 2 is 4
   the second time that the WHILE-WEND loop runs, and so on.

4. The fourth line tells the computer to add one to the value of the variable
   I, so now I represents the number 1 + 1, or 2.

5. The fifth line tells the computer to check whether the Boolean expression I < 5 is true. If it's true, the program skips to the sixth line. If it's
   not true (if I represents the number 1, 2, 3, or 4), the program returns to
   the top of the loop on the second line. The computer repeats the loop
   four times to print out the following:

```
The square of 1 is 1
The square of 2 is 4
The square of 3 is 9
The square of 4 is 16
```

6. The sixth line tells the computer that the program is at an end.

*wrong
—where's
the proof
reader?*

Exiting a WHILE-WEND loop prematurely

Normally the only way to exit out of a WHILE-WEND loop is to wait until a certain condition becomes true. However, Liberty BASIC (like many other programming languages) also allows you to exit out of a loop prematurely using
the magic EXIT WHILE command as follows:

```
I = 1
WHILE I <= 10
  PRINT "This is I = "; I
  IF I = 5 THEN EXIT WHILE
  I = I + 1
WEND
END
```

Normally this WHILE-WEND loop would repeat ten (10) times but the IF I = 5 THEN EXIT WHILE command tells the program to stop after the program has looped only five (5) times.

The EXIT WHILE command can be useful to make sure a WHILE-WEND loop eventually stops running, but make sure that you don't exit out of a loop sooner than you really want to.

Endless loops #1: Failing to modify the Boolean expression inside the loop

One of the trickiest parts of using a loop is avoiding an endless loop. An *endless loop* occurs whenever the Boolean expression of a loop never changes to tell the computer to stop running the instructions inside the loop as in the following program:

```
I = 1
WHILE I < 5
 PRINT "This loop never ends."
WEND
END
```

This loop never stops because the value of I never changes. Thus the Boolean expression I < 5 always remains true, so the WHILE-WEND loop keeps running the instructions between the WHILE and WEND commands. In this case, the program just keeps printing, This loop never ends.

To fix this problem, you need to insert a command inside the WHILE-WEND loop that changes the variable in the Boolean expression such as inserting the command I = I + 1, as shown in the following example:

```
I = 1
WHILE I < 5
 PRINT "This loop eventually ends."
 I = I + 1
WEND
END
```

Endless loops are a common bug that keeps a program from working correctly. You can often recognize an endless loop if a program never responds to anything you try to do and you can't do anything except shut your computer off and start all over again.

Endless loops #2: Failing to initialize a Boolean expression outside the loop

Another variation of the endless loop occurs if you forget to define the value of a variable outside the WHILE-WEND loop, as in the following program:

```
WHILE I < 5
  I = 1
  PRINT "This loop never ends."
  I = I + 1
WEND
END
```

In this example, the value of variable I is always set to one (1) at the beginning of the WHILE-WEND loop and then gets incremented to two (2) at the end of the WHILE-WEND loop. But each time the WHILE-WEND loop runs, the value of I is reset to one (1) so the Boolean expression I < 5 always remains true, and thus the loop never ends.

The correct way to use the preceding WHILE-WEND loop is to place the statement I = 1 right in front of the WHILE-WEND loop, as in the following example:

```
I = 1
WHILE I < 5
  PRINT "This loop will eventually end."
  I = I + 1
WEND
END
```

In this example, the value of the I variable is set to one (1) before the computer runs the WHILE-WEND loop. Once inside the WHILE-WEND loop, the value of I steadily increases until the value of I is equal to 5, which makes the Boolean expression I < 5 false; therefore, the WHILE-WEND loop ends.

To avoid endless loops in your program, always remember the following two points:

✔ Initialize all variables that make up a Boolean expression right before a WHILE-WEND loop. This makes sure that your variable starts out with a value that you intended.

✔ Make sure that the variable of the Boolean expression changes inside the WHILE-WEND loop. This makes sure that your loop eventually ends.

Looping a Fixed Number of Times

A conditional loop, such as the WHILE-WEND loop, stops repeating itself only if a certain condition becomes true or false. So the number of times that a loop repeats can vary from one moment to the next.

Sometimes, however, you may need to loop a specific number of times. Although you can still use a conditional loop, you may prefer to use another type of loop known as the FOR-NEXT loop, which in Liberty BASIC looks as follows:

```
FOR counter = start TO end
 ' One or more instructions
NEXT
```

This loop tells the computer to repeat a fixed number of times the instructions between the FOR and NEXT commands. The start and end values determine the number of repeats. A typical FOR-NEXT loop looks as follows:

```
FOR I = 1 TO 10
 PRINT "The square of "; I; " is "; I * I
NEXT
END
```

If you run this program, here's what happens:

1. The first line creates the variable I and tells the computer to keep repeating the command 10 times.

2. The second line tells the computer to print The square of 1 is 1. Each time that this line runs, the value of I is different, so the final output from the program looks as follows:

```
The square of 1 is 1
The square of 2 is 4
The square of 3 is 9
The square of 4 is 16
The square of 5 is 25
The square of 6 is 36
The square of 7 is 49
The square of 8 is 64
The square of 9 is 81
The square of 10 is 100
```

3. The third line tells the computer to go back to the second line.

4. The fourth line tells the computer that the program is at an end.

more

If the start value is less than the end value, the `FOR-NEXT` loop doesn't run at all, as in the following example:

```
FOR counter = 8 TO 2
   ' This doesn't work at all
NEXT
```

Counting with different numbers

syntax

Most `FOR-NEXT` loops count from 1 to another fixed value, such as 10. The `FOR-NEXT`, however, loop can count from any number to any other number, as in the following example:

```
FOR I = 8 TO 14
   PRINT "The value of I ="; I
NEXT
END
```

This loop repeats seven times and prints the following:

```
The value of I = 8
The value of I = 9
The value of I = 10
The value of I = 11
The value of I = 12
The value of I = 13
The value of I = 14
```

You can also use negative numbers for the start and end values, as follows:

```
FOR counter = -5 TO 3
   ' One or more instructions
NEXT
```

Unless you have a good reason for choosing different numbers to start and end, a good idea is to always start at number 1. Using 1 as the starting point simply makes determining how many times the `FOR-NEXT` loop repeats easier for you or someone else.

Counting in increments

A `FOR-NEXT` loop counts by one. In the following example, the loop runs four times:

```
FOR counter = 1 TO 4
   ' One or more instructions
NEXT
```

If you like, you can use the following STEP command to make the FOR-NEXT loop count in any increments other than one:

```
FOR counter = 1 TO 4 STEP increment
 ' One or more instructions
NEXT
```

If, for example, you want to count by twos, you can use the following FOR-NEXT loop:

```
FOR I = 1 TO 8 STEP 2
  PRINT "The value of I = "; I
NEXT
```

If you run this program, the FOR-NEXT loop doesn't repeat eight times, but rather four times and prints this:

```
The value of I = 1
The value of I = 3
The value of I = 5
The value of I = 7
```

You can make a FOR-NEXT loop count backward by using a negative number for the increment value, which is the only time that you can have the start value greater than the end value, as shown in the following example:

```
FOR I = 6 TO -8 STEP -3
  PRINT "The value of I = "; I
NEXT
```

If you run this program, the FOR-NEXT loop repeats five times, printing the following results:

```
The value of I = 6
The value of I = 3
The value of I = 0
The value of I = -3
The value of I = -6
```

How the FOR-NEXT loop looks in a C program

Because many people eventually graduate to programming in C, here's a glimpse at how a FOR-NEXT loop looks in a C program:

```
main ()
{
  int counter;
  for (counter = 1; counter <=
    5; counter++) {
  printf ("The square of %d is
    %d\n", counter, counter *
    counter);
  }
}
```

This FOR-NEXT loop tells the computer, "Create an integer variable, counter, and set its value to 1 (counter = 1). Then keep incrementing the value of counter by 1 (counter++) until the Boolean expression (counter <= 5) becomes false. Then stop looping." (This FOR-NEXT loop repeats itself exactly five times.)

If the C version of the FOR-NEXT loop looks a bit cryptic, that's because it is. Now you know why learning the fundamentals of programming is much easier if you learn BASIC rather than C.

Exiting a FOR-NEXT loop prematurely

The FOR-NEXT loop repeats a fixed number of times. However, there may be times when you want to exit out of the FOR-NEXT prematurely. To do this, you can use the magic EXIT FOR command as follows:

```
FOR I = 1 to 10
  PRINT "This is I = "; I
  IF I = 5 THEN EXIT FOR
NEXT
END
```

Normally this FOR-NEXT loop would repeat ten (10) times but the IF I = 5 THEN EXIT FOR command tells the program to stop after the program has looped only five (5) times.

Part III

Advanced Programming with Liberty BASIC

The 5th Wave   By Rich Tennant

MARKETING MISSTEPS:
The Magic-Eye GUI

I don't see it.

It looks like File Manager to me.

I see the opening screen for DOOM.

I'm getting a headache.

In this part . . .

In this part you find all the fancy things you can do with Liberty BASIC — create graphics, make sounds, save data on a floppy disk or hard drive, create a real Windows user interface, and much more. After you understand these more advanced features of Liberty BASIC, you can create useful and interesting programs that rival the features that you find in commercial-quality software.

To maximize your programming skills, make sure that you type and run the many Liberty BASIC programs that sprinkled throughout each chapter. And keep your eyes open for all the different ways to write the same program in both Liberty BASIC and other languages such as C/C++, Pascal, or Java. The more that you use Liberty BASIC to help you master general programming principles now, the easier you can migrate to another language such as C/C++ later.

Chapter 11

Writing Large Programs by Using Subprograms

*P*rogramming is not so much a hard science as it is a creative art form. The ultimate goal of programming is to write the smallest possible program that uses the least amount of computer resources (memory, hard drive space, and so on) while accomplishing as much as possible.

Although some people are naturally talented at writing small, tight, fast code (to use the lingo of the programming community), most people need guidelines to help them write programs.

Small programs are easy to write and read. But if you're writing a large program that consists of several thousand lines of instructions, guess what? You'd better organize your program carefully from the start, or you may waste lots of time writing a large program that doesn't work.

Breaking the Bad Programming Habits of the Past

In the old days, people wrote programs without any advance planning, which is like trying to write a novel by sitting down at a word processor and typing continuously until you're done. You can possibly write a decent novel that way, but you're more likely to create an unreadable mess.

Similarly, programmers used to write programs by typing commands into the computer just to get something to work. After they had a simple program that worked, they started adding new instructions into the program.

Unfortunately, programmers often didn't add new instructions with any planning or organization. Some programmers added new instructions in the beginning of a program; others put new instructions at the end; and still others sprinkled new instructions throughout the program's existing instructions so that determining where the new instructions began and the old ones ended was nearly impossible.

One reason programmers used to write programs that were hard to read is because they could use a special programming command, the GOTO command. The GOTO command tells the computer to jump to another part of the program. GOTO LabelOne, for example, tells the computer to suddenly jump to the part of the program that LabelOne identifies.

The GOTO command encouraged programmers to write programs that told the computer to jump from one place in the program to another to find instructions. Programs that use the GOTO command are like a novel in which page 2 tells you to jump to page 349, page 349 tells you to jump to page 34, page 34 tells you to jump to page 125, and so on.

Because bouncing from one part of a program to another can prove as confusing as trying to untangle strands of spaghetti, writing programs in this manner became known as *spaghetti coding*.

Consider, for example, the following Liberty BASIC program:

```
GOTO [LabelOne]
[LabelFour]
 PROMPT "How much money do you have"; MyCash
 GOTO [LabelThree]
[LabelTwo]
 END
[LabelOne]
GOTO [LabelFour]
[LabelThree]
 PRINT "You owe me = "; MyCash * .95
 GOTO [LabelTwo]
```

Trying to figure out what this program does is confusing because the instructions are jumbled. But the following breakdown shows you how the program works:

1. The first line tells the computer to jump to the part of the program that the label [LabelOne] (which happens to be on the seventh line of the program) identifies.

2. The computer jumps to the seventh line in the program, which contains the label [LabelOne].

3. The eighth line in the program tells the computer to jump to the part of the program that the label [LabelFour] (which happens to be the second line of the program) identifies.

4. The computer jumps to the second line in the program, which contains the label [LabelFour].

5. The third line displays a Prompt dialog box that asks, How much money do you have? on-screen and waits for the user to type a number, which the program stores in the variable MyCash.

6. The fourth line tells the computer to jump to the part of the program that the label [LabelThree] (which happens to be the ninth line in the program) identifies.

7. The computer jumps to the ninth line in the program, which contains the label [LabelThree].

8. The tenth line prints, You owe me = and follows it with the value of MyCash multiplied by .95.

9. The eleventh line tells the computer to jump to the part of the program that the label [LabelTwo] (which happens to be the fifth line of the program) identifies.

10. The computer jumps to the fifth line of the program, which contains the label [LabelTwo].

11. The sixth line tells the computer that the program is at an end.

The preceding GOTO program is equivalent to the following simple program:

```
PROMPT "How much money do you have:"; MyCash
PRINT "You owe me ="; MyCash * .95
END
```

In the early days of computer programming, structures such as IF THEN and SELECT CASE statements didn't exist. (See Chapter 9 for more information about IF THEN statements.) For many years, the GOTO command was the only way programmers had to tell the computer to skip over certain instructions or follow a different set of instructions. Although you can still use the GOTO command, you should avoid using GOTO commands whenever possible.

Introducing Structured Programming

You never find one "right" way to write a program, but programmers have created different ways to write programs that are at least well organized. One popular way to write a program is known as *structured programming*, and its main idea is to organize your program by using only three types of instructions (none of which resembles the GOTO command). If you use only the following three instructions, you ensure that you and other people can easily read and understand your program:

- Sequential instructions
- Branching instructions
- Looping instructions

The following sections describe each of these types of instructions.

Sequential instructions

The simplest way to organize instructions in a program is to place them *sequentially*, or one after another, as in the following example:

```
PROMPT "How much stuff did you steal last year"; Amount
TaxesOwed = Amount * .95
PRINT "This is how much tax you owe ="; TaxesOwed
END
```

Unfortunately, you can't write every program as one big list of instructions. If the computer needs to make a decision, your program may need to choose between two or more different sets of instructions. Programs that must make a choice are said to *branch*.

Branching instructions

Branching instructions (such as the IF THEN statement) provide two or more different instructions for the computer to follow, based on a certain condition. (For more information about IF THEN statements and other types of branching statements, see Chapter 9.) The following program, for example, calculates two different taxes owed, depending on whether you're a politician:

```
PROMPT "How much stuff did you steal last year"; Amount
TaxesOwed = Amount * .95
PROMPT "Are you a professional criminal (Y or N)"; Answer$
IF (Answer$ = "N") THEN
  PRINT "This is how much tax you owe ="; TaxesOwed
ELSE
  PRINT "Lawyers and politicians don't need to pay taxes."
END
```

Branching instructions offer two or more alternative sets of instructions for the computer to follow. As a result, branching instructions are harder to read than instructions that you organize sequentially because you must determine which set of instructions the computer may follow at any given time.

Looping instructions

Sometimes the computer may need to repeat certain instructions. Rather than type the same instructions over and over, you can use a loop, such as a FOR-NEXT or a WHILE-WEND loop.

A FOR-NEXT loop repeats a fixed number of times. A WHILE-WEND loop repeats itself while a certain condition remains true. Thus the number of times that a WHILE-WEND loop repeats itself can range from zero to infinity. (See Chapter 10 for more information about looping.)

The following program, for example, asks for a password, checks to see whether the user types the correct password (which is the string "open"), and repeats these instructions until the user types the correct password:

```
PROMPT "What is the password"; Password$
WHILE Password$ <> "open"
  PRINT "Wrong password, moron. Try again."
  PROMPT "What is the password"; Password$
WEND
PRINT "You typed the correct password!"
END
```

Loops can prove harder to read than sequential instructions and branching instructions because you can't always tell how many times a loop repeats itself. Essentially, a loop is a shortcut so that you don't need to type a long series of sequential instructions in your program. (For more information about loops, see Chapter 10.)

Putting structured programming into practice

The reason for organizing your program in chunks of sequential, branching, and looping instructions is to make how your program works easier for others to understand. If they can understand how your program works, they can modify and improve on it later.

Just because you write a program, don't be so sure that you can understand it later. If you write a program consisting of several thousand lines of instructions, you're likely to forget how certain parts of the program work — especially if you put the program aside and work on another project for awhile. So writing programs that are easy to understand is crucial for your own benefit and for the benefit of any other programmer whose job is to fix or modify programs that you write.

To see how structured programming can make a program easier to read, look at the following program, which consists of sequential, branching, and looping instructions:

```
'Sequential instructions
PRINT "This program prints a message, of your"
PRINT "choosing, on the screen."
PROMPT "What message do you want to appear"; Message$
PROMPT "Display message in all UPPERCASE (type U) or
          lowercase (type l)?"; WhatCase$

'Branching instructions
IF WhatCase$ = "U" THEN
 Message$ = UPPER$(Message$)
END IF
IF WhatCase$ = "l" THEN
 Message$ = LOWER$(Message$)
END IF

'Looping instructions
FOR I = 1 TO 15
 PRINT SPACE$(I + 4); Message$
NEXT
END
```

Think of sequential, branching, or looping instructions as the building blocks of any program. If you write a program that uses only sequential, branching, and looping instructions, your program will be easier for you (or anyone else) to read and edit at a later date.

Writing Modular Programs

If you're really ambitious, you can write a large program as one huge list of instructions. The larger your program is, however, the harder reading, writing, and understanding the program become. Writing a large program as one set of instructions is like trying to build a house out of sand. Most likely, one part of the structure (such as a wall) is weaker than the rest of the structure and will eventually cause the whole thing to collapse.

Rather than create one huge program, programmers create a bunch of smaller programs and paste them together (sort of like using bricks to build a house). That way, if one part of the program doesn't work, you can unplug that portion, rewrite or replace it, and leave the rest of your program unaffected.

In the computer world, little programs that make up part of a larger program are known as *subprograms*. Subprograms are also known as *modules*, hence the term *modular programming*.

Every modular program contains at least one subprogram, known as the *main program*. The main program usually does nothing more than tell the computer which subprograms to use next to accomplish a specific task.

A subprogram typically solves a single task, such as multiplying two numbers or verifying that the user types a correct password. For really complicated programs, you may have several subprograms that themselves break down into several smaller subprograms.

Suppose, for example, that you want to write a program to break into another computer. The overall task is simply as follows:

Break into another computer.

Of course, you can't tell the computer just to break into another computer because it doesn't know how to do it. You must tell the computer, in specific detail, exactly how to do what you want it to do. This task means defining the overall goal of the program by using smaller tasks, as follows:

1. Find the phone number of the target computer.

2. Guess a password to access the system.

3. After gaining access, beep to notify the user.

Ideally, you can solve each task by using a separate subprogram that's completely independent of any other part of the program. After you get each subprogram to work correctly, you can paste all the subprograms together to create a larger working program.

Programmers use subprograms for the following two reasons:

- **To make writing large programs easier:** By writing a bunch of small programs that perform a specific task, you can paste together a bunch of subprograms to make a much larger program.

- **To store repetitive instructions in a single location:** Sometimes you need to run the same set of instructions over and over again. Rather than write these instructions each time that you need them, you can write them just once and store them in a subprogram that any other part of your program can run at any time.

The main advantage of breaking a large program into subprograms is so that you can easily modify a large program just by modifying one or more of its smaller subprograms. Because small programs are easier to understand and modify than large ones, subprograms can help make your program more reliable.

To create a subprogram in Liberty BASIC, you need to perform the following tasks:

- Write any subprogram instructions after the END command in your main program.

- Identify the start of your subprogram with a unique name, enclosing it in square brackets [like this].

- Identify the end of your subprogram by using the RETURN command, which tells the computer to return back to the part of the program that was running before the subprogram ran.

You can choose any name for your subprogram, but a good idea is to choose a descriptive name. If your subprogram prints a warning message to the user, for example, you may want to name your subprogram [warning].

The RETURN command identifies the end of your subprogram and tells the computer to return back to the main program.

So a typical subprogram may look as follows in Liberty BASIC:

```
Main program instructions
Main program instructions
END

[subprogram]
Subprogram instructions
Subprogram instructions
RETURN
```

At this point, the computer totally ignores your subprogram because the computer starts at the top, beginning with the first instruction, and follows each succeeding instruction until it reaches the END command, which tells the computer to stop running the program before it can reach any of the instructions that your subprogram stores.

So if you want the computer to run your subprogram instructions, you must use the GOSUB command, such as in the following line:

```
GOSUB [Subprogram name]
```

This command does nothing more than tell the program to jump to the subprogram that the label in brackets identifies. If you want your subprogram to run, you must insert a GOSUB command somewhere in your main program as follows:

```
Main program instructions1
GOSUB [subprogram]
Main program instructions2
END

[subprogram]
Subprogram instructions
Subprogram instructions
RETURN
```

In the above example, the Main program instructions1 run and then the GOSUB command starts the subprogram running. After the subprogram instructions run, the RETURN command returns the computer to the line immediately following the GOSUB command. This makes the computer run the Main program instructions2 until it stops at the END command.

To see a real program that you can type and try yourself, take a look at the following example:

```
NOMAINWIN
PROMPT "What is your password?"; password$
IF password$ = "open" THEN
  NOTICE "You typed a valid password."
ELSE
  NOTICE "Invalid password."
  GOSUB [hackeralert]
END IF
END

[hackeralert]
PROMPT "Are you a hacker? (Y or N)?"; answer$
IF answer$ = "Y" THEN
  NOTICE "The police are on their way to pick you up now."
ELSE
  NOTICE "Then you must just be incompetent."
END IF
RETURN
```

In this example, the main program instructions start with line one (NOMAINWIN) and stop with line nine (END). The subprogram, [hackeralert], starts on line 11 ([hacker alert]) and stops on line 18 (RETURN). The only time that the [hackeralert] subprogram runs is if you type an incorrect password in the first Prompt dialog box that asks, What is your password?

Ideally, you want to make all your subprograms small enough to fit on a single screen. The smaller your subprograms are, the easier they are to understand, debug, and modify.

If you use subprograms in a Liberty BASIC program, you're essentially dividing a larger program into smaller parts, although you still save everything into a single file with a name such as PACMAN.BAS or BLACKJACK.BAS.

Be aware that programming languages often use similar terms to represent different items. If you divide a large program into smaller parts, for example, BASIC calls these smaller parts *subprograms*. But what BASIC calls a subprogram, the C language calls a *function*. So if you use a different language, make sure that you use the correct terms for that particular language; otherwise, you may get confused in talking to other programmers.

Using Subroutines

In Liberty BASIC, you can create subprograms, which are miniature programs that perform a specific task. Unfortunately, subprograms work exactly the same every time that they run.

For more flexibility, you may want to create subprograms that can accept data and calculate a new result, basing it on the data that it receives. You may, for example, want to create a subprogram that multiplies two numbers together. In most cases, you don't want to multiply the same two numbers every time that the subprogram runs. Instead, the subprogram is more useful if you can feed it a different number each time and have the subprogram spit back an answer based on the number that it receives.

In most programming languages such as C/C++, Java, or Pascal, you can create the following two different types of subprograms:

✔ **Subroutines:** These types of subprograms contain instructions that accept data and use that data for performing certain tasks, such as verifying that the user types a correct password or moving the cursor as the user moves the mouse.

✔ **Functions:** These types of subprograms calculate and return a single value, such as calculating the cube of a number or counting the number of words in a sentence. In Liberty BASIC, the COS(*x*) and SIN(*x*) commands are examples of a function.

Defining a subroutine

A subroutine consists of the following two or three parts:

✔ The subroutine's name

✔ One or more instructions that you want the subroutine to follow

✔ Any data that you want the subroutine to use (optional)

In Liberty BASIC, a subroutine looks as follows:

```
SUB SubroutineName Data
 ' One or more instructions
END SUB
```

If a subroutine doesn't need to accept data from the main program or another subprogram, you can omit the Data portion of the subroutine, as in the following example:

```
SUB SubroutineName
 ' One or more instructions
END SUB
```

Passing data to a subroutine

A subroutine acts like a miniature program that performs one or more tasks. Although a subroutine is part of a bigger program, some subroutines can act independently from the rest of the program. You may, for example, have a subroutine that does nothing but display a message on-screen. If a subroutine can act independently from the rest of the program, you need to define only a name for your subroutine and any instructions that you want the subroutine to follow, as in the following example:

```
SUB SubroutineName
 PRINT "This subroutine doesn't use any data."
END SUB
```

The preceding example of a subroutine is similar to a subprogram in Liberty BASIC. As a program runs the preceding subroutine, the subroutine merrily follows its instructions without using any data from any other part of the program.

But in many cases, a subroutine requires outside data to accomplish a given task, such as checking to see whether the user types a valid password. If your subroutine needs data from another part of your program, you need to create a variable to store this data, as in the following example:

```
SUB SubroutineName Variable
  ' One or more instructions here
END SUB
```

As another part of the program tells this subroutine to run, it "passes" data to this subroutine, in much the same way that a person may pass a baton to another person. After a subroutine receives data that another part of the program passes to it, the subroutine uses variables (which it traps inside parentheses) to "hold" any data that another part of the program sends to it.

The list of variables, which accepts outside data for a subroutine, is known as a *parameter list*.

Each variable inside a subroutine's parameter list specifies one chunk of data, such as a number or string. If another part of the program passes your subroutine two chunks of data, the subroutine's parameter list must contain exactly two variables to hold this data. The following subroutine example uses three variables in its parameter list:

```
SUB SubroutineName Variable1, Variable2, Variable3
  ' One or more instructions here
END SUB
```

Make sure that you declare string variables by using the dollar sign ($) and number variables without the dollar sign. The following example uses a string and a number variable in its parameter list:

```
SUB SubroutineName Name$, Age
  ' One or more instructions here
END SUB
```

The first line of the preceding subroutine defines the name of the subroutine (which is SubroutineName) and creates two variables, Name$ and Age. The Name$ variable represents a string, and the Age variable represents an integer.

Calling a subroutine

After you create a subroutine, the final step is to actually run the instructions inside the subroutine. Normally, the subroutine sits around and does absolutely nothing (much like a politician) until the computer specifically tells the subroutine to run its instructions. In technical terms, as you tell the subroutine to run its instructions, you're *calling a subroutine.* Essentially, you're saying, "Hey, stupid subroutine! Start running your instructions now!"

If you want to run the subroutine `BurnOutMonitor,` you must use the `CALL` command. Many versions of BASIC enable you to use one of the following two methods:

```
CALL BurnOutMonitor
```

If the `BurnOutMonitor` subroutine needs you to pass data to it for it to run, you just tack on the data to pass to the subroutine as follows:

```
CALL BurnOutMonitor 45
```

If you use the `CALL` command, make sure that you spell your subroutine correctly, including upper and lowercase letters. Liberty BASIC assumes that a subroutine by the name of `DisplayMessage` is completely different from a subroutine with the name `displaymessage`.

To help you understand subroutines better, try the following Liberty BASIC program. Notice that the subroutine appears after the `END` command. This program asks for a name (such as Bill McPherson) and then displays that name to a Notice dialog box by using either the string `Bill McPherson must be a moron` or `Bill McPherson sounds like an idiot to me.`

```
NOMAINWIN
PROMPT "Give me the name of someone you hate:"; enemy$
CALL DisplayMessage enemy$
END

SUB DisplayMessage stuff$
  X = INT(RND(1) * 2) + 1
  IF X = 1 THEN
    NOTICE stuff$ + " must be a moron."
  ELSE
    NOTICE stuff$ + " sounds like an idiot to me."
  END IF
END SUB
```

Liberty BASIC interprets the preceding program as follows:

1. The first line prevents the main window from appearing.

2. The second line displays a Prompt dialog box that reads, `Give me the name of someone you hate:`. After the user types a name, the `enemy$` variable stores this name.

3. The third line calls the subroutine `DisplayMessage` and "passes" it the data that the variable `enemy$` stores. When the subroutine `Display Message` runs, it runs all the lines of the program starting from line five (`SUB DisplayMessage stuff$`) to line 12 (`END SUB`).

4. The fourth line ends the program.

5. The fifth line is the start of the `DisplayMessage` subroutine that accepts a string and stores it in the variable `stuff$`.

6. The sixth line creates a random number, either 1 or 2, and stores this value into the variable `X`.

7. The seventh through eleventh lines display two different Notice dialog boxes, using the name that the `stuff$` variable stores.

8. The twelfth line marks the end of the subroutine. When the computer reaches this line, it returns back to the main program starting with the line immediately following the `CALL DisplayMessage` command. In this case, it returns the computer back to line four, where the program ends.

Exiting prematurely from a subroutine

Normally a subroutine runs from start to finish. However, you may want to exit a subroutine before it finishes running. To do this, you just need to insert the magic `EXIT SUB` command such as:

```
NOMAINWIN
PROMPT "Give me the name of someone you hate:"; enemy$
CALL DisplayMessage enemy$
END

SUB DisplayMessage stuff$
  X = INT(RND(1) * 2) + 1
  IF X = 1 THEN
    EXIT SUB
  ELSE
    NOTICE stuff$ + " must be a moron."
  END IF
END SUB
```

Note that the `EXIT SUB` command simply tells Liberty BASIC to stop running the function and ignore any commands that come after the `EXIT SUB` command. In the above example, the `EXIT SUB` command has a 50 percent chance of running.

Using Functions

A *function* is a specialized subprogram that does nothing but calculate and return a single value. If you want to calculate the cube of a number (which is the same number multiplied by itself three times), for example, you can use the following instructions:

```
Cube = Number * Number * Number
```

But if you must calculate the cube of a number in several places throughout your program, you must type the formula `Number * Number * Number` in each place in your program. As you know, this practice is tedious and likely to create errors, especially if you want to modify the program later.

Defining a function

Rather than type similar instructions multiple times (using slightly different numbers), you can store instructions in a function. Then you pass data to the function, and the function spits back a single value. A function consists of the following four parts:

- ✔ A name
- ✔ One or more instructions for the function to calculate a single value
- ✔ One line that assigns a value (or an expression that represents a value) to the function name
- ✔ Any data that you want the function to use

A typical function in Liberty BASIC looks as follows:

```
FUNCTION FunctionName(Data)
 ' One or more instructions
 FunctionName = value
END FUNCTION
```

Don't leave a space between the function name and the left parenthesis, or Liberty BASIC doesn't run your program.

Passing data to a function

Nearly all functions need to receive data from another part of your program. As another part of a program runs (or *calls*) a function, it needs to send (or *pass*) data to that function. To make sure that the function receives any data that another part of the program passes to it, you need to specify one or more variables in parentheses, as in the following example:

```
FUNCTION FunctionName(Variable)
 ' One or more instructions here
 FunctionName = value
END FUNCTION
```

The preceding function can receive one chunk of data (such as a string or number) that another part of the program passes to it.

If your function needs to receive two or more chunks of data that another part of the program passes to it, just separate the variable names with commas, as in the following example:

```
FUNCTION FunctionName(Variable1, Variable2, Variable3)
 ' One or more instructions here
 FunctionName = value
END FUNCTION
```

Don't forget to define the type of data that the function accepts — for example, strings or numbers. (See Chapter 8 for more information about strings.) A complete declaration of variables may look as follows:

```
FUNCTION FunctionName(Note$, Salary)
 ' One or more instructions here
 FunctionName = value
END FUNCTION
```

The first line of the preceding function defines the name of the function (which is FunctionName) and creates two variables, Note$ and Salary. The Note variable represents a string, and the Salary variable represents a single-precision value such as 3.14.

Calling a function

Of course, you want to use the function that you create in your program. A function represents a single value, such as an integer or a double-precision number, so you can treat the function name as a variable.

Suppose, for example, that you have a function that you call Cube, as in the following example:

```
FUNCTION Cube(Number)
Cube = Number * Number * Number
END FUNCTION
```

You can treat this function as you do any other variable, as the following examples show:

```
PRINT Cube(3)
```

or

```
MyValue = Cube(3)
```

The following breakdown shows how the computer interprets the first example, `PRINT Cube (3)`:

1. The `PRINT Cube(3)` line tells the computer to run the function named Cube and "pass" it the number 3 as data. Print on-screen whatever value the Cube function calculates using the number 3.

2. Right away, the computer searches for the function Cube. The first line in the Cube function tells the computer that the function's name is Cube and it needs an integer, which the variable Number represents — and in this case, it represents the number 3.

3. The second line in the Cube function tells the computer to multiply the value that the Number variable represents three times and to assign this value to the function name of Cube. In this case, the value that the Number variable represents is 3, so the value of Cube is 3 * 3 * 3, or 27.

4. The third line in the Cube function tells the computer it's the end of the function, so go back to the part of the program that originally called the Cube function. In this case, the computer goes back to the instruction `PRINT Cube(3)`.

5. Because the value of `Cube(3)` is actually 27, the computer reinterprets the instruction `PRINT Cube(3)` to actually mean `PRINT 27`. Thus the number 27 appears on-screen.

The complete Liberty BASIC program that calls the Cube function might look like this:

```
NOMAINWIN
PROMPT "Type a number:"; mynumber
NOTICE "This is the cube = "; Cube(mynumber)
END

FUNCTION Cube(Number)
  Cube = Number * Number * Number
END FUNCTION
```

Exiting prematurely from a function

A *function* acts like a miniature program that runs from start to finish. However, there may be some cases when you want to exit a function before it finishes running. To do this, you just need to insert the magic EXIT FUNCTION command such as:

```
NOMAINWIN
PROMPT "Type a number:"; mynumber
NOTICE "This is the cube = "; Cube(mynumber)
END

FUNCTION Cube(Number)
  EXIT FUNCTION
  Cube = Number * Number * Number
END FUNCTION
```

Note that the EXIT FUNCTION command simply tells Liberty BASIC to stop running the function and ignore any commands that come after the EXIT FUNCTION command. For more flexibility, you may want to use an IF-THEN statement to determine if a function should stop prematurely, such as:

```
FUNCTION Cube(Number)
  IF (Condition = TRUE) THEN EXIT FUNCTION
  Cube = Number * Number * Number
END FUNCTION
```

The above example simply checks to see if a certain condition is true; then it exits the function prematurely, which means that sometimes the entire function may run and sometimes it may exit prematurely.

Passing Data by Value or by Reference

When a subroutine or function needs data, your main program can pass it data in one of two ways:

- By value
- By reference

Obviously these two terms mean nothing to most people, so the plain-English translation means that if you pass data to a subroutine or function by value, your program actually creates two separate copies of the same data; one copy stays with the main program and a second copy gets used by the subroutine or function itself. Anything the subroutine or function does to the data remains isolated within that subroutine or function.

In the following code, the main program passes the data enemy$ to the MakeMessage subroutine function by value (which is the default method that Liberty BASIC passes data to a subroutine or function).

If you type the name **Bobby Lee** at the Prompt dialog box, the main program stores the string Bobby Lee into the enemy$ variable. When the main program passes the data by value to the MakeMessage subroutine, the MakeMessage subroutine creates a second copy of that same data, but stores it in a new variable called stuff$. At this time, both the enemy$ and stuff$ variable contain the string Bobby Lee.

The MakeMessage subroutine then modifies the value of the stuff$ variable. But because the main program originally passed the data by value, these changes never get returned back to the main program, so when the main program displays the value of the enemy$ variable, it's just the original string of Bobby Lee as shown, in Figure 11-1.

```
NOMAINWIN
PROMPT "Give me the name of someone you hate:"; enemy$
CALL MakeMessage enemy$
NOTICE enemy$
END

SUB MakeMessage stuff$
  stuff$ = "Bo the Cat hates " + stuff$ + " too!"
END SUB
```

Figure 11-1: When you pass data by value, a subroutine or function can alter data as much as it wants, but that altered data will never be returned back to the main program.

If you pass data from the main program to the subroutine by reference, how-ever, any changes made to the data within the subroutine or function will get passed back to the main program. To specify that you want a subroutine or function to get data passed to it by reference instead of by value, you have to use the magic BYREF command, such as:

```
SUB MakeMessage BYREF stuff$
```

Adding this single BYREF command to the DisplayMessage subroutine lets the subroutine pass any changes made to the data back to the main program, as shown in Figure 11-2.

```
NOMAINWIN
PROMPT "Give me the name of someone you hate:"; enemy$
CALL MakeMessage enemy$
NOTICE enemy$
END

SUB MakeMessage BYREF stuff$
   stuff$ = "Bo the Cat hates " + stuff$ + " too!"
END SUB
```

Figure 11-2: When you pass data by reference using the BYREF command, any changes that the subroutine or function makes to the data get passed back to the main program.

Chapter 12

Drawing Pictures and Making Noise

In This Chapter

▶ Making a graphics control

▶ Toying with turtle graphics

▶ Drawing circles and boxes

▶ Adding sound

*I*n the old days, computer programs printed data on a single strip of paper that consisted of one long scroll. So after computers eventually got monitors, most programs still displayed information on-screen the same as if they were printing on a scrolling piece of paper. Only after monitors were around for a while did programmers realize that they could write programs that use fancy graphics, color, and sound.

So in this chapter, you can learn different ways to make your Liberty BASIC programs more colorful and visually appealing. After you add graphics and sound to your program, people will naturally find your program more interesting and (sometimes) easier to use.

Creating a Graphics Control

Before you can create and display graphics, you must create a *graphics control,* which is any window or part of a window that can display graphics on the screen. You can create a graphics control in the following two ways:

✔ Create a separate graphics window

✔ Create a graphics box inside an existing window

To create a separate graphics window, just use the OPEN command, as in the following example:

```
OPEN "My Drawing Area" FOR Graphics AS #graphWin
```

The main difference between a graphics window and an ordinary window is that a graphics window displays graphics (hence its name) while an ordinary window displays text.

If you don't want to create a separate graphics window, you can create a graphics box inside an ordinary window. To create a graphics box inside a window, you need to use the following two commands:

```
GRAPHICBOX #main.graph, 10, 10, 150, 150
OPEN "Ordinary Window" FOR Window AS #main
```

The GRAPHICBOX command works as follows:

```
GRAPHICBOX #Windowhandle.boxname, xpos, ypos, width, height
```

Here's what's happening in that command:

1. The GRAPHICBOX command tells the computer to create a box for displaying graphics. This box appears inside the window that the #Windowhandle name identifies.

2. The boxname portion identifies this graphic box with a unique name.

3. The xpos and ypos variables define the X and Y position of the graphic box, measuring from the upper-left corner of the window that #Windowhandle identifies.

4. The width and height variables measure the width and height of the graphics box.

After you create a graphics window or graphic box, you're ready to start giving commands to display graphics on-screen.

Using Turtle Graphics

Turtle graphics get their name from the idea of putting an imaginary robotic turtle with a pen in the middle of your screen. To draw something, your program must tell the robotic turtle when to put its pen down and when to move in a certain direction to draw a line. To stop drawing, you must tell the robot to lift up its pen.

The LOGO programming language uses the idea of turtle graphics extensively to teach children the fundamentals of programming.

The four basic commands for drawing pictures by using turtle graphics in Liberty BASIC (or any other programming language that allows turtle graphics) are as follows:

1. Lift up the pen from the paper (to stop drawing).
2. Lower the pen down to the paper (to start drawing).
3. Move forward a distance that you specify (which draws a line if the pen is down).
4. Turn a number of degrees that you specify in any direction.

By stringing together a list of commands for moving, turning, lifting, and lowering the pen, you can make the imaginary robotic turtle on-screen draw a variety of interesting designs ranging from single lines and rectangles to geometric patterns and shapes.

Liberty BASIC includes special commands for creating turtle graphics, as follows:

- UP: Lifts the pen up (don't draw).
- DOWN: Lowers the pen down (draw).
- HOME: Moves the turtle (pen) in the center of the graphics area.
- GO: Moves forward in the current direction.
- GOTO: Goes to a position that you specify. This draws a line if the pen is down.
- PLACE: Goes to a position that you specify but without drawing, even if the pen is down.
- TURN: Turns the turtle clockwise a specific number of degrees.
- NORTH: Causes the turtle to point north (straight up).
- POSXY: Returns the X and Y coordinates of the turtle's current location.

To see how turtle graphics work, try the following program to draw a flag (or the number 4, depending on your perspective) in the middle of the screen, as shown in Figure 12-1:

Figure 12-1:
Using turtle
graphics
to draw
a simple
design.

```
NOMAINWIN
WindowHeight = 300
WindowWidth = 250

OPEN "Graphics window" FOR Graphics AS #main

PRINT #main, "HOME"
PRINT #main, "DOWN"
PRINT #main, "NORTH"
PRINT #main, "GO 35"
PRINT #main, "TURN 225"
PRINT #main, "GO 25"
PRINT #main, "TURN 225"
PRINT #main, "GO 20"
PRINT #main, "FLUSH"

PRINT #main, "trapclose [quit]"
WAIT

[quit]
CONFIRM "Are you sure you want to quit?"; quit$
IF quit$ = "no" THEN WAIT
CLOSE #main
END
```

Here's what's happening in the preceding program:

1. The first line tells the computer not to display the main window.

2. The second and third lines define the height (300) and width (250) of
   the window that the fourth line creates.

3. The fourth line of code creates a graphics window containing the text Graphics window in the title bar. The window handle of #main identifies this window.

4. The fifth line of code moves the turtle to the home position, which is in the center of the window.

5. The sixth line tells the turtle to put the pen down and get ready to start drawing.

6. The seventh line tells the turtle to point north, which is up.

7. The eighth line tells the turtle to move 35 pixels in the direction the turtle is currently facing, which is north or up.

8. The ninth line tells the turtle to turn 225 degrees to the right.

9. The tenth line tells the turtle to go 25 pixels forward.

10. The eleventh line tells the turtle to turn 225 degrees to its right.

11. The twelfth line tells the turtle to go 20 pixels forward.

12. The thirteenth line gives the turtle the FLUSH command, which is a special command for making sure that the turtle graphics remain in the window even if the user resizes or moves the window.

13. The fourteenth line uses the trapclose command to tell the computer that after the user closes the program, the computer needs to find instructions to shut down at the [quit] label.

14. The fifteenth line tells the computer to wait for the user to do something.

15. The sixteenth (the one with [quit]) through nineteenth lines tell the computer what to do after the user closes the program. In this case, a Confirm dialog box appears to make sure that the user really wants to quit. If so, the program closes the window that the #main handle identifies.

16. The twentieth line marks the end of the program.

If you don't use the flush command, your turtle graphics may disappear completely if the user resizes the graphics window.

Rather than type separate turtle graphics commands on each line, you can cram together multiple turtle graphics commands by separating them with a semicolon. Typing these commands takes up a lot of space, as the following example demonstrates:

```
PRINT #main, "HOME"
PRINT #main, "DOWN"
PRINT #main, "NORTH"
PRINT #main, "GO 35"
PRINT #main, "TURN 225"
```

To save space, you can cram all the preceding lines together, as follows:

```
PRINT #main, "HOME; DOWN; NORTH; GO 35; TURN 225"
```

Another way to break up one long line into smaller, easier-to-read short lines is to use the underscore (_) character, which tells Liberty BASIC, "If you see the underscore character, treat the following line as if it's tacked on to the end of the line containing the underscore character."

So instead of writing the following:

```
PRINT #main, "HOME; DOWN; NORTH; go 35; TURN 225"
```

You can divide this line into smaller, separate lines, as in the following example:

```
PRINT #main, "HOME; DOWN; _
NORTH; GO 35; TURN 225"
```

For a faster way to draw a line, use the GOTO command following a DOWN command, as follows:

```
PRINT #MAIN, "DOWN; GOTO x y"
```

This line tells the computer to put down the pen and draw a line from the current turtle (pen) position to the X and Y coordinates that x and y, respectively, define.

Defining line thickness

For variety, you can alter the thickness of your lines. To change line thickness, use the SIZE command, as follows:

```
PRINT #Windowhandle, "size X"
```

Here's what's happening in this example:

1. The #Windowhandle portion defines the graphics window to adjust the thickness of the next lines that turtle graphics draw.

2. The size X command defines line thickness, where X is a number such as 3 or 8. If you don't use the size command, the default thickness of a line is one (1).

To see how changing the thickness of a line works, try the following program, which creates two parallel lines of line thickness: five (5) and ten (10):

```
NOMAINWIN
WindowHeight = 300
WindowWidth = 250

OPEN "Graphics window" FOR Graphics AS #main

PRINT #main, "HOME; DOWN; NORTH"
PRINT #main, "SIZE 5"
PRINT #main, "GO 35; TURN 90; UP; GO 35; TURN 90"
PRINT #main, "SIZE 10"
PRINT #main, "DOWN; GO 35"
PRINT #main, "FLUSH"

PRINT #main, "trapclose [quit]"
WAIT

[quit]
CONFIRM "Are you sure you want to quit?"; quit$
IF quit$ = "no" THEN WAIT
CLOSE #main
END
```

Defining line colors

Because drawing black lines can get tedious after a while, you may want to change the color of your lines. To change colors, you just need to use the COLOR command, as follows:

```
PRINT #Windowhandle, "COLOR color"
```

Here's what's happening in this example:

1. The #Windowhandle portion defines the graphics window to change the color of lines that turtle graphics draw.

2. The COLOR color command defines the color of the line, where color is one of the following: black, blue, brown, cyan, darkblue, darkcyan, darkgray, darkgreen, darkpink, darkred, green, lightgray, palegray, pink, red, white, and yellow.

To see how changing the color of a line works, try the following program, which adds color to two parallel lines:

```
NOMAINWIN
WindowHeight = 300
WindowWidth = 250

OPEN "Graphics window" FOR Graphics AS #main

PRINT #main, "HOME; DOWN; NORTH"
PRINT #main, "COLOR green"
PRINT #main, "GO 35; TURN 90; UP; GO 35; TURN 90"
PRINT #main, "COLOR pink"
PRINT #main, "DOWN; go 35"
PRINT #main, "FLUSH"

PRINT #main, "trapclose [quit]"
WAIT

[quit]
CONFIRM "Are you sure you want to quit?"; quit$
IF quit$ = "no" THEN WAIT
CLOSE #main
END
```

Drawing Circles

Because drawing individual lines can become tiresome, you may want to tell Liberty BASIC to draw circles instead. To draw a circle, you can use the CIRCLE command as in the following example:

```
PRINT #Windowhandle, "CIRCLE R"
```

Here's what's happening in this example:

1. The #Windowhandle portion defines the graphics window in which the circle that turtle graphics draws appears.

2. The CIRCLE R command tells the computer to draw a circle, at the current position of the turtle (pen), with a radius that R defines, where R is a number such as 35 or 90.

If you want to draw your circle in a specific color, you can use the COLOR command prior to the CIRCLE command, as follows:

```
PRINT #Windowhandle, "COLOR darkpink; CIRCLE R"
```

You can also fill in your circle with a specific color by using the BACKCOLOR command prior to using the CIRCLEFILLED command, as follows:

```
PRINT #Windowhandle, "BACKCOLOR yellow; CIRCLEFILLED R"
```

To see how turtle graphics can create circles, try the following program, which draws two circles, as shown in Figure 12-2:

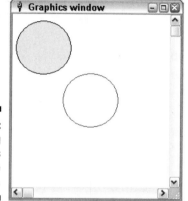

Figure 12-2:
Drawing
two circles
using turtle
graphics.

```
NOMAINWIN
WindowHeight = 300
WindowWidth = 250

OPEN "Graphics window" FOR Graphics AS #main

PRINT #main, "HOME; DOWN"
PRINT #main, "COLOR red; CIRCLE 40"
PRINT #main, "PLACE 45 50"
PRINT #main, "COLOR darkblue; BACKCOLOR yellow; CIRCLEFILLED
          40"
PRINT #main, "FLUSH"

PRINT #main, "trapclose [quit]"
WAIT

[quit]
CONFIRM "Are you sure you want to quit?"; quit$
IF quit$ = "no" THEN WAIT
CLOSE #main
END
```

The seventh line in the preceding program uses the PLACE command, which moves the turtle (pen) position without drawing a line.

Drawing Boxes

Just as you can draw circles, Liberty BASIC also enables you to draw boxes. To draw a box, you can use the BOX command as in the following example:

```
PRINT #Windowhandle, "BOX x y"
```

Here's what's happening in this example:

1. The #Windowhandle portion defines the graphics window where turtle graphics draws the box.

2. The BOX x y command tells the computer to draw a box where the current turtle (pen) position defines one corner of the box and the x and y coordinates define the location of the opposite corner.

If you want to draw your circle in a specific color, you can use the COLOR command prior to the BOX command, as follows:

```
PRINT #Windowhandle, "COLOR red; BOX x y"
```

You can also fill in your circle with a specific color by using the BACKCOLOR command prior to using the BOXFILLED command, as in the following example:

```
PRINT #Windowhandle, "BACKCOLOR pink; BOXFILLED x y"
```

To see how turtle graphics can create boxes, try the following program, which draws two boxes.

```
NOMAINWIN
WindowHeight = 300
WindowWidth = 250

OPEN "Graphics window" FOR Graphics AS #main

PRINT #main, "HOME; DOWN"
PRINT #main, "COLOR red; BOX 190 190"
PRINT #main, "PLACE 45 50"
PRINT #main, "COLOR darkblue; BACKCOLOR pink; BOXFILLED 80
        80"
```

```
PRINT #main, "FLUSH"

PRINT #main, "trapclose [quit]"
WAIT

[quit]
CONFIRM "Are you sure you want to quit?"; quit$
IF quit$ = "no" THEN WAIT
CLOSE #main
END
```

Displaying Text

Besides drawing lines, circles, and boxes, you can also create text in a graphics window. To display text in a graphics control, you just need to move the turtle (pen) to the location where you want the text to appear and then print the text with a backslash in front, which the following program accomplishes:

```
NOMAINWIN
WindowHeight = 300
WindowWidth = 250

OPEN "Text graphics window" FOR Graphics AS #main

PRINT #main, "HOME"
PRINT #main, "\This is an"
PRINT #main, "\example of text"
PRINT #main, "FLUSH"

PRINT #main, "trapclose [quit]"
WAIT

[quit]
CONFIRM "Are you sure you want to quit?"; quit$
IF quit$ = "no" THEN WAIT
CLOSE #main
END
```

The backslash character (\) displays the text and causes a new line to print, as shown in Figure 12-3. That way, you can display multiple lines of text without needing to move the turtle (pen) each time.

For variety, you can add color to your text or to the background. To change the color of your text, use the COLOR command, as follows:

```
PRINT #main, "HOME"
PRINT #main, "COLOR red"
PRINT #main, "\This is an"
PRINT #main, "\example of text"
PRINT #main, "FLUSH"
```

The second line in the preceding example tells the computer to display text in red.

If you want to change the backdrop on which your text appears, use the BACKCOLOR command instead, as follows:

```
PRINT #main, "HOME"
PRINT #main, "BACKCOLOR red"
PRINT #main, "\This is an"
PRINT #main, "\EXAMPLE OF TEXT"
PRINT #MAIN, "FLUSH"
```

The second line in the preceding example displays text against a red background.

Figure 12-3:
Displaying text in a graphics window by using turtle graphics.

Making Sounds

Many programs use sound for a variety of reasons, such as alerting a user that something's gone wrong or playing soothing music in the background while the program's running. Sound can make your program more interesting to use.

Making a beeping noise

At the most primitive level of sound-making, Liberty BASIC can make a simple (and annoying) beeping noise by using a special BEEP command as follows:

```
PROMPT "How many beeps do you want to hear"; Answer
FOR I = 1 TO Answer
 BEEP
NEXT
END
```

You often use the BEEP command as a warning message to the user, such as if the user presses the wrong key or tries to choose an invalid command.

Playing WAV files

Because the BEEP command is simplistic and relatively limited, Liberty BASIC also provides the PLAYWAVE command, which can play WAV files that you can download off the Internet or record on your own computer.

Windows includes several WAV files in the C:\Windows\Media directory.

To use the PLAYWAVE command, you need to specify which WAV file you want to play and how you want it to play. The three choices for playing a WAV file are as follows:

- ✔ SYNC: Temporarily halts your program until the WAV file finishes playing.

- ✔ ASYNC: Enables your program to continue running while the WAV file continues playing.

- ✔ LOOP: Plays the WAV file over and over again until your program gives the computer the PLAYWAVE "" command to shut the WAV file off.

The PLAYWAVE command looks as follows:

```
PLAYWAVE filename, mode
```

So if you want to play the tada.wav file that you store in the C:\Windows\Media directory, you can use the following command:

```
PLAYWAVE "C:\Windows\Media\tada.wav", SYNC
```

In this example, the tada.wav file plays, temporarily halting your program until the WAV file finishes playing.

Make sure that you specify the correct directory where the PLAYWAVE command can find your WAV file.

To see how a real Liberty BASIC program may work, try the following on your own computer:

```
NOMAINWIN
FILEDIALOG "Pick a .WAV file to play.", "*.wav", filename$
PLAYWAVE filename$, SYNC
END
```

The following steps tell you how the preceding program works:

1. The first line tells Liberty BASIC not to display the main window.

2. The second line displays a dialog box, enabling the user to choose a WAV file to play.

3. The third line plays the WAV file that the user chooses from the dialog box that appears as a result of Line 2 of the program.

4. The fourth line ends the program.

Chapter 13

Saving and Retrieving Stuff in Files

*E*very program needs to accept data from an outside source (such as from a person banging away on the keyboard) and then spit it back out again in some useful format (such as in a neatly printed report). To store data temporarily, programs use variables, which store data in the computer's memory. As soon as the program ends, the computer wipes out the data in memory to make room for another program.

But what if you want to store data on a more permanent basis? Many computer games, for example, save the highest score to give future players a goal to beat. If a program stores data on a hard drive, the program saves the data in a file separate from the program file.

Storing Stuff in Text Files

The simplest data that a program can save is text, which consists of nothing more exciting than letters, numbers, and symbols (such as #, ~, <, or &) from the keyboard. Any file that contains only text is known as a *text file*. If you want to store, write, or retrieve data from a text file, you always must start reading the text file from the beginning. As a result, text files are sometimes known as *sequential files*.

Because text files contain only letters, numbers, and symbols, you can share text files among different computers, such as any computer running Windows, Linux, or the Macintosh operating system. If you use the Save As command in your favorite word processor, you find an option to save your document as a text file. Just remember that saving a word-processing document as a text file removes all the document's formatting, such as underlining or special fonts.

Creating a new text file

Before you can store any data in a text file, you (obviously) must create that text file first. To create a text file, you use the following Liberty BASIC command:

```
OPEN "Filename" FOR OUTPUT AS #Handle
```

Here's what's happening in the preceding example:

1. The OPEN command tells the computer, "Create a new text file and give it the name that "Filename" specifies, which can represent a filename (such as STUFF.TXT) or a drive, directory, and filename (such as C:\ WINDOWS\STUFF.TXT)."

2. The FOR OUTPUT portion of the command tells the computer, "Get ready to start outputting data into the newly created text file that "Filename" identifies."

3. The #Handle is any nickname that you choose to represent the text file you just created.

If you want to create a file that you call STUFF.TXT and save it on a floppy disk (the A drive), use the following command:

```
OPEN "A:\STUFF.TXT" FOR OUTPUT AS #Secrets
```

This line tells Liberty BASIC to create the text file STUFF.TXT on the A drive and assign it the name #Secrets.

Any time that you use the OPEN command to create a new text file or to open an existing text file, you must eventually use the CLOSE command to shut the text file. If you don't use the CLOSE command eventually, your program may cause the computer to crash.

Putting stuff in a text file

After you create a text file, you can use the PRINT command to stuff data into that text file. If you use the PRINT command, Liberty BASIC normally displays that data on-screen, so you must tell Liberty BASIC to store the data in your text file instead by using the handle of the text file, as in the following command:

```
PRINT #Secrets, "This line gets stored in the text file."
```

This command tells Liberty BASIC, "Look for a text file that the name #Secrets identifies and stuff that text file with the line, This line gets stored in the text file."

Putting it all together, you have a program similar to the following example:

```
OPEN "A:\STUFF.TXT" FOR OUTPUT AS #Secrets
PRINT #Secrets, "This line gets stored in the text file."
CLOSE #Secrets
END
```

This Liberty BASIC program tells the computer to do the following:

1. The first line tells the computer, "Open a text file on the A drive and call this text file STUFF.TXT. Then give it the handle #Secrets."

2. The second line tells the computer, "Look for a file that the #Secrets handle identifies and stuff it with the line, This line gets stored in the text file."

3. The third line tells the computer, "Close the text file that the #Secrets handle identifies."

4. The fourth line tells the computer that the program is at an end.

To see whether this program really stores the line This line gets stored in the text file. inside the text file STUFF.TXT, run the Windows Explorer program from within Windows and double-click the STUFF.TXT file to view its contents.

Adding new stuff to an existing text file

If you use the OPEN command, as in the following example, Liberty BASIC knows that you're ready to store data:

```
OPEN "A:\STUFF.TXT" FOR OUTPUT AS #Secrets
```

This line of code tells Liberty BASIC, "Make a new text file with the name STUFF.TXT on the A drive and get ready to store data in it."

But what happens if the STUFF.TXT file already exists? Then the OPEN command tells Liberty BASIC, "Wipe out any data that the STUFF.TXT text file currently contains and get ready to store new data in it."

If you want to save any data that a text file currently stores but you still want to add new data to the text file, you must use the APPEND command, as follows:

```
OPEN "A:\STUFF.TXT" FOR APPEND AS #Secrets
```

If you've already run the previous Liberty BASIC program that creates a STUFF. TXT file, try running the following program to see how you can add new data to a text file without wiping out any existing data:

```
OPEN "A:\STUFF.TXT" FOR OUTPUT AS #Secrets
PRINT #Secrets, "This line gets stored in the text file."
CLOSE #Secrets
OPEN "A:\STUFF.TXT" FOR APPEND AS #NewStuff
PRINT #NewStuff, "New data gets appended to existing data."
CLOSE #NewStuff
END
```

Retrieving data from a text file

Of course, storing data inside a text file is nice just as long as you need to use that data again. Fortunately, Liberty BASIC includes a command to retrieve any data that you store in a text file. That way, you can display it on-screen again.

To retrieve data from a text file, you use the INPUT command with the OPEN command, as follows:

```
OPEN "A:\STUFF.TXT" FOR INPUT AS #Retrieve
```

Then you use the INPUT command to read each line that the text file stores, as follows:

```
INPUT #FileHandle, Variable$
```

In this example, #FileHandle represents the file handle that you previously used with the OPEN command, and Variable$ is the name of a string variable that temporarily stores the line that you're retrieving from the text file.

If all this stuff sounds too complicated, just run the following program to see how this procedure works:

```
OPEN "A:\STUFF.TXT" FOR OUTPUT AS #myfile
INPUT "What is your name? "; Name$
PRINT #myfile, Name$
CLOSE #myfile
OPEN "A:\STUFF.TXT" FOR INPUT AS #file2
LINE INPUT #file2, YourName$
```

```
PRINT "This is the name you stored in the text file = ";
              YourName$
CLOSE #file2
END
```

The INPUT command retrieves only one line at a time, starting from the first line that the text file contains. Because text files usually have two or more lines of data, you use a loop and a special EOF (which stands for *End Of File*) command to retrieve every line that you store inside a text file.

To see how this procedure works, try running the following program, which stuffs three lines of text in a text file and then retrieves it:

```
OPEN "A:\STUFF.TXT" FOR OUTPUT AS #ufo
PRINT #ufo, "Isn't this exciting?"
PRINT #ufo, "Another line bites the dust."
PRINT #ufo, "The last line in the text file."
CLOSE #ufo
OPEN "A:\STUFF.TXT" FOR INPUT AS #bigfoot
I = 1
WHILE EOF(#bigfoot) = 0
  LINE INPUT #bigfoot, OneLine$
  PRINT "Line #" + STR$(I) + ": " + OneLine$
  I = I + 1
WEND
CLOSE #bigfoot
END
```

The WHILE WEND loop may look a bit strange to you; for more information on loops, refer to Chapter 10. Take a closer look to see how it works in the following example:

```
OPEN "A:\STUFF.TXT" FOR INPUT AS #bigfoot
I = 1
WHILE EOF(#bigfoot) = 0
  INPUT #bigfoot, OneLine$
  PRINT "Line #" + STR$(I) + ": " + OneLine$
  I = I + 1
WEND
CLOSE #bigfoot
```

Here's what's happening in the preceding example:

1. The first line of the preceding code tells the computer, "Open up the text file STUFF.TXT, assign it a file handle of #bigfoot, and get ready to read data from it."

2. The second line tells the computer, "Create the variable I and set its value to 1."

3. The third line tells the computer, "A WHILE-WEND loop starts here," which tells the computer to keep looping until it reaches the end of the file (EOF) for a file with the nickname #bigfoot (which is the STUFF.TXT file that the first line identifies as file #bigfoot). The moment that it reaches the end of the file, the program sets the value of EOF(#bigfoot) to a nonzero value.

4. The fourth line tells the computer, "Read a line from a file that I'm identifying as file #bigfoot and store this line in the variable OneLine$." After the INPUT command, the computer automatically jumps to the next line in the text file.

5. The fifth line tells the computer, "Print the line that the OneLine$ variable stores." To make the printed output look nice, this fifth line prints the text Line #: following it with the value of I and the text that the OneLine$ variable stores.

6. The sixth line tells the computer, "Take the value that the I variable stores and add 1 to it."

7. The seventh line tells the computer, "The WHILE-WEND loop is at an end."

8. The eighth line tells the computer, "Close the file with the nickname #bigfoot."

Storing Stuff in Random-Access Files

Text files are handy for storing and retrieving one line of text at a time, but if you want to retrieve just the last line in a text file, the computer must read each line of text from the start of the text file to the end just to find the last line.

To solve this problem, programmers created something known as *random-access files*. Unlike text files, which cram data in one huge file, random-access files divide a large file into smaller parts (known as *records*), each of which holds a single chunk of data. Each chunk of data is known as a *field*. That way, if you want to retrieve a chunk of data from the end of a random-access file, you can just jump to the last part of the random-access file directly without needing to read the entire file as you'd need to do if you store the data in a text file. Figure 13-1 shows the difference between the way a computer stores data in a text file versus a random-access file.

The main advantage of a random-access file is that it can retrieve data more efficiently than a text file.

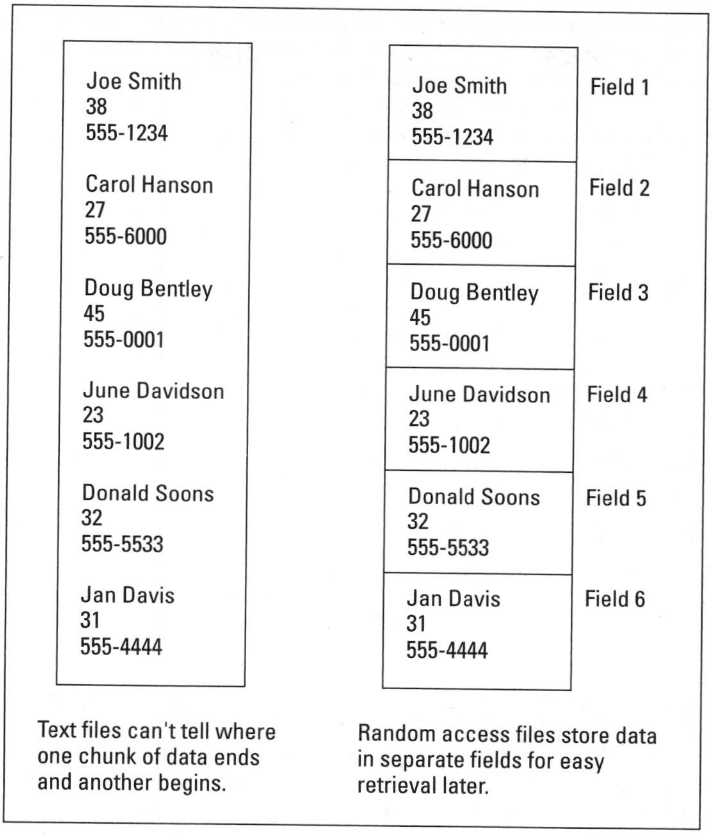
Joe Smith
38
555-1234
Carol Hanson
27
555-6000
Doug Bentley
45
555-0001
June Davidson
23
555-1002
Donald Soons
32
555-5533
Jan Davis
31
555-4444
Text files can't tell where one chunk of data ends and another begins.
Joe Smith
38
555-1234
Field 1
Carol Hanson
27
555-6000
Field 2
Doug Bentley
45
555-0001
Field 3
June Davidson
23
555-1002
Field 4
Donald Soons
32
555-5533
Field 5
Jan Davis
31
555-4444
Field 6
Random access files store data in separate fields for easy retrieval later.

Figure 13-1: Text files store data sequentially from start to finish, whereas random-access files store data in discrete chunks.

Creating a new random-access file

You often use random-access files to store one or more related chunks of data, such as a person's name, address, employee ID, and phone number. To store this data in a random-access file, you need to define the following items:

- How many different categories of information you want to store, such as a person's name, address, and age.
- How many characters you want to allocate for each chunk of data. You may, for example, want to allocate up to 15 characters for a person's name but only 2 characters for a person's age.

After you define how many characters to allocate for each chunk of data, you need to total this number to define the total length of all this data by using the `FIELD` command, as in the following example:

```
FIELD #filehandle, X AS name$, Y AS age
```

This line tells Liberty BASIC, "Each field contains one person's name and age, where the name can run up to `X` characters in length and the age can run up to `Y` characters in length." Because the `FIELD` command also specifies the file handle to store this data in, you must use the `FIELD` command immediately following an `OPEN` command, as in the following example:

```
OPEN "Filename" FOR RANDOM AS #FileHandle LEN = Size
```

Here's what's happening in the preceding example:

1. The `OPEN` command tells the computer, "Create a new random-access file and give it the name that `"Filename"` specifies, which can represent a filename (such as `TRASH.DAT`) or a drive, directory, and filename (such as `C:\WINDOWS\TRASH.DAT`)."

2. The `FOR RANDOM` command tells the computer, "Get ready to start shoving data into the newly created random-access file that `"Filename"` identifies."

3. The `#FileHandle` can be any nickname that you use to identify the actual file in which to store the data. Although you just defined a name for your random-access file, Liberty BASIC needs to identify the file by a nickname or handle as well.

4. The `LEN = Size` command tells the computer, "This is the total length of each record." (If the computer knows the exact length of each record, it knows how many bytes to skip over in trying to retrieve information from the middle of a random-access file.)

To create the file `TRASH.DAT`, which stores a name (15 characters long) and an age (2 characters long), you can use the following command:

```
OPEN "A:\TRASH.DAT" FOR RANDOM AS #garbage LEN = 17
```

This command tells the computer to create the random-access file `TRASH.DAT` on the A drive, assign it a file handle of `#garbage`, and define each record as exactly 17 characters in length.

If you use the `OPEN` command to create a new random-access file or open an existing random-access file, you must eventually use the `CLOSE` command to shut the text file. If you don't use the `CLOSE` command after using an `OPEN` command, your program may cause the computer to crash.

Saving data into a random-access file

After you go through the hassle of creating a random-access file, the next step is knowing how to stuff data into that random-access file.

To put something inside a random-access file, use the following command:

```
PUT #Filehandle, Recordnumber
```

In this example, `#Filehandle` represents the number that you assign to the random-access file by using the `OPEN` command, and `Recordnumber` is the order in which you want to store the data in the random-access file. (Record number 1 is the first chunk of data in the file; record number 2 is the second; and so on.)

Putting it all together, you have a program similar to the following example:

```
OPEN "a:\stuff.dat" FOR random AS #losers LEN = 25
FIELD #losers, 15 AS name$, 2 AS age$, 8 AS phone$
FOR I = 1 TO 3
  PROMPT "Type a name:"; name$
  PROMPT "What is this person's age?"; age$
  PROMPT "What is this person's phone number:"; phone$
  PUT #losers, I
NEXT I
CLOSE #losers
END
```

This Liberty BASIC program tells the computer to do the following:

1. The first line tells the computer, "Open the random-access file `STUFF.DAT` on the A drive, identify it by a nickname as `#losers`, and get ready to store records that are a total of 25 characters in length."

2. The second line tells the computer, "Create a record for the random-access file that the `#losers` nickname identifies. Each record consists of a name (which takes up 15 characters), an age (which takes up 2 characters) and a phone number (which takes up to 8 characters). The total of 15 plus 2 plus 8 equals 25, which is why the first line allocates record lengths of 25 characters."

3. The third line starts a `FOR-NEXT` loop to ask the user for data three times.

4. The fourth through sixth lines display a Prompt dialog box and ask for a person's name, age, and phone number.

5. The seventh line uses the PUT command to store the person's name, age, and phone number into the random access file that the #losers handle identifies. The first time the FOR-NEXT loop runs, the value of I equals one, so the program stores the first name, age, and phone number in record number one. The second time the FOR-NEXT loop runs, the value of I equals two, so it stores the second batch of data in record number two, and so on.

6. The eighth line marks the end of the FOR-NEXT loop.

7. The ninth line tells the computer, "Close the file that the handle #losers identifies."

8. The tenth line tells the computer, "This line ends the program."

If you run this program, nothing appears on-screen. To see whether this program really stores any data into the random-access file STUFF.DAT, you need to eventually retrieve the data from the random-access file, which you find out how to do in the following section.

Retrieving data from a random-access file

After storing data in a random-access file, you can yank it back out again by using the following command:

```
GET #Filehandle, Recordnumber
```

In this command, #Filehandle represents the file number that you previously used with the OPEN command; Recordnumber represents the record that you want to retrieve (which can be 1 to retrieve the first record in the random-access file, 2 to retrieve the second record, and so on).

The previous statements make sense after you run the following program and see for yourself how to yank out data that a random-access file stores. Add commands near the bottom of the previous Liberty BASIC program as follows:

```
OPEN "a:\stuff.dat" FOR random AS #losers LEN = 25
FIELD #losers, 15 AS name$, 2 AS age$, 8 AS phone$
FOR I = 1 TO 3
  GET #losers, I
  PRINT "Name = "; name$
  PRINT "Age = "; age$
  PRINT "Phone = "; phone$
  PRINT
NEXT I
CLOSE #losers
END
```

If you ran the previous Liberty BASIC program, in the section "Saving data into a random access file," to store three names, ages, and phone numbers into the file STUFF.DAT, you can use the above Liberty BASIC commands to retrieve data out of the STUFF.DAT file:

1. The first line tells the computer, "Open the random-access file STUFF.DAT on the A drive, identify it by a nickname as #losers, and get ready to store fields that are a total of 25 characters in length."

2. The second line tells the computer, "Create a field for the random-access file that the #losers nickname identifies. Each field consists of a name (which takes up 15 characters), an age (which takes up 2 characters) and a phone number (which takes up 8 characters). The total of 15 plus 2 plus 8 equals 25, which is why the first line allocates field lengths of 25 characters."

3. The third line starts a FOR-NEXT loop to retrieve three fields out of a random-access file.

4. The fourth line uses the GET command to retrieve records from the random-access file that the handle #losers identifies. The first time that the GET command runs, the value of I is one, so the GET command retrieves data from the first record. The second time the GET command runs, the value of I is two, so the GET command retrieves data from the second record, and so on.

5. The fifth through eighth lines print the data that the GET command retrieves out of each field.

6. The ninth line marks the end of the FOR-NEXT loop.

7. The tenth line tells the computer, "Close the file that the handle #losers identifies."

8. The eleventh line tells the computer, "This line is the end of the program."

One main advantage of random-access files is the capability to selectively retrieve information from specific records. Try the following Liberty BASIC program, which asks you which record to retrieve data from (1, 2, or 3) and then retrieves and prints data from that record on-screen:

```
OPEN "a:\stuff.dat" FOR random AS #losers LEN = 25
FIELD #losers, 15 AS name$, 2 AS age$, 8 AS phone$
PROMPT "What record do you want to retrieve data from?";
          fieldnum
GET #losers, fieldnum
PRINT "Name = "; name$
PRINT "Age = "; age$
PRINT "Phone = "; phone$
PRINT
CLOSE #losers
END
```

Saving and Retrieving Data in a Binary File

Text files can be convenient for storing long strings of information, but they can be painfully cumbersome in retrieving data. Random-access files make retrieving data simple but at the expense of having to organize every chunk of data into records. In case you want to store long bits of information with the convenience of retrieving them quickly, you can save data in a binary file.

Creating a new binary file

Before you can store any data in a binary file, you must first create that binary file. To create a binary file, you use the following Liberty BASIC command:

```
OPEN "Filename" FOR BINARY AS #Handle
```

This is what the above Liberty BASIC command tells the computer:

1. The OPEN command tells the computer, "Create a new file and give it the name that "Filename" specifies, which can represent a filename (such as STUFF.BIN) or a drive, directory, and filename (such as C:\WINDOWS\ STUFF.BIN)."

2. The FOR BINARY portion of the command tells the computer, "Get ready to start outputting data into the newly created binary file that "Filename" identifies."

3. The #Handle is any nickname that you choose to represent the binary file you just created.

If you want to create a file called STUFF.BIN and save it on a floppy disk (the A drive), use the following command:

```
OPEN "A:\STUFF.BIN" FOR BINARY AS #Secrets
```

This line tells Liberty BASIC to create the binary file STUFF.BIN on the A drive and assign it the name #Secrets.

Any time that you use the OPEN command to create a new binary file or to open an existing binary file, make sure you use the CLOSE command to shut the binary file. If you don't use the CLOSE command eventually, your program may cause the computer to crash.

Saving stuff in a binary file

After you create a binary file, you can stuff it with data by using the PRINT command. If you use the PRINT command, Liberty BASIC normally displays that data on-screen, so you must tell Liberty BASIC to store the data in your binary file instead by using the handle of that binary file, as in the following command:

```
PRINT #Secrets, "This line gets stored in the binary file."
```

This command tells Liberty BASIC, "Look for a binary file that the name #Secrets identifies and stuff that binary file with the line, This line gets stored in the binary file."

Putting it all together, you can create a program similar to the following example:

```
OPEN "A:\STUFF.BIN" FOR BINARY AS #Secrets
PRINT #Secrets, "This line gets stored in the binary file."
CLOSE #Secrets
END
```

This Liberty BASIC program tells the computer to do the following:

1. The first line tells the computer, "Open a binary file on the A drive and call this binary file STUFF.BIN. Then give it the handle #Secrets."

2. The second line tells the computer, "Look for a file that the #Secrets handle identifies and stuff it with the line, This line gets stored in the binary file."

3. The third line tells the computer, "Close the binary file that the #Secrets handle identifies."

4. The fourth line tells the computer that the program is at an end.

If you run this program, it simply creates a binary file on your disk but you won't see anything on the screen.

Changing stuff in a binary file

When you store data in a binary file, you can overwrite that data at any time by using something magical called a *file pointer*. Because binary files store data as a continuous stream of bytes, the file pointer lets you point at the part of the file that contains the data you want to overwrite.

To find the current location of the file pointer, you have to create a variable and assign it the value of the file pointer's position with the LOC command such as:

```
FilePointer = LOC(#Filename)
```

So if #Filename represents a binary file that contains the string, "I love programming with Liberty BASIC," the value of the FilePointer variable initially would be 38 (the total number of characters in the "I love programming with Liberty BASIC" string).

To move the file pointer, you have to use the SEEK command, such as:

```
SEEK(#Filename), NewPosition
```

This command tells Liberty BASIC, "Move the file pointer to the location specified by NewPosition." So if the value of NewPosition is 3, the file pointer will now point to the third character stored in the binary file. If you stored the string "I hate copycat publishers," in a binary file, the third position would point to the letter *h*, which is the first letter of the word "hate".

To overwrite data in a binary file, you just have to move the file pointer to the location where you want to overwrite the data and then use the ordinary PRINT command such as:

```
SEEK(#MyStuff), 3
PRINT #MyStuff, "despise copycat publishers."
```

If the #MyStuff handle represented a binary file that contained the string, "I hate copycat publishers," then the above two commands would first move the file pointer to the third position and then overwrite the third position and the rest of the file with the string "despise copycat publishers."

Be careful when overwriting data in a binary file. Say you have the following string stored in a binary file, "I like cats," and use the following code:

```
SEEK(#MyStuff), 1
PRINT #MyStuff, "'m tired."
```

This is what your original binary file contains:

```
I like cats.
```

And this is what the overwritten binary file contents now look like:

```
I'm tired.s.
```

Note that the extra *s* and period remain because the new string doesn't completely overwrite the old data in the binary file.

Retrieving stuff from a binary file

Storing data in a binary file is nice, but eventually you may want to retrieve that data out again. To retrieve data from a binary file, you have to move the file pointer to anywhere in the file where you want to start retrieving data, then use the INPUT command such as:

```
SEEK #MyFile, 0
INPUT #MyFile, RetrieveMe$
```

In this example, the SEEK #MyFile, 0 command simply moves the file pointer to the beginning of the binary file. If you only wanted to retrieve part of the data in a binary file, you could move the file pointer to a different location such as 8 or 12. #MyFile represents the file handle that you previously used with the OPEN command and RetrieveMe$ is the name of a string variable that temporarily stores the string you stored in that binary file.

If you're retrieving numeric data stored in a binary file, you would use a numeric variable name that doesn't have the dollar sign ($) after it, such as:

```
INPUT #MyFile, RetrieveMe
```

To see how to store, overwrite and retrieve data in a binary file, take a look at this example:

```
OPEN "STUFF.BIN" FOR BINARY AS #myfile
PRINT #myfile, "Welcome back home!"
SEEK #myfile, 0
INPUT #myfile, txt$
PRINT "Current Data in binary file: "; txt$
SEEK #myfile, 8
PRINT #myfile, "to my world!"
SEEK #myfile, 0
INPUT #myfile, txt$
PRINT "New Data in binary file: ";txt$
CLOSE #myfile
END
```

Here's what's happening in the preceding example:

1. The first line tells the computer, "Open up the binary file STUFF.BIN, assign it a file handle of #myfile."

2. The second line tells the computer to store the string, `"Welcome back home!"` in the binary file.

3. The third line tells the computer to move the file pointer to the beginning of the binary file.

4. The fourth line tells the computer, "Read all the data out of the binary file represented by the `#myfile` handle and store the result in a variable called `txt$`."

5. The fifth line tells the computer, "Print the current contents of the binary file in the main window, which means Liberty BASIC prints the string, `"Welcome back home!""`

6. The sixth line tells the computer, "Move the file pointer to the eight position in the binary file."

7. The seventh line tells the computer, "Starting with the eighth position in the binary file, overwrite the data and replace it with the string, `"to my world!""`

8. The eighth line tells the computer, "Move the file pointer back to the front of the binary file."

9. The ninth line tells the computer, "Read all the data from the binary file represented by the handle `#myfile`, and store it in a variable called `txt$`."

10. The tenth line tells the computer, "Print the contents of the binary file in the main window."

11. The eleventh line tells the computer, "Close the binary file represented by the `#myfile` handle."

12. The twelfth line tells the computer, "This is the end of the program. Now it's safe for Microsoft Windows to crash without losing any of my valuable data."

Chapter 14

Creating a User Interface

· ·

· ·

A s the name implies, a *user interface* acts as the middleman between the user and your program. A user gives commands through your program's user interface, which passes those commands to the part of your program that actually does the work. Then your program passes data back to the user interface to display on-screen for the user to see.

Designing a Window

The most common element of a Windows program is a window, which is nothing more than a rectangle that appears on-screen. A window has the following two purposes:

✔ To display your program's commands, such as pull-down menus or command buttons, so that the user can use them to make selections or input information into the program

✔ To display information on-screen for the user to see, such as a graph of a stock price or text that the user types

Creating a new window

To create a window, you need to use the OPEN command and define the text that you want to appear in the window titlebar, as the following example shows:

```
NOMAINWIN
OPEN "Titlebar text" FOR Window AS #1
PRINT #1, "trapclose [quit]"
WAIT

[quit]
CONFIRM "Are you sure that you want to quit?"; quit$
IF quit$ = "no" THEN WAIT
CLOSE #1
END
```

This program tells Liberty BASIC to do the following:

1. The first line tells Liberty BASIC not to display the main window.

2. The second line uses the OPEN command to create a new window, display the Titlebar text string in the title bar of the window, and assign the nickname #1 to represent the window that you just created.

3. The third line tells the computer to follow the instructions following the [quit] label if the user tries to close the program. This line uses the PRINT command to detect when the user tries to close the window identified by the #1 nickname, but doesn't actually print anything on the screen.

4. The fourth line uses the WAIT command to tell your program to wait for the user to do something.

5. The fifth line is the [quit] label.

6. The sixth line displays a Confirm dialog box that asks, Are you sure that you want to quit? The CONFIRM command automatically displays a Yes and No command button in the dialog box. If the user clicks the Yes button, the program stores a value of "yes" in the quit$ variable. If the user clicks the No button, it stores a value of "no" in the quit$ variable.

7. The seventh line checks to see whether the value of the quit$ variable equals "no." If so, it runs the WAIT command to wait for the user to do something.

8. The eighth line closes the window that the nickname #1 identifies. This line runs only if the user clicks the Yes button in the Confirm dialog box that the sixth line displays.

9. The ninth line marks the end of the program.

When you run this program, a window appears on-screen and waits for you to click its close box before the program stops running.

Any time that you use the OPEN command to create a new window, you must eventually use the CLOSE command to shut the window. If you don't use the CLOSE command eventually, your program may cause the computer to crash.

Defining the size and location of a window

Each time that you create a window, Liberty BASIC may display that window on a different part of the screen. If you want to specify the exact location where you want your window to appear, you can use the UpperLeftX and UpperLeftY commands, which define how far from the left (the X coordinate) and the top edge (the Y coordinate) the upper-left corner of your window appears on-screen, as shown in Figure 14-1. If you want your window to appear exactly 225 pixels from the top and 139 pixels from the left edge of the screen, for example, you can use the following program:

```
NOMAINWIN
UpperLeftX = 139
UpperLeftY = 225
OPEN "Titlebar" FOR Window AS #1
PRINT #1, "trapclose [quit]"
WAIT

[quit]
CONFIRM "Are you sure you want to quit?"; quit$
IF quit$ = "no" THEN WAIT
CLOSE #1
END
```

The UpperLeftX and UpperLeftY commands define how far the window appears from the left and top edges, respectively. If you want to define the exact size of your window, you can use the WindowHeight and WindowWidth commands to define a size measured in pixels, as follows:

```
NOMAINWIN
UpperLeftX = 139
UpperLeftY = 225
WindowWidth = 550
WindowHeight = 275
OPEN "Titlebar" FOR Window AS #1
PRINT #1, "trapclose [quit]"
WAIT

[quit]
CONFIRM "Are you sure you want to quit?"; quit$
IF quit$ = "no" THEN WAIT
CLOSE #1
END
```

Title bar

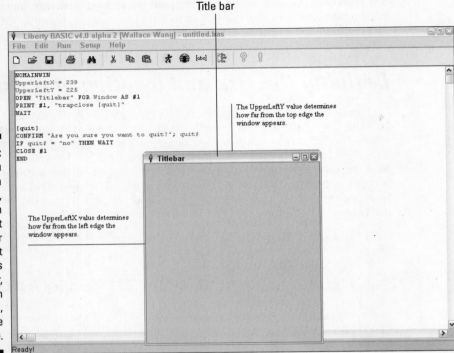

Figure 14-1: After you create a window, you can define text to appear in that window's title bar, location on-screen, and the window size.

You must define the size and location of a window before using the OPEN command that actually creates the window on-screen.

Adding color to a window

Liberty BASIC also enables you to choose the background color for your window by using the BackgroundColor$ command and to set its value to one of the following colors:

White	Darkblue
Black	Red
Lightgray (or Palegray)	Darkred
Darkgray	Pink
Yellow	Darkpink
Brown	Green
Blue	Darkgreen
Cyan	Darkcyan

If you want to create a window with a pink background, you can use the following commands:

```
NOMAINWIN
UpperLeftX = 139
UpperLeftY = 225
WindowWidth = 550
WindowHeight = 275
BackgroundColor$ = "Pink"
OPEN "Titlebar" FOR Window AS #1
PRINT #1, "trapclose [quit]"
WAIT

[quit]
CONFIRM "Are you sure you want to quit?"; quit$
IF quit$ = "no" THEN WAIT
CLOSE #1
END
```

Putting Pull-Down Menus in a Window

Most windows provide *pull-down menus* so that users can pick a command. To create a pull-down menu, you need to use the MENU command to define the following:

✔ Menu title (typical menu titles are File, Edit, and Help)

✔ Menu commands that appear on the menu, under the menu title (such as Edit, Print, or Cut)

✔ A label to tell your program which instructions to follow after a user chooses a particular menu command

A typical menu command may look as follows:

```
MENU #WindowHandle, "Menu Title", "Command1", [command1]
```

In this example, #WindowHandle refers to the nickname of the window where you want the menu to appear, Menu Title appears at the top of the window, and Command1 appears after the user clicks the title of the pull-down menu. To show you a real-life example, take a look at the following program:

```
NOMAINWIN
MENU #1, "&File", "&Open", [asOpen], "&Print", [asPrint],
        "E&xit", [quit]
OPEN "Menu Example" FOR Window AS #1
PRINT #1, "trapclose [quit]"
WAIT

[quit]
```

```
CONFIRM "Are you sure that you want to quit?"; quit$
IF quit$ = "no" THEN WAIT
CLOSE #1
END

[asOpen]
NOTICE "Open command chosen"
WAIT

[asPrint]
NOTICE "Print command chosen"
WAIT
```

This program works as follows:

1. The first line tells Liberty BASIC not to display the main window.

2. The second line defines a pull-down menu that appears in the window that the file handle #1 designates. The menu title is File and the commands that appear underneath are Open, Print, and Exit.

   If you want a letter in a menu title or command to appear underlined, put an ampersand character (&) in front of that letter, such as &Print. Any underlined letter acts as a shortcut or accelerator key so that the user can choose that menu title by pressing Alt plus the underlined letter, such as Alt+F for the File menu. After selecting a menu, the user can then type the underlined letter in a command, such as *X*, to choose that menu command — for example, Exit.

3. The third line tells the computer, "Create a window with the text Menu Example in the title bar and identify this window by its file handle of #1."

4. The fourth line tells the computer to follow the instructions following the [quit] label if the user tries to close the program.

5. The fifth line tells the computer to wait for the user to choose a command.

6. The sixth line is the [quit] label.

7. The seventh line displays a Confirm dialog box that asks, "Are you sure that you want to quit?" If the user clicks the Yes button, the program stores a value of "yes" in the quit$ variable. If the user clicks the No button, it stores a value of "no" in the quit$ variable.

8. The eighth line checks to see whether the value of the quit$ variable equals "no". If so, it runs the WAIT command to wait for the user to do something.

9. The ninth line closes the window that the nickname #1 identifies. This line runs only if the user clicks the Yes button in the Confirm dialog box that the seventh line displays.

10. The tenth line marks the end of the program.

11. The eleventh line identifies the label [asOpen]. After the user chooses the Open command from the File menu, the computer jumps to this line to look for further instructions to follow.

12. The twelfth and thirteenth lines tell the computer, "Display a Notice dialog box with the message, Open command chosen. Then wait for the user to do something else."

13. The fourteenth line identifies the label [asPrint]. After the user chooses the Print command from the File menu, the computer jumps to this line to look for further instructions to follow.

14. The fifteenth and sixteenth lines tell the computer, "Display a Notice dialog box with the message, Print command chosen. Then wait for the user to do something else."

To define additional menus for a window, as shown in Figure 14-2, just use multiple MENU commands, as in the following example:

```
NOMAINWIN
MENU #1, "&File", "&Open", [asOpen], "&Print", [asPrint],
     "E&xit", [quit]
MENU #1, "&Help", "&Contents", [asContents], "&About",
     [asAbout]
OPEN "Menu Example" FOR Window AS #1
PRINT #1, "trapclose [quit]"
WAIT

[quit]
CONFIRM "Are you sure that you want to quit?"; quit$
IF quit$ = "no" THEN WAIT
CLOSE #1
END

[asOpen]
NOTICE "Open command chosen"
WAIT

[asPrint]
NOTICE "Print command chosen"
WAIT

[asContents]
NOTICE "Contents command chosen"
WAIT

[asAbout]
NOTICE "About command chosen"
WAIT
```

Each time that you create additional menu commands, you need to create instructions (which a [label] identifies) for the computer to follow whenever the user chooses those commands.

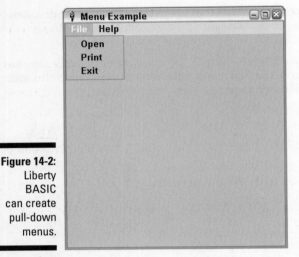

Figure 14-2:
Liberty
BASIC
can create
pull-down
menus.

Making Pop-Up Menus

In addition to pull-down menus, many programs also offer *pop-up menus* that appear next to the mouse pointer when you right-click the mouse. To create a pop-up menu in Liberty BASIC, you need to use the POPUPMENU command, as follows:

```
POPUPMENU "command1", [label1], "command2", [label2]
```

To make the POPUPMENU easier to understand, place each command and label on a separate line and use the underscore character (_) at the end of each line. The underscore character tells Liberty BASIC that additional instructions appear on the following line. You can use the underscore character to divide long lines of commands into shorter, separate lines, such as you see in the following example:

```
POPUPMENU _
"command1", [label1], _
"command2", [label2], _
"command3", [label3]
```

Here's what the preceding commands do:

1. The POPUPMENU command tells the computer, "Create a pop-up menu next to the current position of the mouse pointer."

2. The "command1" and "command2" text are the actual commands that appear on the pop-up menu. You can add additional commands so that your pop-up menus can display 5, 7, or 15 different commands.

3. The [label1] and [label2] labels identify instructions for the computer to follow if the user chooses a particular menu command. So if the user chose "command1", the computer immediately follows the instructions that the [label1] label identifies.

If you want to add a horizontal line to separate commands on your pop-up menu, just use the vertical line character (|) in place of a command and omit any label following the | character, as shown in the example below.

```
POPUPMENU _
"command1", [label1], _
|, _
"command3", [label3]
```

To see how pop-up menus work, try the following program, as shown in Figure 14-3. Notice how the vertical line character creates a horizontal line to separate commands on the pop-up menu.

```
NOMAINWIN
POPUPMENU _
    "Destroy the planet", [one], _
    "Poison the environment", [two], _
    | ,_
    "Get elected to political office", [three]

NOTICE "Nothing selected."
END

[one]
NOTICE "Launching missiles now."
END

[two]
NOTICE "Spilling oil into the oceans."
END

[three]
NOTICE "Fooled the public once more."
END
```

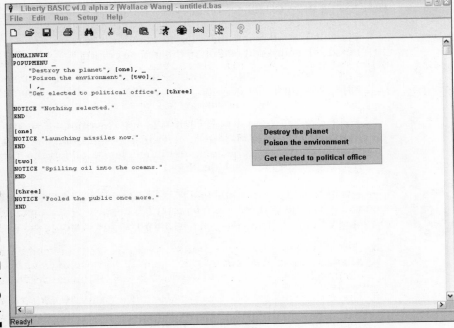

Figure 14-3:
Pop-up
menus can
provide
additional
options for
users to
choose.

Putting Controls in a Window

Although you commonly use pull-down menus to get commands from the user,
you may also want to add command buttons, check boxes, radio buttons, and
text boxes to a window. In placing such controls as command buttons on a
window, you need to define the following:

- A name to identify the control
- Text to appear on the control
- A label to identify instructions for the computer to follow after the
  user chooses that particular control
- The width and height of the control
- The position of the control

Creating a command button

A command button usually appears on-screen as a gray rectangle containing
a label such as OK or Cancel. To create a command button, you need to use
the BUTTON command, as follows:

```
BUTTON #Windowhandle.buttonname, "Button text",
        [branchLabel], UL, xpos, ypos, width, height
```

If you omit the width and height, the button automatically adjusts to the size of the text that you want to appear on the button.

Here's how the following command works:

1. The BUTTON command tells the computer, "Create a command button inside the window that the nickname #Windowhandle identifies."

2. The buttonname portion tells the computer, "Identify this button by this unique name."

3. The Button text portion is the text that actually appears on the button.

4. The [branchLabel] portion identifies a label to which the computer jumps to find instructions to follow after the user clicks the button.

5. The UL portion tells the computer, "Position the command button by using the *upper-left* corner of the window." Instead of using UL, you can also use UR (upper-right), LL (lower-left), or LR (lower-right).

6. The xpos and ypos portions represent the X and Y position of the button's location, which you measure in pixels from the upper-left (UL), upper-right (UR), lower-left (LL), or lower-right (LR) edge of the window.

7. The width and height portions define the width and height of the button.

To see how this button works in a real-life example, run the following program, the results of which are shown in Figure 14-4:

```
NOMAINWIN
WindowHeight = 200
WindowWidth = 250
BUTTON #main.mybutton, "E&xit", [quit], LL, 10, 10, 45, 25
OPEN "Command button example" FOR WINDOW AS #main
PRINT #main, "trapclose [quit]"
WAIT

[quit]
CONFIRM "Are you sure you want to quit?"; quit$
IF quit$ = "no" THEN WAIT
CLOSE #main
END
```

As an alternative to creating a command button, Liberty BASIC also enables you to use a bitmap image as a button. To turn a bitmap image into a button, you need to use the BMPBUTTON command, as follows:

```
BMPBUTTON #Windowhandle.buttonname, "bitmap filename",
          [branchLabel], UL, xpos, ypos
```

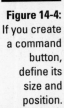

Figure 14-4:
If you create
a command
button,
define its
size and
position.

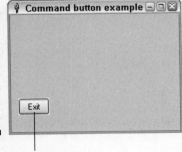

Command button

Here's what the preceding command does:

1. The BMPBUTTON command tells the computer, "Create a button out of a bitmap image and display this image inside the window that the nickname #Windowhandle identifies."

2. The buttonname portion tells the computer, "Identify this bitmap button by this unique name."

3. The "bitmap filename" portion defines the directory and filename of the bitmap image that you want to use, such as C:\Liberty\face.bmp.

4. The [branchLabel] portion identifies a label to which the computer jumps to find instructions to follow after the user clicks the bitmap button.

5. The UL portion tells the computer, "Position the bitmap button by using the *upper-left* corner of the window." Instead of using UL, you can also use UR (upper-right), LL (lower-left), or LR (lower-right).

6. The xpos and ypos portions represent the X and Y position of the bitmap button's location, which you measure in pixels from the upper-left (UL), upper-right (UR), lower-left (LL), or lower-right (LR) edge of the window.

To see how this button works in a real-life example, try running the following program:

```
NOMAINWIN
WindowWidth = 400
BMPBUTTON #main.picturebtn, "vwsignon.bmp", [Exit], UL, 10,
          40
OPEN "Bitmap Button Example" FOR WINDOW AS #main
PRINT #main, "trapclose [quit]"
WAIT

[quit]
CONFIRM "Are you sure you want to quit?"; quit$
IF quit$ = "no" THEN WAIT
CLOSE #main
END
```

Displaying text

Sometimes you may want to display text inside a window to display a message or give instructions to the user. In Liberty BASIC, text that the user can't change is known as *static* text, which you can create by using the STATICTEXT command, as follows:

```
STATICTEXT #Windowhandle.staticname, "Static text", xpos,
           ypos, width, height
```

Here's what the preceding command does:

1. The STATICTEXT command tells the computer, "Display text inside a window that the nickname #Windowhandle identifies. Identify the static text by the name staticname."

2. The "Static text" portion tells the computer, "Display inside the window whatever text appears inside double quotes."

3. The xpos and ypos portions represent the X and Y position of the static text's location, which you measure in pixels from the upper-left edge of the window.

4. The width and height portions represent the width and height of the static text, which you also measure in pixels.

You can change text inside static text by using the PRINT command, as follows:

```
PRINT #Windowhandle.staticname, "New text"
```

To try out a real program, try the following example:

```
NOMAINWIN
STATICTEXT #main.static, "Old text", 10, 10, 75, 25
BUTTON #main.mybutton, "Change", [change], LL, 10, 10, 45, 25
OPEN "Real-life example" FOR Window AS #main
PRINT #main, "trapclose [quit]"
WAIT

[change]
PRINT #main.static, "New text"
WAIT

[quit]
CONFIRM "Are you sure you want to quit?"; quit$
IF quit$ = "no" THEN WAIT
CLOSE #main
END
```

This program displays static text in a window that reads Old text. After you click the Change command button, the static text changes and displays New text.

Creating a check box

Sometimes you may want to give the user several options to choose. To do so, you can create check boxes that display a box for the user to click, along with a label to describe the option, as shown in Figure 14-5.

Check boxes

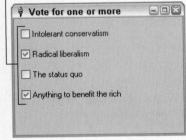

Figure 14-5:
Check
boxes offer
multiple
choices.

To create a check box, you need to use the CHECKBOX command, as follows:

```
CHECKBOX #Windowhandle.boxname, "Check box text", [set],
        [reset], xpos, ypos, width, height
```

Here's what the preceding command does:

1. The CHECKBOX command tells the computer, "Create a check box inside the window that the nickname #Windowhandle identifies."

2. The boxname portion tells the computer, "Identify this check box by this unique name."

3. The "Check box text" portion defines the text that appears next to the check box.

4. The [set] label defines instructions to follow if the user chooses the check box. The [reset] label defines instructions to follow if the user clears the check box.

5. The xpos and ypos portions represent the X and Y positions of the check box's location, which you measure in pixels from the upper-left edge of the window.

6. The width and height portions represent the width and height of the check box, which you also measure in pixels.

To see how a check box works in a real-life example, try running the following program (which appears in Figure 14-4):

```
NOMAINWIN
WindowWidth = 250
WindowHeight = 200
CHECKBOX #1.check1, "Intolerant conservatism", [set],
        [reset], 10, 10, 250, 25
CHECKBOX #1.check2, "Radical liberalism", [set], [reset], 10,
        40, 250, 25
CHECKBOX #1.check3, "The status quo", [set], [reset], 10, 70,
        250, 25
CHECKBOX #1.check4, "Anything to benefit the rich", [set],
        [reset], 10, 100, 250, 25
OPEN "Vote for one or more" FOR Window AS #1
PRINT #1, "trapclose [quit]"
WAIT

[set]
NOTICE "Are you sure you live in a democracy?"
WAIT

[reset]
NOTICE "Good move!"
WAIT

[quit]
CONFIRM "Are you sure you want to quit?"; quit$
IF quit$ = "no" THEN WAIT
CLOSE #1
END
```

The value of a check box is either set (if the check box contains a check mark) or reset (if the check box is empty). To determine the value of a check box, you can use the following two commands:

```
PRINT #1.cboxname, "value?"
INPUT #1.cboxname, result$
```

The PRINT command retrieves the value from the check box that cboxname identifies, and the INPUT command stores the value (either set or reset) in the variable result$.

Creating a radio button

Unlike check boxes, which enable you to choose multiple options that the check boxes list, radio buttons enable you to choose only one option at a time. To create a radio button, you need to use the RADIOBUTTON command, which works nearly identically as the CHECKBOX command, as follows:

```
RADIOBUTTON #Windowhandle.radioname, "Radio button text",
        [set], [reset], xpos, ypos, width, height
```

To see how radio buttons work, try running the following program, as shown in Figure 14-6. After you click the command button containing the label Check radio button 1, an Information dialog box pops up to tell you the value of the first radio button.

```
NOMAINWIN
WindowWidth = 250
WindowHeight = 200
RADIOBUTTON #1.radio1, "Intolerant conservatism", [set],
        [reset], 10, 10, 250, 25
RADIOBUTTON #1.radio2, "Radical liberalism", [set], [reset],
        10, 40, 250, 25
RADIOBUTTON #1.radio3, "The status quo", [set], [reset], 10,
        70, 250, 25
RADIOBUTTON #1.radio4, "Anything to benefit the rich", [set],
        [reset], 10, 100, 250, 25
BUTTON #1.button1, "Check radio button 1", [test], LL, 50, 3
OPEN "Vote for one or more" FOR Window AS #1
PRINT #1, "trapclose [quit]"
WAIT

[test]
PRINT #1.radio1, "value?"
INPUT #1.radio1, test$
NOTICE "The value of radio button 1 is "; test$
WAIT

[set]
WAIT

[quit]
CONFIRM "Are you sure you want to quit?"; quit$
IF quit$ = "no" THEN WAIT
CLOSE #1
END
```

The value of a radio button is either set (if you choose the radio button) or reset (if the radio button is empty). To determine the value of a radio button, you can use the following two commands:

```
PRINT #1.radiobuttonname, "value?"
INPUT #1.radiobuttonname, result$
```

The PRINT command retrieves the value from the radio button that the radio buttonname identifies, and the INPUT command stores the value (either set or reset) in the variable result$.

Radio buttons

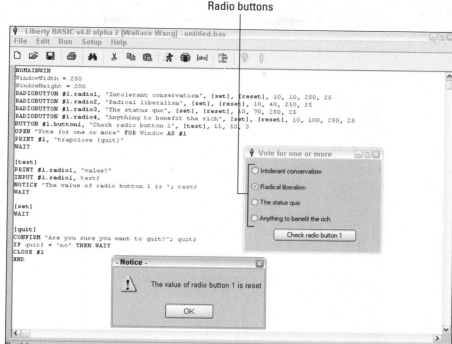

Figure 14-6:
Radio
buttons
force a user
to choose
one option
out of many.

Creating text boxes

Text boxes provide a box that can both display text and enable the user to type text. To create a text box, you need to use the TEXTBOX command, as follows:

```
TEXTBOX #Windowhandle.textboxname, xpos, ypos, width, height
```

Here's what the preceding command does:

1. The TEXTBOX command tells the computer, "Create a text box inside the window that the nickname #Windowhandle identifies."

2. The textboxname portion tells the computer, "Identify this text box by this unique name."

3. The xpos and ypos portions represent the X and Y positions of the text box's location, which you measure in pixels from the upper-left edge of the window.

4. The width and height portions represent the width and height of the text box, which you also measure in pixels.

If you want to insert text into a text box, you need to use the PRINT command and identify the window handle, the name of the text box, and the text that you want to insert, as follows:

```
PRINT #1.text1, "This text appears in the text1 text box."
```

To retrieve the text from a text box, you need to use the following two commands:

```
PRINT #1.text1, "!contents?"
INPUT #1.text1, stuff$
```

To show you how text boxes work, try the following program, which displays a text box and a menu that gives you the option of clearing the text box and displaying the contents of the text box in a Notice dialog box:

```
NOMAINWIN
WindowWidth = 250
WindowHeight = 200
TEXTBOX #1.text1, 25, 25, 200, 100
MENU #1, "&Options", "&Clear text box", [clear], _
    "&Display text from text box", [display], _
    "E&xit", [quit]
OPEN "Text box example" FOR Window AS #1
PRINT #1.text1, "Initial text."
PRINT #1, "trapclose [quit]"
WAIT

[clear]
PRINT #1.text1, ""
WAIT

[display]
PRINT #1.text1, "!contents?"
INPUT #1.text1, stuff$
NOTICE "Text in text box = " + stuff$
WAIT

[quit]
CONFIRM "Are you sure that you want to quit?"; quit$
IF quit$ = "no" THEN WAIT
CLOSE #1
END
```

Creating list boxes

To offer users multiple choices, you can use either check boxes or radio buttons. List boxes are especially handy for displaying numerous items that are cumbersome to list individually as multiple check boxes or radio buttons. In addition, list boxes help eliminate input errors because the user just clicks on a choice rather than typing something in (and risking misspelling a word).

To create a list box, you need to use the LISTBOX command this way:

```
LISTBOX #Windowhandle.listboxname, array$(), [action], xpos,
        ypos, width, height
```

Here's what the preceding command does:

1. The LISTBOX command tells the computer, "Create a list box inside the window that the nickname #Windowhandle identifies."

2. The listboxname portion tells the computer, "Identify this list box by this unique name."

3. The array$ portion represents a string *array* that contains all the items that you want to display in the list box. To learn more about arrays, see Chapter 16.

4. The [action] portion represents the instructions for the computer to follow the moment that the user chooses an item from the list box.

5. The xpos and ypos portions represent the X and Y positions of the list box's location, which you measure in pixels from the upper-left edge of the window.

6. The width and height portions represent the width and height of the list box, which you also measure in pixels.

To choose an item in a list box, users must double-click that item. If you want users to choose an item in a list box by single-clicking, however, you need to use the following command:

```
PRINT #handle.listboxname, "singleclickselect"
```

This command tells the computer, "Let the user single click to choose any item that appears in the list box identified by listboxname."

After the user selects an item in a list box, you can use the following two commands to identify what the user chose:

```
PRINT #1.listbox1, "selection?"
INPUT #1.listbox1, selected$
```

To see how list boxes work, try the following program, which displays two list boxes, as shown in Figure 14-7. Because the top list box is smaller than the total number of items, this list box automatically adds a vertical scroll bar so that users can scroll through all the options. The top list box enables the user to single-click an item because of the following command:

```
PRINT #1.list1, "singleclickselect"
```

On the other hand, the bottom list box forces users to double-click to select an item.

```
NOMAINWIN
array$(0) = "Mystery meat"
array$(1) = "Cat food"
array$(2) = "Something pink and artificially preserved"
array$(3) = "Liquid mush"
array$(4) = "Sugar and artificial coloring"

WindowWidth = 300
WindowHeight = 240

LISTBOX #1.list1, array$(), [Action1], 40, 10, 216, 40
LISTBOX #1.list2, array$(), [Action2], 40, 100, 216, 70
OPEN "Here are your choices for dinner tonight" FOR Window AS
      #1
PRINT #1.list1, "singleclickselect"
PRINT #1, "trapclose [quit]"
WAIT

[Action1]
PRINT #1.list1, "selection?"
INPUT #1.list1, selected$
NOTICE "You chose = " + selected$
WAIT

[Action2]
PRINT #1.list2, "selection?"
INPUT #1.list2, selected$
NOTICE "You chose = " + selected$
WAIT

[quit]
CONFIRM "Are you sure you want to quit?"; quit$
IF quit$ = "no" THEN WAIT
CLOSE #1
END
```

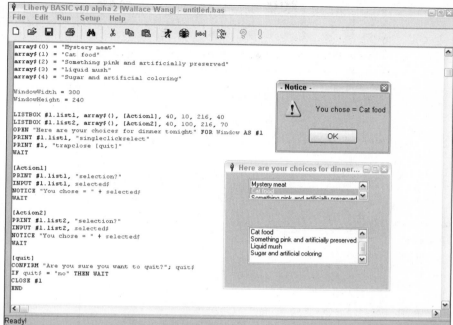

Figure 14-7:
List boxes
can display
multiple
options to
a user in
a small
amount
of space.

Creating combo boxes

Combo boxes act like list boxes but they take up even less room on-screen. After the user clicks a combo box, a drop-down list of options appears for the user to choose among, as shown in Figure 14-8. As a result, combo boxes are sometimes referred to as drop-down list boxes.

To create a combo box, you need to use the COMBOBOX command, which is nearly identical to the LIST BOX command, as follows:

```
COMBOBOX #Windowhandle.comboboxname, array$(), [action],
         xpos, ypos, width, height
```

After the user selects an item in a combo box, you can use the following two commands to identify what the user chose:

```
PRINT #1.combobox1, "selection?"
INPUT #1.combobox1, selected$
```

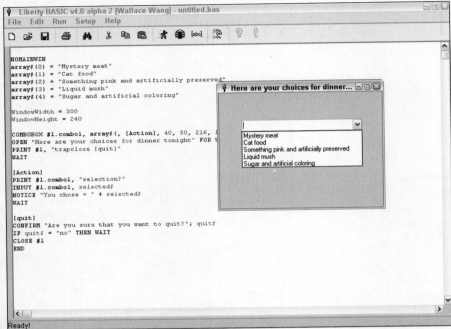

Figure 14-8:
Combo
boxes
display
a drop-
down list.

To see how combo boxes work, try the following program:

```
NOMAINWIN
array$(0) = "Mystery meat"
array$(1) = "Cat food"
array$(2) = "Something pink and artificially preserved"
array$(3) = "Liquid mush"
array$(4) = "Sugar and artificial coloring"

WindowWidth = 300
WindowHeight = 240

COMBOBOX #1.combo1, array$(, [Action], 40, 50, 216, 100
OPEN "Here are your choices for dinner tonight" FOR Window AS
        #1
PRINT #1, "trapclose [quit]"
WAIT

[Action]
PRINT #1.combo1, "selection?"
INPUT #1.combo1, selected$
```

```
NOTICE "You chose = " + selected$
WAIT

[quit]
CONFIRM "Are you sure that you want to quit?"; quit$
IF quit$ = "no" THEN WAIT
CLOSE #1
END
```

Creating group boxes

Group boxes do nothing more than surround other controls, as shown in Figure 14-9. This can be especially useful when you want to separate groups of radio buttons or check boxes. To create a group box, use the following command:

```
GROUPBOX #Windowhandle, "Groupbox text", xpos, ypos, width,
        height
```

To see how group boxes work, try the following program:

```
NOMAINWIN
WindowWidth = 250
WindowHeight = 200
GROUPBOX #1, "Your choices are", 5, 5, 225, 120
RADIOBUTTON #1.radio2, "Radical liberalism", [set], [reset],
        10, 30, 150, 15
RADIOBUTTON #1.radio3, "The status quo", [set], [reset], 10,
        60, 150, 15
RADIOBUTTON #1.radio4, "Anything to benefit the rich", [set],
        [reset], 10, 90, 150, 15
BUTTON #1.button1, "Exit program", [quit], LL, 50, 1
OPEN "Vote for one or more" FOR Window AS #1
PRINT #1, "trapclose [quit]"
WAIT

[set]
WAIT

[quit]
CONFIRM "Are you sure you want to quit?"; quit$
IF quit$ = "no" THEN WAIT
CLOSE #1
END
```

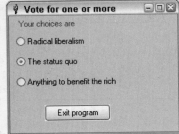

Figure 14-9:
A group box organizes multiple controls such as radio buttons.

Chapter 15

Debugging Programs

*N*obody writes programs that work 100 percent correctly all the time. The problem is that programming means giving the computer extremely detailed instructions. Give the computer one wrong instruction or one misplaced instruction, make one wrong assumption or omit one necessary instruction, and the computer has no idea what to do next, which can cause your program to fail or, in programming lingo, to *crash*.

If a program doesn't work correctly, programmers never say, "My program has a problem." Instead, programmers use their own lingo and say, "My program has a *bug*." Although eliminating all bugs from a program is impossible, Liberty BASIC (and many other language compilers) provides special features to help you track down the obvious bugs and wipe them out so that your program works well enough for people to actually use it.

Anatomy of a Computer Bug

Computer bugs tend to fall into the following three categories:

✔ **Syntax errors:** This type of error occurs if you spell something wrong or type a command incorrectly, such as misspelling PRINT as PRRINT or typing too many commas.

✔ **Run-time errors:** These errors occur if your program runs into something unexpected, such as if you ask the user to input an age and the user types a negative number.

✔ **Logic errors:** These bugs occur if your instructions don't work as you intend them to, but the computer performs these flawed instructions anyway, creating unpredictable results.

Although bugs riddle every program, most bugs are relatively harmless or cause only minor problems, such as displaying a menu incorrectly at unpredictable times. Bugs that keep a program from working at all are more serious. Any bug that keeps a company from shipping (and selling) a program is known as a *showstopper*.

Syntax Errors

Syntax errors are often misspellings of valid commands or omissions (or misplacement) of crucial characters such as a comma or a left parenthesis. If you misspell a BASIC command such as PRINT, Liberty BASIC is usually smart enough to highlight the line where the *syntax error* occurs so that you can fix it later. If Liberty BASIC finds a syntax error, it highlights the line causing the problem and displays a message in the bottom left corner of the screen, as shown in Figure 15-1.

Syntax error in code

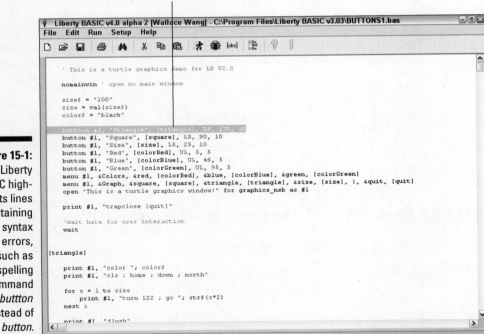

Figure 15-1:
Liberty
BASIC high-
lights lines
containing
syntax
errors,
such as
misspelling
a command
as *buttton*
instead of
button.

Error message

The Destruction of Mariner 1

Syntax errors are usually caught because they give an invalid command to the computer, which immediately keeps the program from running at all. The worst syntax errors, however, are those that somehow give a valid but unintended command to the computer. Thus, the program keeps working — but not the way you want it to.

Back in 1962, NASA sent the Mariner 1 probe to study Venus, but before the rocket carrying the probe could make its way into outer space, it veered off course and NASA had to prematurely detonate the rocket. According to one story, the program was supposed to contain a FOR NEXT loop that told the computer to loop three times, as in the following example:

```
FOR I = 1, 3
```
But instead of a comma, the programmer had accidentally typed in a period, as follows:

```
FOR I = 1.3
```
So instead of telling the computer to loop three times, this command told the computer to set the value of the variable I to 1.3. The end result was that this error managed to give the computer a valid but incorrect command, causing NASA to lose a multimillion dollar rocket and payload as a result.

Although syntax errors usually prevent a program from working at all, watch out for your own misspellings because the computer will assume that you know what you're doing, even if you make a mistake. Especially troublesome are those times that you misspell a variable name. Consider, for example, the following program:

```
PROMPT "How many times do I need to tell you no"; Answeer$
PRINT "Your reply = "; Answer$
END
```

The preceding program asks the user, "How many times do I need to tell you no?" Then the program stores whatever the user types into the variable Answeer$ (the misspelling of Answer$). Because Liberty BASIC considers Answer$ and Answeer$ as two completely different variable names, the Answer$ variable doesn't contain any data. If you run this program, it doesn't print out what the user types, simply because of a single misspelling.

Liberty BASIC can detect syntax errors in misspelled commands, but it cannot detect misspelled variable names. If you insert a space between a function or subroutine name and any parentheses that follow it, Liberty BASIC may treat that as a syntax error, too, although it won't necessarily tell you so.

Besides misspelling a variable name, watch out for mixing upper- and lowercase letters in variable names. Liberty BASIC considers the variable Answer$ as completely different from the variable answer$ simply because one starts with an uppercase letter A and the second one doesn't.

Death from the Therac-25

The Therac-25 was a radiation-therapy machine designed to adminster radiation doses to patients. To prevent excessive doses of radiation, the Therac-25 included a safety mechanism that relied completely on its software to prevent any problems — but the software contained a fatal run-time error.

The Therac-25 offered two modes of operation: X-ray and electron beam. If the technician accidentally selected the X-ray mode first, the Therac-25 would select a high-intensity energy level. If the technician then switched to electron-beam mode right away without completing the X-ray mode, the Therac-25 would maintain its higher energy intensity level for electron-mode operation, which meant delivering a fatal radiation burn to any unlucky patient lying underneath.

Only after several people suffered severe radiation burns at the hands of the Therac-25 did someone finally discover this hidden run-time error, but by then, it was too late for all the people who'd already been irreparably burned by the Therac-25 and its supposedly fail-safe software safety mechanism.

Because a single misspelling of a variable name can mess up your program, many programmers take shortcuts and choose short, cryptic variable names. Don't take this route! The time that you save in using short variable names is lost in comparison with the time that you need to decipher what those short variable names represent.

Such errors can prove hard to detect because a misspelling can still enable the program to run, albeit incorrectly. Anytime that your program runs but doesn't seem to work right, start looking for misspellings or missing elements such as quotation marks, commas, upper and lowercase variable names, and parentheses, any of which may cause the program to fail.

Run-Time Errors

Run-time errors are sneaky little bugs that hide in programs. A program may work correctly right up until it receives data that the programmer never expected, such as a negative number that the user types for his year of birth. Unfortunately, the only time that you can find run-time errors is after they cause the program to crash.

Because run-time errors occur only after your program receives data that it doesn't know how to handle, the best way to hunt down run-time errors is to run your program over and over, feeding the program extreme values of different data each time.

If your program asks the user to input an age, for example, type a huge number (such as 60,000). Then type zero. Finally, type a negative number such as –9,489. By testing extreme ranges of values, you can often smoke out run-time errors before you release your program for actual use.

Fun with Logic Errors

Of all the types of bugs that can infest your program, none is more insidious than a *logic error*. Syntax errors can prove fairly easy to find because you just need to look for misspellings or places where you may have forgotten to type a character, such as a closing parenthesis. Similarly, you can often find run-time errors by testing your program by using extreme values of data.

Logic errors, however, occur even after you write your instructions perfectly — except for the fact that they're the *wrong* instructions. Because you assume that the instructions you write are correct, to find and correct a logic error, you must examine these instruction line by line to see whether they're missing a step or simply solving the wrong problem altogether.

Because logic errors can prove so difficult to find, Liberty BASIC provides special debugging features to help make this task a little easier. The two main ways to examine a program for logic errors are by *stepping* and *tracing*.

The Sinking of the *H.M.S. Sheffield*

The trouble with eradicating all logic bugs from a program is that you must examine your entire program for mistaken assumptions. Although programs may work perfectly fine during testing, they may encounter unexpected situations in the real world, causing the programs to fail catastrophically.

One prominent example of a logic bug occurred during the Falkland Islands War between Great Britain and Argentina. The British destroyer the *H.M.S. Sheffield* used an advanced computer air-defense system designed to protect the ship from air and missile attack. To prevent this air-defense system from shooting down its own

missiles, the computers were programmed to allow certain "friendly" missiles to fly unmolested through its defenses. These "friendly" missiles included all the types of missiles that the British Navy used, which included the French-built Exocet antiship missile.

Unfortunately for the British, Argentina had also bought Exocet anti-ship missiles from the French, so when the Sheffield's computers detected the incoming Exocet missiles, they assumed the missiles were "friendly" and allowed them to pass uncontested through the Sheffield's air defense system — and right into the Sheffield, sinking the ship with several direct hits.

Stepping line by line

Stepping involves running through your program line by line and watching to see how your program works. The moment that you spot the program doing something wrong, you know exactly which line in your program is making the mistake.

To step through a Liberty BASIC program, follow these steps:

1. **Load the program that you want to step through line by line.**

2. **Choose Run➪Debug, press Alt+F5, or click the Debug icon on the toolbar.**

   A Debugging window appears, as shown in Figure 15-2. If the main window also appears, you may need to close or move it out of the way to see the Debugging window.

3. **Click one of the following:**

   ✓ **Step Into:** Runs your program line-by-line so you can see what it's doing at each instruction.

   ✓ **Step Over:** Runs your program line-by-line but doesn't highlight any lines buried inside subroutines or functions.

   ✓ **Step Out:** In case you used the Step Into command to view code inside a subroutine or function, the Step Out command lets you quickly jump out of a subroutine or function without having to go through every single line in that particular subroutine or function.

   ✓ **Animate:** Runs your entire program, line by line, which you can halt at any time by clicking the Stop icon. To start running your program again, click the Resume icon.

   ✓ **Stop:** Temporarily halts program execution so you can examine the current status of your program such as the value of the different variables.

   ✓ **Resume:** Starts executing your program again after you have clicked the Stop icon.

   Liberty BASIC runs your program until it finds another TRACE command.

To help you study how a small chunk of your program works, click the mouse on a line in your program and then choose Code ➪ Run to Line. Liberty BASIC runs all the instructions up to the line that you clicked on and shows you the values of all of your variables in the top pane of the Debugging window.

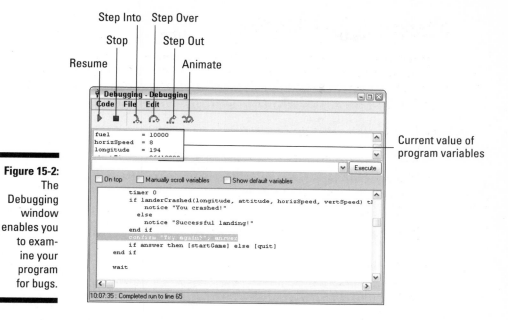

Figure 15-2:
The
Debugging
window
enables you
to exam-
ine your
program
for bugs.

Tracing through your program

Stepping through an entire program line by line can prove tedious and time-consuming, especially if you already have an idea of which part of your program may hide a bug. Instead of stepping through your whole program, line by line from the beginning, you can use tracing instead.

To use tracing in your program, follow these steps:

1. **Open the program that you want to debug.**

2. **Type the** TRACE **command at the point in your program where you want to start debugging.**

    In using the TRACE command, you have the following three options:

    - TRACE 0 runs your program from start to finish and stops only if you're fast enough to click the Stop button in the Debugging window.

    - TRACE 1 runs your program line by line, giving you a chance to click the Stop button in the Debugging window at any time.

    - TRACE 2 runs your program line by line in the Debugging window.

3. **Choose Run⇨Debug, or press Alt+F5.**

   The Debugging window appears. Depending on the TRACE command you typed in your program (such as TRACE 0 or TRACE 2), your program may run quickly or wait for you to click one of the Step icons to examine your program line by line.

4. **When you're done studying your program, click the Run icon in the Debugging window.**

   Liberty BASIC runs your program until it finds another TRACE command.

You can add multiple TRACE commands anywhere you need to put them in your program. The TRACE commands have no effect on the running of your program. Use TRACE commands only if you're debugging a program.

Part IV
Dealing with Data Structures

The 5th Wave   By Rich Tennant

"It's a ten step word processing program. It comes with a spell-checker, grammar-checker, cliche-checker, whine-checker, passive/aggressive-checker, politically correct-checker, hissy-fit-checker, pretentious pontificating-checker, boring anecdote-checker and a Freudian reference-checker."

In this part . . .

As you write a program, your program needs to store data in the computer's memory. Of course, your program can't just toss data anywhere in the computer's memory; if it did that, the memory would become as disorganized as a closet where you randomly throw clothes onto a heap.

To help organize the computer's memory, programs store data in something known as a *data structure*. A data structure is nothing more than a technical term that describes how computer programs organize data so that you can easily store and retrieve information. The simplest data structure is a simple variable that holds one chunk of information. A more complicated data structure comprises arrays, records, linked lists, and objects. You get to know all of them in this part of the book.

Chapter 16

Storing Stuff in Arrays

· ·

· ·

*I*f you want to store data temporarily, you must use a variable with a descriptive name, such as PhoneNumber, MovieRating, or FirstName. After you create a variable name to hold data, you normally also need to define what type of data the variable can hold, such as a string, integer, or single-precision number.

But sometimes you may want to store a list of nearly identical data. If you write a program to store the names of all the people in your class, for example, you may need to create a series of nearly identically named variables just to hold their names, as the following example shows:

```
Name1$ = "Patrick DeGuire"
Name2$ = "Jordan Preston Wang"
Name3$ = "Michael Elizondo"
Name4$ = "Bo the Cat"
```

Naturally, this method is clumsy, and any time that programmers run into a problem that threatens to make programming harder than necessary, they come up with a solution to avoid the problem. In this case, the solution that programmers developed is known as an *array*. Think of an array as a list — something like the one shown in Figure 16-1.

Figure 16-1:
An array stores items by the array's name and the item's position in the array.

DIM MyArray(5) AS STRING				
MyArray(1)	MyArray(2)	MyArray(3)	MyArray(4)	MyArray(5)

Making an Array

An ordinary variable can hold only one chunk of data at a time, such as a number or a name. The moment that you try to store another chunk of data in a variable, the variable immediately erases the old data and saves the new data.

Unlike ordinary variables, an array is a single variable name that can hold one or more chunks of data, as long as each chunk of data represents the same data type, such as string, integer, single-precision, and so on. To make an array, you must define it by using the DIM command, as follows:

```
DIM ArrayName(Number)
```

In this example, ArrayName is any valid variable name, and Number represents the total number of items that you want to store in the array.

As is true of other variables, an array can hold either numbers or strings. To define your array to hold strings, you need to add the dollar sign ($) symbol to the end of the array name, as follows:

```
DIM ArrayName$(Number)
```

An array consists of the following three parts:

- ✔ A name.

- ✔ A data type that defines the only type of data that the array can hold, such as strings or numbers.

- ✔ A number that defines how many elements the array can hold. (A single element can hold one chunk of data.) This number is sometimes known as the *array index*.

You can define the size of an array using a single number, as follows:

```
DIM CatArray$(45)
```

This creates an array that can hold 45 items, in locations starting with number 1, such as `CatArray$(1)`, and ending with number 45, such as `CatArray$(45)`.

If you need to define several arrays, you can create them all on a single line like this:

```
DIM CatArray$(45), DogArray$(12), BirdArray$(87)
```

This line simply tells the computer to create three different arrays of size 45, 12, and 87. If you want, you can also define your arrays on separate lines, like this:

```
DIM CatArray$(45)
DIM DogArray$(12)
DIM BirdArray$(87)
```

How C/C++, Java, and Visual Basic.NET define arrays

If you define the size of an array in languages such as Liberty BASIC and Pascal, the program numbers the array locations starting with 1. You define an array in Liberty BASIC, for example, as follows:

```
DIM AgeArray(3)
```

In Liberty BASIC, the `AgeArray` consists of three locations: `AgeArray(1)`, `AgeArray(2)`, and `AgeArray(3)`.

But if you define the size of an array in C/C++, Java, or Visual Basic.NET, the program numbers the array locations starting with 0. Consider, for example, the following array as defined in C:

```
int agearray(3)
```

In C, this array consists of three locations: `agearray(0)`, `agearray(1)`, and `agearray(2)` but never has a location numbered 3. To make matters even more confusing, the command DIM agearray(3) in Visual Basic.NET actually creates an array with four elements: agearray(0), agearray(1), agearray(2), and agearray(3). So if you program in C/C++, Java, or Visual Basic.NET, you need to remain aware of these subtle difference so that your arrays in C/C++, Java, and Visual Basic.NET work the way that you expect.

Storing (and Retrieving) Data in an Array

After you first create an array, it's completely empty. Because an array can hold multiple chunks of data, you need to specify the location in the array in which you want to store your data.

Suppose, for example, that you create an array to hold five different integers, as follows:

```
DIM IQArray(5)
```

Normally, to stuff the number 93 into a variable, you just use a command such as the following:

```
MyVariable = 93
```

But because an array can hold multiple chunks of data, you must specify the location in the array in which you want to store the data. If you want to store data in the first location in the array, you use the following command:

```
IQArray(3) = 93
```

This command tells the computer to store the number 93 in the second element of the `IQArray` array.

If you try to store data in a location in the array that already contains data, Liberty BASIC simply wipes out the old data and replaces it with the new data.

To retrieve data out of an array, you assign a variable of the correct data type to a specific array location, as follows:

```
YourIQ = IQArray(3)
```

If you previously stored the number 93 in the third location of `IQArray`, the value of the `YourIQ` variable is 93 as well.

Arrays can store multiple chunks of data, so programmers use loops to make storing and retrieving data from an array easy. Without a loop, you'd need to specify the exact location in an array to store (or retrieve) data, as in the following example:

```
NameArray$(1) = "Mike Ross"
NameArray$(2) = "Bill McPherson"
NameArray$(3) = "John Smith"
```

You can, however, specify the array location by using a variable within a WHILE-WEND or FOR-NEXT loop, as follows:

```
FOR I = 1 TO 3
  NumberArray(I) = 125
NEXT I
```

The FOR-NEXT loop stores the number 125 in the first, second, and third locations of NumberArray.

To see how to store and retrieve data in an array, try the following program:

```
DIM NameArray$(3)
FOR I = 1 TO 3
  PROMPT "Type the name of someone you hate:"; Enemy$
  NameArray$(I) = Enemy$
NEXT I
FOR I = 1 TO 3
  PRINT NameArray$(I) + " sounds like the name of a moron."
NEXT I
END
```

Here's how the computer runs the preceding program:

1. The first line creates the array NameArray, which can hold three different strings.

2. The second line starts a FOR-NEXT loop that runs three times.

3. The third line displays a Prompt dialog box that tells the user, "Type the name of someone you hate." Whatever name the user types the program stores in the Enemy$ string variable.

4. The fourth line tells the computer, "Store the value of the Enemy$ string variable into the NameArray. The first time that this FOR-NEXT loop runs, store the value of the Enemy$ string variable in NameArray$(1). The second time, store the Enemy$ string variable in NameArray$(2). The third time, store the Enemy$ string variable in NameArray$(3)."

5. The fifth line marks the end of the FOR-NEXT loop.

6. The sixth line starts a second FOR-NEXT loop that runs three times.

7. The seventh line prints the value of NameArray plus the string " sounds like the name of a moron." The first time, it prints the value that it's storing in NameArray$(1); the second time, it prints the value in NameArray$(2); and the third time, it prints it in NameArray$(3).

8. The eighth line marks the end of the FOR-NEXT loop.

9. The ninth line tells the computer that the program is at an end.

Making a Multidimensional Array

The simplest arrays are nothing more than a single list of items, as in the following example:

```
DIM PetArray$(5)
```

This command creates an array that can hold five strings (refer to Figure 16-1). In programming lingo, any array that holds a single list of data is known as a *one-dimensional array*. A one-dimensional array uses a single number to define its size, as follows:

```
DIM ArrayName(X)
```

Liberty BASIC can also create two-dimensional arrays by defining two sizes. The code for a two-dimensional array looks as follows:

```
DIM ArrayName(X, Y)
```

This command creates a two-dimensional array, as shown in Figure 16-2.

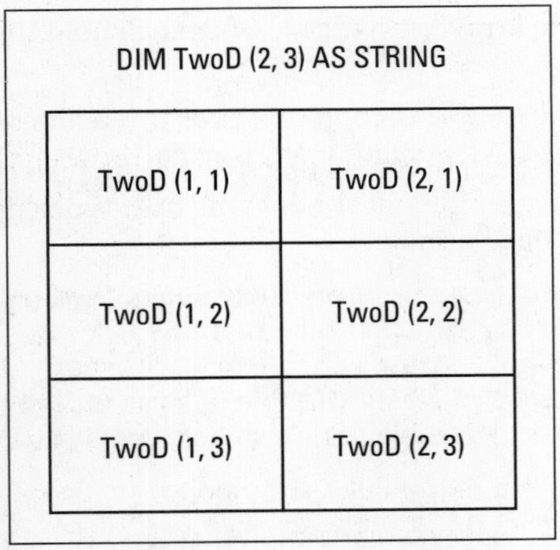

Figure 16-2:
A two-dimensional array uses two numbers to define the size of the array.

DIM TwoD (2, 3) AS STRING	
TwoD (1, 1)	TwoD (2, 1)
TwoD (1, 2)	TwoD (2, 2)
TwoD (1, 3)	TwoD (2, 3)

The following is an example of a two-dimensional array:

```
DIM VictimArray(10, 9) AS STRING
```

This command creates a two-dimensional array that can hold 90 (or 10 * 9) strings.

Although Liberty BASIC supports only one- or two-dimensional arrays, other programming languages enable you to create multidimensional arrays. To create a three-dimensional array in other languages, such as Visual Basic, you must define three sizes, as in the following array (see also Figure 16-3):

```
DIM ArrayName(X, Y, Z)
```

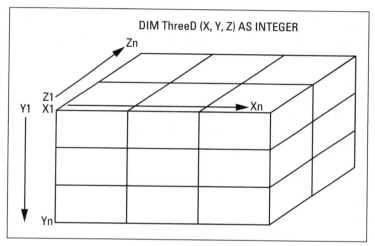

DIM ThreeD (X, Y, Z) AS INTEGER

Figure 16-3:
A three-dimensional array requires three numbers to define the size of the array.

Storing and retrieving data by using multidimensional arrays requires identifying the X, Y, and Z locations of the array in which you want to store your data.

To see a two-dimensional array that can store up to six strings, try the following program:

```
DIM VictimArray$(2, 3) AS STRING
FOR I = 1 TO 2
  FOR J = 1 TO 3
    PROMPT "Who do you want to hurt"; Enemy$
    VictimArray$(I, J) = Enemy$
  NEXT J
NEXT I
PROMPT "Type X location of the array item that you want to
          print, such as 1"; X
PROMPT "Type Y location of the array item that you want to
          print, such as 1"; Y
PRINT VictimArray$(X, Y) + " deserves to be hurt the most."
END
```

This program asks you to type six names. Suppose that you type the following six names, in this order:

```
Mike Ross
Bill McPherson
Jon Markey
Bobby Lee
Tom Clark
Roger Smith
```

The following order is the one in which the program stores these names:

```
VictimArray$(1, 1) = Mike Ross
VictimArray$(1, 2) = Bill McPherson
VictimArray$(1, 3) = Jon Markey
VictimArray$(2, 1) = Bobby Lee
VictimArray$(2, 2) = Tom Clark
VictimArray$(2, 3) = Roger Smith
```

If the program says, "Type X and Y locations of the array item that you want to print, such as 1, 3," and you type **2, 1**, the program prints the following:

```
"Bobby Lee deserves to be hurt the most."
```

Because storing and retrieving data in a multidimensional array can become confusing, consider using multidimensional arrays only if absolutely necessary.

Creating Dynamic Arrays

In most programming languages, you can create only a *static array*. A static array is a fixed size and poses the following two potential problems:

- ✔ After you define the array size, you can't change the array size later to make it smaller (if you make the array too big) or larger (if you make the array too small).

- ✔ A static array always requires a certain amount of memory, regardless of whether the array contains any data or is empty.

Despite these problems, static arrays are often suitable for most programs. If you want the capability to resize an array while your program is running, however, or to completely erase all data in an array to free up memory, you may want to consider creating something known as a *dynamic array*.

The main advantage of a dynamic array is that you can resize it or completely erase it (thus freeing up memory) while the program is running. The disadvantage is that you must write specific commands to do so.

Unlike some programming languages (such as older versions of BASIC such as GW-BASIC), Liberty BASIC always creates dynamic arrays so that you can change the size of your array after you create it. To change the size of an array, just use the REDIM command, as in the following example:

```
REDIM VictimArray$(44)
```

This command tells the computer to take the existing array, VictimArray$, and change its size so that it can hold 44 items.

If you change the size of an array, Liberty BASIC erases all the data stored in that array.

Resizing a dynamic array enables you to change the size of the array but not the data type. If your original array held strings, your newly resized array must also hold strings.

After you resize a dynamic array, you can stuff new data into it. To see how dynamic arrays can work, try the following program:

```
DIM LoserArray$(3)
FOR I = 1 TO 3
  PROMPT "Who is incompetent"; MyBoss$
  LoserArray$(I) = MyBoss$
NEXT I
FOR J = 1 TO 3
  PRINT LoserArray$(J)
NEXT J
REDIM LoserArray$(7)
LoserArray$(7) = "Bobby Lee"
PRINT LoserArray$(7) + " is a pathetic character."
END
```

Here's how the computer runs the preceding program:

1. The first line creates the array LoserArray, which can hold three different strings.

2. The second line starts a FOR-NEXT loop that runs three times.

3. The third line displays a Prompt dialog box that asks the user, "Who is incompetent?" Any name that the user types the program stores in the MyBoss$ string variable.

4. The fourth line tells the computer, "Store the value of the MyBoss$ variable in LoserArray."

5. The fifth line marks the end of the FOR-NEXT loop.

6. The sixth line starts a FOR-NEXT loop that runs three times.

7. The seventh line prints the contents of the LoserArray. The first time the FOR-NEXT loop runs, it prints the first name that you type; the second time, it prints the second name that you type; and the third time, it prints the third name that you type. At this point, the LoserArray holds only three items.

8. The eighth line marks the end of the FOR-NEXT loop.

9. The ninth line erases everything that you're currently storing in LoserArray and resizes LoserArray so that it can now hold seven (7) items.

10. The tenth line stores the string Bobby Lee in the seventh location in LoserArray.

11. The eleventh line prints the contents of LoserArray(7), which is the string Bobby Lee, and combines it with the string, " is a pathetic character." The entire PRINT statement displays, Bobby Lee is a pathetic character.

12. The twelfth line tells the computer that the program is at an end.

You can resize multidimensional arrays, but you can't change the number of dimensions. If you create a two-dimensional array, for example, you can't resize it to a one-dimensional array.

Dynamic and multidimensional arrays may be nice, but they can still hold only one type of data, such as numbers or strings. To avoid this limitation, many other programming languages include an array-like structure called a *collection*. Essentially, a *collection* is an array that can hold any type of data. So one part of the collection may hold a number, another part of the collection may hold a string, and so on. Think of a collection as a super-flexible version of an array.

Chapter 17

Lumping Related Data in Records

An array can prove handy for storing data of the same type (such as strings or integers) in a list, but sometimes you may need to store a variety of related data that consists of both strings and numbers. Because you can't store different data types in an array — see Chapter 16 for more information about arrays — you must use a different data structure known as a *record*.

Data structure is a fancy term for something that can hold information such as words or numbers. The simplest data structure is a variable, which can hold one chunk of data. A more complicated data structure is an array, which can hold a list of data as long as all the information shares the same data type (such as integers or strings).

A record stores related data under a single variable name. If, for example, you want to store the names, addresses, and phone numbers of all your friends (and enemies), you create several different variables, as the following example shows:

```
Name1$ = "Bo Katz"
Address1$ = "123 Main Street"
Phone1$ = "555-1234"
Salary1 = 55000
Name2$ = "Roger Wilco"
Address2$ = "948 Manchester Road"
Phone2$ = "555-4587"
Salary2 = 29000
```

The more names, addresses, and phone numbers that you need to store, the more separate variables you must create. Because this process is confusing, programmers create records as a way to simplify storing related data under a single variable name. Essentially, records allow you to group related data together and manipulate that record instead of the individual chunks of data, such as names, addresses, phone numbers, and salary as separate variables.

Liberty BASIC doesn't support records, so the program examples in this chapter are written in QBASIC, just so you can see how a different BASIC dialect implements records as data structures. Don't worry about running any of these sample programs. Just study them and try to understand the general principles behind them.

Creating a Record

A record consists of a name and one or more variables.

If, for example, you want to create a record to store names, addresses, and phone numbers, you use the following code:

```
TYPE RecordName
    FullName AS STRING * 15
    Address AS STRING * 25
    Phone AS STRING * 14
    Salary AS SINGLE
END TYPE
```

This record definition tells the computer to do the following:

1. The first line tells the computer, "This is the beginning of the record `RecordName`."

2. The second line creates a `FullName` variable that can hold a string up to 15 characters long.

3. The third line creates an `Address` variable that can hold a string up to 25 characters long.

4. The fourth line creates a `Phone` variable that can hold a string up to 14 characters long.

5. The fifth line creates a `Salary` variable that can hold a single-precision number.

6. The sixth line tells the computer, "This is the end of the record `RecordName`."

After you first create a record, you can't use it immediately. In technical terms, a record is a *user-defined data type*. Before you can use a record, you must create a variable to hold the information that you want to store in your record, in much the same way that you create a variable to hold an integer or string.

The following bit of code shows that you must first define your record and then create a variable to represent your record:

```
TYPE EmployeeRecord
  FullName AS STRING * 15
  Address AS STRING * 25
  Phone AS STRING * 14
  Salary AS SINGLE
END TYPE
DIM Workers AS EmployeeRecord
```

The DIM command in the preceding example tells the computer, "Create the variable Workers that can hold data that the record EmployeeRecord defines."

Only after you define a variable to represent your record can you start stuffing data into the record.

Manipulating Data in Records

To add data to and retrieve data from a record, you need to specify the following two items:

✔ The variable name that represents the record

✔ The variable name inside the record in which you want to store data or from which you want to take data

Storing data in a record

To store data in a record, you need to specify both the variable name (which represents a record) and the specific record variable to use, as in the following example:

```
RecordVariable.Variable = Data
```

Suppose that you had a record definition like the following example:

```
TYPE BomberInfo
  NickName AS STRING * 16
  MissionsFlown AS INTEGER
  Crew AS INTEGER
END TYPE
```

You define a variable to represent this record as follows:

```
DIM B17 AS BomberInfo
```

Then, if you want to store a string in the `NickName` variable, you use the following command:

```
B17.NickName = "Brennan's Circus"
```

This command tells the computer, "Look for the variable `B17` and store the string `"Brennan's Circus"` in the `NickName` variable."

Retrieving data from a record

You can retrieve stored data by specifying both the record's variable name and the specific variable that contains the data that you want to retrieve, as follows:

```
Variable = RecordVariable.Variable
```

Suppose, for example, that you have the following record definition and a variable to represent that record:

```
TYPE BomberInfo
  NickName AS STRING * 15
  MissionsFlown AS INTEGER
  Crew AS INTEGER
END TYPE
DIM B24 AS BomberInfo
```

See how C creates records

Different languages use different ways to create identical data structures. The C programming language creates a record (known as a *structure* in the C language) as shown in the following example:

```
struct bomberinfo {
  char nickname[15]
  int missionsflown
  int crew
} B24;
```

This bit of C code creates the structure (or record) bomberinfo. The bomberinfo structure can store a nickname up to 15 characters, an integer in the variable missionsflown, and another integer in the variable crew. In addition, this code also creates the variable B24 that represents this structure.

If you're already storing data in the B24 record, you can retrieve it by using the following commands:

```
GetName = B24.NickName
GetHistory = B24.MissionsFlown
GetCrew = B24.Crew
```

Using Records with Arrays

Although a record can store several related chunks of data under a single variable name, records by themselves aren't very good at storing lists of related data, such as a list of names, addresses, and phone numbers. To solve this problem, you can create an array that contains a record by using the following command:

```
DIM ArrayName(Number) AS RecordType
```

Refer to Chapter 16 for more information about arrays.

Because an array is nothing more than a list representing a specific data type, you can define an array to represent a record as follows:

```
TYPE GulliblePeople
 FullName AS STRING * 15
 CashAvailable AS SINGLE
END TYPE
DIM PotentialVictims(3) AS GulliblePeople
```

This chunk of code tells the computer to do the following:

1. The first line creates the record `GulliblePeople`.

2. The second line creates a `FullName` string variable that can hold up to 15 characters.

3. The third line creates a `CashAvailable` variable that can hold a single-precision number.

4. The fourth line marks the end of the `GulliblePeople` record.

5. The fifth line creates an array that can hold three records based on the `GulliblePeople` record. (You can refer to Figure 16-1, in Chapter 16, to see a representation of this array.)

To see a real-life example of how records work, study the following QBASIC program:

```
TYPE GulliblePeople
 FullName AS STRING * 15
 CashAvailable AS SINGLE
END TYPE
DIM PotentialVictims(2) AS GulliblePeople

FOR I = 1 TO 2
 PRINT "Type the name of someone you want to con:"
 INPUT PotentialVictims(I).FullName
 PRINT "How much money do you think you can get?"
 INPUT PotentialVictims(I).CashAvailable
NEXT I
PRINT
PRINT "Here is your list of future con victims:"

FOR I = 1 TO 2
 PRINT PotentialVictims(I).FullName
 PRINT PotentialVictims(I).CashAvailable
NEXT I
END
```

This program asks that you type in two names and two numbers. The first name you store in PotentialVictims(1).FullName, and the first number you store in PotentialVictims(1).CashAvailable. The second name you store in PotentialVictims(2).FullName, and the second number you store in PotentialVictims(2).CashAvailable.

Liberty BASIC doesn't support records, so you won't be able to get the above BASIC program to run under Liberty BASIC.

Chapter 18

Linked Lists and Pointers

. . . .

In This Chapter

▶ Pointing at data

▶ Understanding how linked lists work

▶ Creating linked lists

▶ Making data structures with linked lists

. . . .

*W*hen you create an array, you must specify a size for it. If you make your array too small, your program won't have enough room to store data unless you increase the array size. Make the array too large, however, and you waste your computer's valuable memory.

As a compromise, programmers developed something known as a *linked list*. Like an array, a linked list can store a list of items. But unlike an array, a linked list can grow or shrink as you need it to, so you never need to decide how much space to allocate ahead of time.

Some languages, such as BASIC, can't create a linked list. Although you can't make or use linked lists in Liberty BASIC, you still need to know about them. Linked lists are a common data structure that many other programming languages use, such as Java and C/C++.

Starting with a Pointer

An array contains a fixed number of storage units for holding data. If you design an array to hold five numbers but it needs to hold only two numbers, you're wasting space in the computer's memory. For small arrays, this situation isn't much of a problem. But if you're using a large, multidimensional array, the large amount of memory that the array consumes can actually keep your program from working on computers that don't contain enough memory.

Another problem is that you can't easily rearrange data in an array. Suppose, for example, that you have an array containing a list of first names, like the array shown in Figure 18-1. If you want to rearrange the names alphabetically, you must take all the data out and put it back in the array in alphabetical order.

Figure 18-1:
To rearrange data in an array, empty out the array and then put data back in.

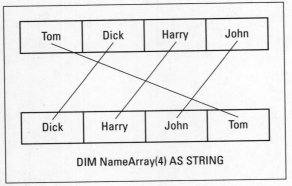

DIM NameArray(4) AS STRING

To solve both these problems, programmers create linked lists. A linked list can grow and shrink depending on the amount of data that you store in it, so it uses memory more efficiently than an array does.

In addition, although an array is like a box that you divide into sections so that it can hold data, a linked list is more like a collection of separate boxes (known as a *node*) that you can tie together, as shown in Figure 18-2.

Figure 18-2:
A linked list consists of nodes that contain data and a pointer to the next node in the list.

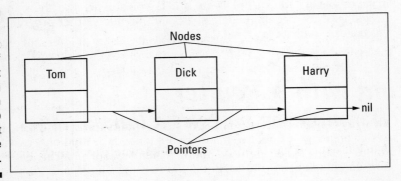

The pointer that the last node of a linked list stores points to a special value known as *nil*. A nil value represents the end of the linked list.

Unlike in an array, you don't need to remove data just to rearrange it in a linked list. Instead, you can rearrange the data in a linked list by simply rearranging the order of the pointers, as shown in Figure 18-3.

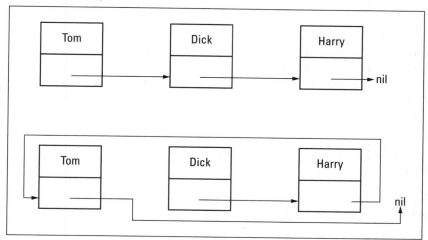

Figure 18-3:
To rearrange data in a linked list, you just need to rearrange a pointer.

Although variables normally contain numbers or strings, a pointer contains a *memory address*, which works much like a mailing address. By reading the memory address, the computer can find its way to the next chunk of data that you're storing in a node.

Pointers are a main part of C/C++ programming. Because a pointer represents a memory address, you can really mess up your C/C++ programs if even one pointer contains the wrong memory address. If this happens, your program can directly manipulate your computer's memory, which is like randomly probing your brain with a long, sharp needle. Using pointers incorrectly (like using brain surgery incorrectly) can mess up your computer's memory, causing it to crash, freeze up, or simply act erratically.

Defining the parts of a linked list

A linked list consists of one or more nodes, where each node contains the following:

- A pointer that points to the next node in your linked list
- A record for storing data in the linked list

Liberty BASIC doesn't offer commands for creating pointers, so the following code examples use the Pascal programming language, which looks enough like English that you can almost certainly understand how it works. If this subject looks too confusing, just browse over the Pascal programs in this chapter and look at the figures in this chapter to get a general idea of how linked lists work.

To create a linked list in Pascal, you must first create a pointer, as follows:

```
TYPE
  PointerName = ^RecordType;
```

This code tells the computer, "Create the data type PointerName. This data type can hold the memory address that defines the location of the record type RecordType."

After creating a pointer to a record, you create the actual record itself. The following record, for example, stores the string variable FullName; a second string variable, Address; and the pointer variable Next:

```
TYPE
  PointerName = ^RecordType;
  RecordType = RECORD
  FullName : string[15];
  Address : string[25];
  Next : PointerName;
  END;
```

After you define a pointer and a record, the third step is to define a variable to represent your record. This variable creates each node of your linked list, as follows:

```
VAR
  Node : PointerName;
```

By putting this code all together, you create a program that looks as follows:

```
PROGRAM LinkedLists;
TYPE
  PointerName = ^RecordType;
  RecordType = RECORD
  FullName : string[15];
  Address : string[25];
  Next : PointerName;
  END;
VAR
  Node : PointerName;
```

The preceding Pascal program tells the computer to perform the following tasks:

1. The first line tells the computer, "This is the beginning of my program that I call `LinkedLists`."

2. The second line contains just the word `TYPE`, which tells the computer, "Get ready to define a pointer and a record."

3. The third line defines the data type `PointerName`, which points to any record by the name of `RecordType`.

4. The fourth line defines the name of the record `RecordType`.

5. The fifth line tells the computer, "Create the variable `FullName`, which can hold up to 15 characters."

6. The sixth line tells the computer, "Create the variable `Address`, which can hold up to 25 characters."

7. The seventh line tells the computer, "Create the variable `Next`, which can point to another record that `RecordType` defines."

8. The eighth line tells the computer, "This line is the end of the record definition `RecordType`."

9. The ninth line contains just the word `VAR`, which tells the computer, "Get ready to define one or more variables."

10. The tenth line tells the computer, "Create the variable `Node`, which represents a pointer to a record that `RecordType` defines." (This variable pointer defines a single node in your linked list.)

Don't worry if linked lists look confusing at this point. The remaining figures in this chapter clarify how linked lists work.

Creating a linked list

After you define a record to hold your data, a pointer to point to each record, and a variable to represent each node in your linked list, you still need to create your linked list. You need to follow three additional steps to create a linked list. The following steps are as shown in Figure 18-4:

1. **Create a node.**

2. **Store data in that node.**

3. **Rearrange pointer to insert a new node in the beginning, middle, or end of the linked list.**

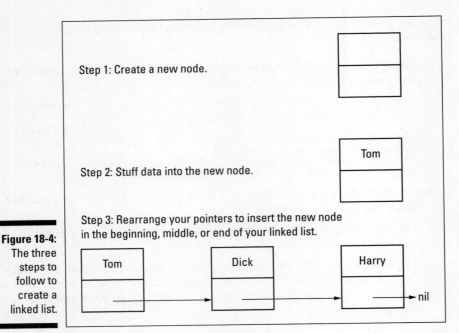

Figure 18-4:
The three
steps to
follow to
create a
linked list.

To see how a Pascal program creates a node and stores data in it, take a look at the following bit of code:

```pascal
PROGRAM LinkedLists;
TYPE
 PointerName = ^RecordType;
 RecordType = RECORD
 FullName : string[15];
 Address : string[25];
 Next : PointerName;
 END;
VAR
 Node : PointerName;
BEGIN
 New(Node);
 Node^.FullName := 'Jonathan Blake';
 Node^.Address := '837 Dead-End Avenue';
 Node^.Next := nil;
END.
```

Starting from the word BEGIN, this program tells the computer to do the following:

If you want to understand the code that appears before the line containing the BEGIN command, refer to the previous section "Defining the parts of a linked list."

1. The BEGIN line tells the computer, "This line is the start of the instructions to follow."

2. The second line creates a new node. At this point, the node contains nothing.

3. The third line stores the name Jonathan Blake in the FullName variable of the node record.

4. The fourth line stores the address 837 Dead-End Avenue in the Address variable of the node record.

5. The fifth line stores the value nil in the Next pointer. A nil value means that the pointer doesn't point to anything. Using a nil value keeps the pointer from accidentally pointing to another part of the computer's memory. If you create a second node, you want the value of Node^.Next to point to this second node.

Managing a linked list

If you store data in an array and you delete a chunk of data in the middle of the array, you wind up with an empty spot in your array. Although that particular location in the array stores nothing, the computer must still allocate memory for that empty part of the array. Even worse, now your array contains an empty gap that you must skip over to find the next chunk of data in the array, as shown in Figure 18-5.

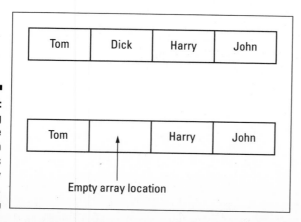

Figure 18-5: Deleting data in the middle of an array leaves an empty gap.

| Tom | Dick | Harry | John |

| Tom | | Harry | John |

Empty array location

Deleting data from a linked list is easy — just follow these two steps:

1. **Rearrange the pointers of the nodes so that they ignore the node containing the data that you want to erase.**

2. **Delete the node containing the data that you want to erase.**

Figure 18-6 illustrates the process of deleting data in a linked list.

Writing the actual instructions to tell the computer to rearrange pointers and delete a node is often fairly lengthy. So although arrays can prove inefficient in terms of memory storage, arrays are much simpler to use and manage. On the other hand, linked lists are more efficient in storing data in memory, but they can become really troublesome to manage because you must write many instructions just to accomplish something as seemingly simple as rearranging a pointer.

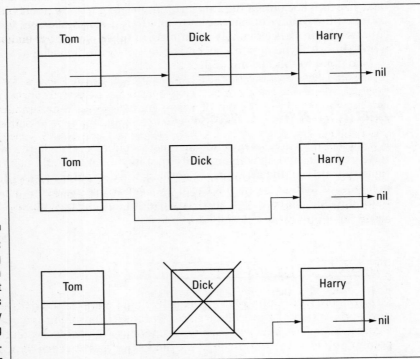

Figure 18-6:
Deleting data in a linked list saves memory by avoiding empty gaps.

Making Data Structures with Linked Lists

The simplest linked list is a *single-linked list*, in which each node contains data and one pointer that points to another node in the linked list (refer to Figure 18-2).

The trouble with a single-linked list is that each node points only to the next node. If you want to find the previous node, you can't. In Figure 18-2, for example, the middle node (containing the name *Dick*) points only to the node containing the name *Harry*. But you can't tell which name appears before Dick. In this case, an array is much simpler, because an array can identify which data appears before and which data appears after a specific array location.

You can arrange linked lists in a variety of ways to create different types of data structures. Because data structures do nothing more than hold data, choosing the right data structure can make your program easier to write. (And choosing the wrong data structure can make your program harder to write.)

A personal organizer program that stores names and addresses, for example, may use a linked list of records. The program can expand or shrink the linked list, depending on the number of names and addresses the user stores. The type of program that you're writing can determine the type of data structure you need (or should use). That's what makes linked lists so powerful — they can create a variety of different data structures.

Don't worry about the details of creating different data structures with linked lists. Just remain aware that different data structures exist — and you usually run into these different data structures later on if you continue learning about computer programming.

Double-linked lists

The problem with a single-linked list is that each node can identify only the next node but not the preceding node. To solve this problem, you can create a *double-linked list*, in which each node contains data and two pointers. One pointer points to the next node in the linked list, and the second pointer points to the previous node in the linked list, as shown in Figure 18-7.

Figure 18-7:
A double-linked list uses two pointers to point at nodes that appear before and after each linked node.

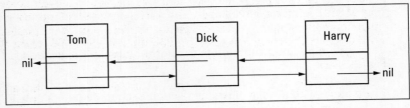

A personal-organizer program is likely to use a double-linked list to enable the user to scroll forward and backward through the linked list to view all the names and addresses that you store in the personal-organizer program.

Creating a double-linked list means writing instructions to manage twice as many pointers, which essentially doubles the chances that you may leave a pointer *dangling* (that is, pointing to a nonexistent node) or pointing to the wrong node. In either case, incorrect pointers can cause subtle, yet serious bugs in your program, so use pointers sparingly.

Circular-linked lists

A typical double-linked list looks like a long rectangle with a beginning and an end (refer to Figure 18-7). But instead of creating an artificial end and beginning, you can link both ends of a single-linked list or a double-linked list to create a *circular-linked list*, as shown in Figure 18-8.

Figure 18-8:
A circular-linked list displays no beginning or ending.

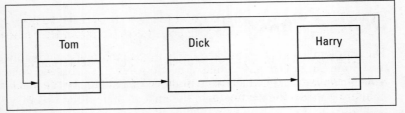

A circular-linked list may prove useful for a presentation program that needs to display information continuously, such as a presentation in a museum kiosk. In this case, the presentation program may display information one screen at a time and then begin again after it reaches the end of the presentation.

Stacks

A *stack* is a special single-linked list that enables you to add and remove nodes only at the beginning of the linked list (see Figure 18-9). In the real world, the most common implementation of a stack occurs as you stack plates. If you want to store a new plate, you simply add it to the top of the stack. If you want to remove a plate, you take it off the top of the stack as well.

One common use for stacks is for calculating formulas by using a method known as *Reverse Polish Notation (RPN)*, which is a method of calculation that many Hewlett-Packard calculators use. If you want to calculate the formula (1 + 2) * 3 by using RPN, you type the following:

```
1  2  +  3  *
```

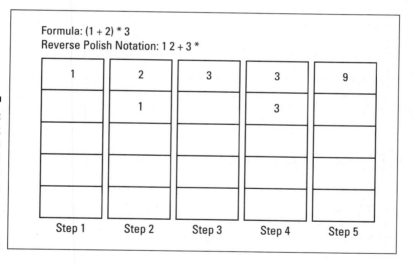

Figure 18-9: A stack adds data to and removes data from the top of a stack (linked list).

Figure 18-9 shows how a stack stores the five steps that you need to calculate the formula (1 + 2) * 3 by using Reverse Polish Notation. Here's how it works:

1. The first step pushes the number 1 to the top of the stack.

2. The second step pushes the number 2 to the top of the stack and pushes the number 1 underneath.

3. The third step pops the number 2 off the stack, pops the number 1 off the stack, and adds the two numbers together to get the number 3. Then it stores the number 3 back on top of the stack.

4. The fourth step pushes the number 3 (from the formula) to the top of the stack and pushes the calculated value of 3 farther down the stack.

5. The fifth step pops the first number 3 off the stack, pops the second number 3 off the stack, and multiplies the two number 3s to get the number 9. Then it stores the number 9 back on top of the stack.

Stacks are often referred to as *LIFO* (which stands for *Last In, First Out*) *linked lists.* This term means that the last data that you store in a stack is the first data that you remove from the stack (just as in stacking and removing plates).

Don't worry if you don't understand the logic behind Reverse Polish Notation. Just understand how stacks work and leave Reverse Polish Notation for the engineers at Hewlett-Packard.

Queues

A *queue* is a special linked list that follows two rules. The first rule is that you can add nodes only to the end of the linked list. The second rule is that you can remove nodes only from the beginning of the linked list.

You often refer to queues as *FIFO* (which stands for *First In, First Out*) *linked lists.* This term means that the first data that you store in the queue is the first data that you remove from the queue. A queue mimics a line of people waiting to board an airplane or see a science-fiction movie. In both cases, the first person (data) put in the queue is the first person (data) who leaves it, as shown in Figure 18-10.

Figure 18-10:
A queue stores new data at the end and removes the oldest data from the front.

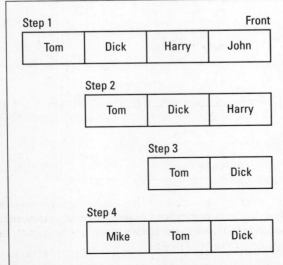

The following steps (along with Figure 18-10) explain how a queue stores and removes data:

1. The first step shows a queue in which the name *John* is first, the name *Harry* is second, the name *Dick* is third, and the name *Tom* is fourth and last.

2. The second step removes John from the queue. Now all the remaining names move closer to the front of the queue.

3. The third step removes Harry from the queue. All the remaining names move closer to the front of the queue.

4. The fourth step adds a new name, *Mike*, to the queue. Because Mike is the newest data adding itself to the queue, its place is at the back of the queue.

Trees

Linked lists don't always need to resemble a linear or circular shape. The most common nonlinear shape for a linked list is a *tree*, in which one node (*the root*) represents the top of the tree with the rest of the nodes (*leaves*) falling underneath the root, as shown in Figure 18-11.

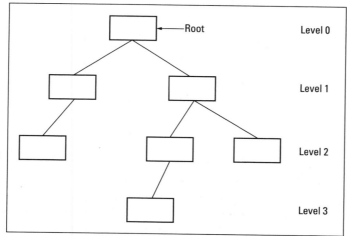

Figure 18-11:
A tree is a nonlinear linked list.

In a tree, a node can point to zero or more nodes. For simplicity, many programmers use a special tree known as a *binary tree*, in which each node can link only to zero, one, or two other nodes.

Programmers often use trees to mimic artificial intelligence in programs, such as in chess-playing programs. A chess-playing program may use a tree in which the root represents a possible move for the first player and the leaf nodes underneath (at level 1) represent potential moves that the second player can make. Then the leaf nodes at level 2 represent potential moves for the first player, and the leaf nodes at level 3 represent potential moves for the second player, and so on.

Graphs

A *graph* is a linked list in which each node can point to one or more nodes without regard to mimicking a certain shape, such as a list. Figure 18-12 shows what a typical graph looks like.

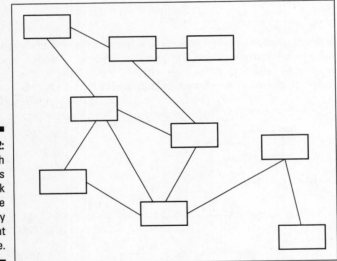

Figure 18-12:
A graph enables nodes to link to one another any way that you choose.

Programmers often use graphs in something known as a *neural network* — a special program that can mimic the way the brain thinks. In a neural network, each node represents a neuron and the links between them represent the synapses linking the neurons.

Graphs, trees, queues, stacks, circular-linked lists, and double-linked lists are just different ways to arrange and use a linked list. The more complicated your programs become, the more you're likely to need these advanced data structures.

Chapter 19

Playing with Object-Oriented Programming

*O*bject-oriented programming is the latest fad (or, to use correct programming lingo, the latest *methodology*) for pursuing the following Holy Trinity of characteristics that programmers want for their software:

✔ Simple and fast to create

✔ Easy to understand and modify

✔ Reliable and error-free

People often abbreviate object-oriented programming as *OOP*, as in "Oops — I don't think that object-oriented programming alone can magically make programming any easier."

Liberty BASIC isn't an object-oriented language, which means that you can't experiment with using objects in Liberty BASIC. Although most versions of BASIC don't support objects, Microsoft has tortured the BASIC dialect in Visual Basic into offering object-oriented programming features. If you want to find out more about object-oriented programming using BASIC, pick up a copy of Visual Basic and a copy of *Visual Basic.NET For Dummies* (written by yours truly and published by Wiley Publishing) today. To show how object-oriented programming works, the examples in this chapter use C++.

The Problem with Software

No matter how powerful a computer is, the software that controls it limits its power. The biggest problem with software is *reliability*. Reliability means that software works without crashing, freezing up, or acting erratically. Software reliability is especially critical with real-time systems, such as airplane navigation systems, computers that host corporate Web sites, and financial trading programs, where losing a single number can mean the loss of billions of dollars.

Of course, reliable software is useless if you can't write it in time. Because of the conflicting demands that companies and programmers finish software on time and make sure that it works reliably, most rush their software out before they can fully test it (which means that it probably doesn't work right), or they delay the software so long that people switch to a competing product. (And those who wait still have no guarantee that the software's going to work correctly, even if it's several years late.)

Whatever fancy new technology, programming language, or programming style may appear, software always faces the twin challenge of working right while reaching users as quickly as possible. This situation means that all software is likely to contain bugs that keep it from working as efficiently as possible.

Ways to Make Programming Easier

In the early days of computers, most programs were fairly small. As a result, programmers often wrote programs with little planning and organization. After finishing the program, they'd run it to see whether it worked. If it didn't work, they simply rewrote the program and tried again.

Such a trial-and-error approach worked fine for writing small programs, but after programs became larger and more complex, rewriting the program over and over made programming tedious and error-prone. The larger the program, the more places bugs could hide, making the program more likely not to work at all.

With today's programs often consisting of a million or more lines of code, the trial-and-error method of writing programs no longer works. Writing a large program without planning or organization is like trying to build a skyscraper without blueprints.

Programmers adopted a new strategy. Instead of trying to write one huge program, they decided to write a bunch of little programs (known as *subprograms*).

The idea was that small programs are easier to write and debug, so you just need to write a bunch of small programs, paste them together, and end up with a larger program that works reliably, as shown in Figure 19-1.

Although the idea of writing small subprograms and pasting them together like building blocks was a sound idea, problems still existed. You may divide a large program into smaller subprograms, but the instructions that you store in one subprogram can still manipulate data that another subprogram uses, as shown in Figure 19-2.

To solve this problem (and solving problems is something that programmers continually strive to do), programmers developed the idea of isolating subprograms in separately compiled files. In this way, subprograms can't mess around with each other's data, and yet they can still work together to create one larger program.

Taking the idea of isolating subprograms into separate and isolated parts (known as *modules* in programming lingo), programmers eventually developed the idea for objects and, hence, the term *object-oriented* programming.

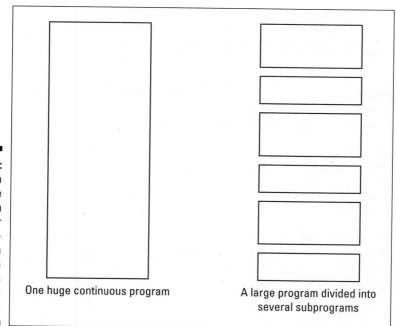

Figure 19-1:
Breaking a large program into smaller subprograms can make programs easier to write.

One huge continuous program

A large program divided into several subprograms

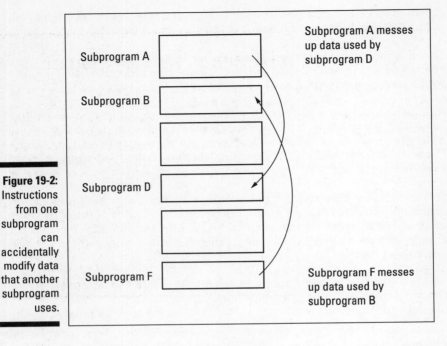

Figure 19-2:
Instructions
from one
subprogram
can
accidentally
modify data
that another
subprogram
uses.

Breaking Programs into Objects

After programmers succeeded in breaking a large program into smaller sub-programs, the next logical step was to isolate both data and the instructions that manipulate that data into an individual unit — in other words, an *object*.

A *program* consists of one or more objects in which each object is a self-contained unit that contains the following two items:

- ✔ Data (also known as *properties*)
- ✔ Instructions (also known as *methods*) for manipulating that data

Because an object doesn't depend on any other part of your program, designing a program by using objects provides the following benefits:

- ✔ **Reliability:** If your program doesn't work, you just need to isolate the bug in a single object and debug that one object instead of trying to debug an entire program that may contain a million lines of code.

- ✔ **Reusability:** Because objects are self-contained units, you can (theoretically) copy an object from one program and plug it into another program, much like making a structure by using building blocks. Reusing objects not only simplifies creating new programs, but also helps create new programs faster because you can reuse objects that already work.

Getting an inheritance from an object

Objects encourage reliability and reusability through a concept known as *inheritance*. The main idea behind inheritance is to encourage programmers to reuse existing code.

In the old days of programming, you could divide a large program into several subprograms. After studying one of your subprograms, you may realize that, with a little modification, you could adapt it to work in a second program. Unfortunately, any time that you modify a program, you take the risk of messing it up so that it doesn't work at all.

To prevent the problem of modifying an existing subprogram and wrecking it by mistake, objects

use inheritance. Inheritance enables you to copy an existing object and then add new code to this new copy without ever modifying any of the existing code inside. Thus the new copy of your object "inherits" all the old data and code, while still enabling you to tack on new code to modify the object for a slightly different purpose.

Inheritance not only protects you from ruining a perfectly good chunk of code by mistake, but it also helps you create programs faster. Copying and modifying an existing object is easier than creating a brand new object from scratch.

In a traditionally designed program, you often store data in one location and the instructions that manipulate that data in another location. Figure 19-3 shows a traditional program divided into subprograms (represented by boxes). Each subprogram can access the data it needs, but can also access data used by another subprogram.

In comparison, an object-oriented program (depicted as ovals in Figure 19-3) lumps data and the instructions that manipulate that data in a single location (known by its official programming term as *encapsulation*). Encapsulation simply keeps one part of a program from messing with data that another part of the program uses.

How to use objects

One of the biggest problems with programming is the need to constantly modify existing programs. People use most programs for years, if not decades. Rather than write a brand new program to replace an existing one, most companies prefer to modify the existing program. The theory is that modifying an existing program (that already works) takes less time and creates a more reliable program than does creating a brand new program.

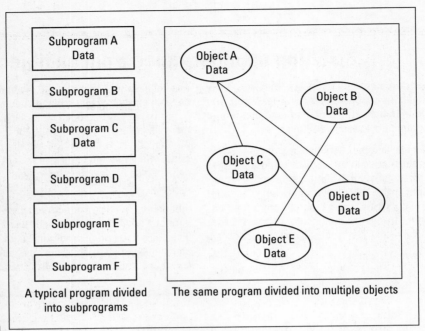

Figure 19-3:
In object-
oriented
programs,
objects
isolate data
from other
objects.

Subprogram A
Data

Subprogram B

Subprogram C
Data

Subprogram D

Subprogram E

Subprogram F

A typical program divided
into subprograms

Object A
Data

Object B
Data

Object C
Data

Object D
Data

Object E
Data

The same program divided into multiple objects

Unfortunately, constantly modifying an existing program can create a program as confusing to read as a novel written one page at a time by 300 different people. In both cases, the overall structure is patched together in so
many different ways that it can prove hard to tell where one part ends and
another part begins.

That's why object-oriented programming looks so appealing. To modify an
object-oriented program, just unplug the object containing the program features that you want to change, rewrite or replace it, and plug it back into the
original program.

Best of all, objects make easy work of identifying which part of the program
you want to update. Suppose, for example, that a video game displays aliens
that pop up on-screen so that you can shoot them in the head. Your job is to
modify the way the aliens look and move on-screen.

If the video game is written in the traditional way of programming (dividing
the program into smaller subprograms), you must figure out which subprogram controls the way the alien looks and which subprogram controls the
way the alien moves. Even if you manage to find which subprograms control
the alien's appearance and movement, you still must worry whether these
subprograms rely on other subprograms lurking somewhere deep within the
bowels of your million-line program. Sound complicated? It is — especially if
you're the one whose job relies on modifying a million-line video game program in less than two weeks.

Hiding and exposing data in an object

Because objects need to communicate with one another, objects can classify their data and instructions into one of three categories: *private*, *public*, and *protected*.

If an object defines data and instructions as private, only that particular object can use that data and instructions. No other object can ever use private data and instructions. (That's why you call them private.)

On the other hand, other objects can use public data and instructions. Objects use public data and instructions to communicate and share data with other objects.

Protected data and instructions work the same as private data and instructions, with one important exception: If you use inheritance to copy an existing object and create a new object, the new object inherits only public and protected data and instructions. Any private data and instructions remain with the old object.

But if the video game is written by using object-oriented programming techniques, your job is much easier. All you need to do is find the object that represents the alien. Inside that object is all the subprograms you need to modify the way the alien looks and moves. Change this single object, plug it back into the original program, and you're done.

How to create an object

The first part to creating an object is to define a *class*, which is similar to a record. (See Chapter 17 for more information about records.) A class defines data and instructions to manipulate that data. After you create a class, you can create one or more objects based on that class to use in your program.

Liberty BASIC doesn't offer commands for creating objects, so the following code examples use the C++ programming language. Don't worry about trying to understand the syntax of C++; just browse the code to get a general idea of how the whole thing works.

The following example shows how to create a class in C++:

```
class monster
{
public:
  int x_coordinate;
  int y_coordinate;
  void moveme(int, int);
  void initialize(int, int);
};
```

This simple C++ code tells the computer to perform the following tasks:

1. The first line tells the computer, "This line starts a new class, `monster`."

2. The second line tells the computer, "This line is the start of the class definition."

3. The third line tells the computer, "Any things that appear on the following lines are public, which means that any part of the program can access them."

4. The fourth line creates the integer variable `x_coordinate`.

5. The fifth line creates the integer variable `y_coordinate`.

6. The sixth line tells the computer, "The object contains a subprogram (or method), `moveme`, that accepts two integer values."

7. The seventh line tells the computer, "The object contains a subprogram, `initialize`, that accepts two integer values."

8. The eighth line defines the end of the class definition.

A *class* isn't an object. To create an object, you must define a variable that represents your defined class.

Writing an object's methods

After you declare the subprograms (or methods) that you want to store in a class, you still need to write the actual instructions that make that subprogram. Suppose you want to use the class definition defined in the preceding section in the following example:

```
class monster
{
public:
  int x_coordinate;
  int y_coordinate;
  void moveme(int, int);
  void initialize(int, int);
};
```

This class defines two subprograms (or methods), `moveme` and `initialize`. To make these methods actually do something, you must write the complete methods directly below the class definition, as follows:

```
void monster::moveme(int new_x, int new_y)
{
 x_coordinate = x_coordinate + new_x;
 y_coordinate = y_coordinate + new_y;
}
void monster::initialize(int init_x, int init_y)
{
 x_coordinate = init_x;
 y_coordinate = init_y;
}
```

The initialize method defines the X coordinate and Y coordinate of any object that you derive from the class `monster`. You use the `moveme` method to move an object's position a certain distance in the X (right and left) direction and Y (up and down) direction.

Creating an object

After you define a class and write any methods that you declare within that class, you still need to define a variable to represent that class. This variable represents the actual object in object-oriented programming.

To create an object, you declare a variable to represent that object. The following program defines an object named `zombie` to represent the `monster` class definition:

```
#include <iostream.h>
class monster
{
public:
 int x_coordinate;
 int y_coordinate;
 void moveme(int, int);
 void initialize(int, int);
};
void monster::moveme(int new_x, int new_y)
{
 x_coordinate = x_coordinate + new_x;
 y_coordinate = y_coordinate + new_y;
}
void monster::initialize(int init_x, int init_y)
{
 x_coordinate = init_x;
 y_coordinate = init_y;
}
void main()
{
```

```
monster zombie;
 zombie.initialize(12, 15);
 cout << "The X-location of the zombie is " <<
 zombie.x_coordinate << "\n";
 cout << "The Y-location of the zombie is " <<
 zombie.y_coordinate << "\n";
 zombie.moveme (34, 9);
 cout << "The new X-location of the zombie is " <<
 zombie.x_coordinate << "\n";
 cout << "The new Y-location of the zombie is " <<
 zombie.y_coordinate << "\n";
}
```

The main C++ program starts with the void main() line. Just examining this portion, line by line, makes the computer do the following:

1. The first line tells the computer, "This line is the start of the C++ program."

2. The second line tells the computer, "This line is the start of all instructions inside the main C++ program."

3. The third line tells the computer, "Create the object zombie and base it on the class definition monster."

4. The fourth line runs the method initialize, which defines the X coordinate (12) and Y coordinate (15) of the zombie object.

5. The fifth line prints the message, The X-location of the zombie is 12.

6. The sixth line prints the message, The Y-location of the zombie is 15.

7. The seventh line runs the moveme method, which moves the zombie object 34 units of measurement in the X direction and 9 units in the Y direction.

8. The eighth line prints the message, The new X-location of the zombie is 46. (That's 12, the original X-location of the zombie as Step 4 defines, plus 34 as Step 7 defines, which equals 46.)

9. The ninth line prints the message, The new Y-location of the zombie is 24. (That's 15, the original Y-location of the zombie as Step 4 defines, plus 9 as Step 7 defines, which equals 24.)

10. The tenth line tells the computer, "This line represents the end of the C++ main program."

Although the C++ program may look confusing, just remember these important points and you're fine:

✔ To create an object, you must define a class first.

✔ A class contains data and instructions (methods) for manipulating the object's data.

Common terms associated with object-oriented programming

Although you aren't likely to become an expert in object-oriented programming from this brief introduction, you can at least understand the purpose behind objects, which is to make modifying and reusing programs easier.

If you plan to continue studying computer programming, you're likely to run into object-oriented programming over and over (or at least until a new programming methodology pops up to make programming easier). To add to your limited knowledge of object-oriented programming, remember the following common object-oriented terms that you're likely to see at one time or another:

- *Encapsulation* means lumping all related data and instructions to manipulate that data in a single location.

- *Inheritance* means passing data and instructions from one object to a second object that derives from the first object.

- *Message* is a subprogram (also known as a *method*) that manipulates the data inside an object.

- *Object* is a collection of data and instructions for manipulating that data, grouped together in a self-contained unit.

Choosing an Object-Oriented Language

After you understand the general principles behind object-oriented programming, you may be eager to start trying it out on your own. Liberty BASIC doesn't support object-oriented programming, so you need to switch to a different programming language. The two types of programming languages that you can choose from are as follows:

- Hybrid object-oriented languages
- True (or pure) object-oriented languages

A *hybrid object-oriented language* simply takes an existing language and slaps object-oriented features on top of it. Some of the more popular hybrid languages include Pascal (as implemented in Delphi), BASIC (as implemented in Visual Basic), and C++.

The main advantage of using a hybrid language is that if you already know how to use a language such as Pascal, BASIC, or C++, you can quickly learn to use the object-oriented features of these languages with a minimum of training, anguish, and experimentation. If you're not quite sure about the benefits of object-oriented programming, you can write a small part of your program using objects and write the bulk of your program using old-fashioned programming methods.

Of course, the main disadvantage of hybrid languages is that they enable programmers to mix traditional and object-oriented programming techniques, which can become an untidy mess. Hybrid languages enable programmers to use none, some, or all object-oriented programming techniques, so using hybrid languages often creates programs that don't take full advantage of objects, destroying the advantage of using objects while making the program harder to read and understand.

That's why many people prefer pure object-oriented languages that force you to use objects right from the start. Some popular pure object-oriented languages include the following:

- SmallTalk
- Eiffel
- C#
- Java

Whether you decide to stick to a conventional language (and use its object-oriented hybrid) or jump straight into a pure object-oriented language, get used to the idea behind breaking your program into objects. Object-oriented programming techniques alone don't make software easier to write and more reliable, but they can make you more aware of the problems in writing software and how object-oriented programming can solve those problems.

In the long run, nobody really cares what language you use, whether you use any object-oriented programming techniques, or whether you write software while sitting in your underwear and listening to Barry Manilow albums at 3 a.m. The important point is to write software on time that works. If you can do that, you can focus on producing results and leave trivial details, such as wearing a tie, dealing with corporate politics, and fighting each other for a cubicle near a window, for your co-workers to worry about.

Part V
Algorithms: Telling the Computer What to Do

The 5th Wave   By Rich Tennant

"We're here to clean the code."

In this part . . .

A program is nothing more than a list of instructions, but you can create instructions in various ways to tell the computer how to perform the same task. If you want to give directions to tell someone how to get from the airport to your house, for example, you probably can tell that person two or three different ways. Each way eventually gets the person to your house, but one way may prove easier, another way may prove faster during the day, and the third way may prove more scenic.

In the world of computer programming, a specific way to accomplish a task is known as an *algorithm*. By choosing the fastest set of instructions (the algorithm), you can make your program faster and more efficient. This part of the book introduces you to several common algorithms for accomplishing different tasks so that you can understand the foundation on which you build most programs.

Chapter 20

Sorting

In This Chapter

▶ Sorting data in many ways

▶ Picking a sorting algorithm

*P*rograms typically accept data from the outside world (such as from someone typing on the keyboard), manipulate that data somehow, and spit that data back out in a format that someone finds useful.

A database is fairly useless if it enables you to store information without enabling you to do anything to rearrange that information. You may, for example, want to rearrange your data alphabetically by last name, numerically by telephone area code, or by some other criterion, such as by those people who're single and earn $75,000 or more every year. Your program needs to know how to sort data.

Although sorting may seem a fairly mundane topic, it can actually get rather complex. That's because whenever a program sorts data, it needs to sort the information as quickly as possible. After all, a program that sorts names and addresses is useless if it takes three hours just to sort 15 names.

So part of computer science centers on studying and developing the most efficient sorting methods (known as *sorting algorithms*) possible. Because many types of programs need to sort data, nearly every programmer needs to know the different sorting algorithms available and how they work. Throughout this chapter, you can type various Liberty BASIC programs and see for yourself exactly how a particular sorting algorithm does its sorting magic.

Computer scientists have created a variety of sorting algorithms — but no single, perfect algorithm that your program should use all the time. The most efficient algorithm depends partly on the data that you want to sort and partly on the data structures that your program uses to store data.

TECHNICAL STUFF

Measuring efficiency with Big-O notation

To measure the efficiency of specific algorithms, computer scientists created something known as *Big-O notation*. Essentially, Big-O notation measures the speed of a particular algorithm (such as a sorting algorithm) based on the number of items it must manage.

If you have an algorithm that sorts a list of names alphabetically, for example, the speed of that algorithm depends on the number of names to search. In Big-O notation, you express this relationship as O(N), where O stands for "order of magnitude" and N stands for the total number of items the algorithm must manage.

The way that programmers determine the Big-O notation of a particular algorithm depends on that algorithm's speed of execution and the number of items it must handle. For example, if an algorithm's speed of execution and number of items (N) it can handle is expressed as N2 + N + 1, the Big-O notation for this algorithm is O(N2).

In calculating the Big-O notation for an algorithm, you choose the fastest-growing item (in this case, N2) and ignore the rest of the expression. (Naturally, if you use the wrong expression to represent your algorithm, your Big-O notation is wrong as well.)

Programmers often use Big-O notation to measure the average and worst-case scenarios as they study how an algorithm behaves while managing a typical number of items and how that same algorithm behaves while managing an extremely large number of items.

Not surprisingly, some algorithms are fast at managing relatively small numbers of items but slow down rapidly if you force them to manage a large number of items. Curiously, other algorithms are very fast and efficient in sorting items that are almost correctly sorted initially but slow if sorting items that you randomly scatter in the list.

Programmers study the average and worst-case scenarios of an algorithm by using Big-O notation to help them choose the algorithm that's best suited for their particular program.

Insertion Sort

Imagine that you're playing cards and the dealer deals the cards to you. As soon as you get two cards, your first inclination is probably to sort those two cards in relation to one another (perhaps by suit or by number). After the dealer gives you a third card, you sort that card in relation to your previous two cards. You sort each additional card that you receive in relation to your previously sorted cards. This method is how an insertion sort works (see Figure 20-1). From the computer's point of view, the insertion sort algorithm works as follows:

1. It compares the first two items in the list and sorts those two items.

2. It looks at the next item in the list and sorts that item in relation to the previously sorted items.

3. It repeats Step 2 for each additional item in the list until it finishes sorting the entire list.

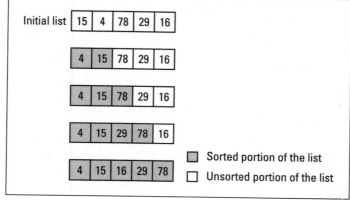

Figure 20-1:
An insertion sort removes one item at a time and sorts it in relation to the previous sorted items in the list.

To see for yourself how the insertion sort algorithm works, try the following program:

```
MaxSize = 5
REDIM MyArray(MaxSize)

FOR I = 1 TO MaxSize
 MyArray(I) = INT(RND(1) * 100) + 1
 PRINT MyArray(I); SPACE$(1);
NEXT I
PRINT "(Initial array)"

FOR ArrayPos = 2 TO MaxSize
 TempValue = MyArray(ArrayPos)
 StopNow = 0
 Count = 1
 Time2Stop = 0
 WHILE (Time2Stop = 0)
   IF TempValue < MyArray(Count) THEN
     FOR J = ArrayPos TO Count STEP -1
       MyArray(J) = MyArray(J - 1)
     NEXT J
     MyArray(Count) = TempValue
     StopNow = 1
     FOR I = 1 TO MaxSize
       PRINT MyArray(I); SPACE$(1);
     NEXT I
     PRINT
   END IF
```

```
   Count = Count + 1
   IF (StopNow = 1) OR (Count = ArrayPos) THEN
     Time2Stop = 1
   END IF
 WEND
NEXT ArrayPos

FOR I = 1 TO MaxSize
 PRINT MyArray(I); SPACE$(1);
NEXT I
PRINT "(Sorted array)"
END
```

A typical output for this program appears as follows:

```
44 4 98 99 26 (Initial array)
4 44 98 99 26
4 26 44 98 99
4 26 44 98 99 )Sorted array)
```

The insertion sort program works as follows:

1. The first through seventh lines create the variable MaxSize, which equals 5; create the array MyArray to hold five integers; generate a random number; create a random number between 1 and 100; store it in the array MyArray; and then print the array on-screen along with the string (Initial array).

2. The eighth line is the start of a FOR-NEXT loop that starts counting from the second item in the array, using the variable ArrayPos.

3. The ninth line creates the variable TempValue and stores the value in the array location that the ArrayPos variable designates. At the beginning of this FOR-NEXT loop, the value of TempValue is equal to the second item in the array.

4. The tenth line creates the variable StopNow and sets its value to zero. You use the StopNow variable later in the program to tell the computer that it's already moved a number to its correctly sorted position in the array.

5. The eleventh line creates the variable Count and sets its value to one. You use the Count variable to locate where in the array to move the number that the TempValue variable stores.

6. The twelfth line creates the variable Time2Stop and sets its value to zero. You use the Time2Stop variable to tell the program when the array is completely sorted.

7. The thirteenth line is the start of a WHILE-WEND statement that checks whether the value that the Time2Stop variable stores is still equal to zero. If so, all the instructions inside the WHILE-WEND statements run.

8. The fourteenth line is the start of an IF THEN statement that checks whether the value that the TempValue variable (which represents the number that you want to sort) stores is less than the value that the array position that the Count variable specifies stores. The first time that this line runs, it checks whether the second item in the list is less than the first item.

9. The fifteenth through seventeenth lines form a FOR-NEXT loop that moves each item in the array down (to the right) one position to make room for inserting the TempValue number in its sorted place in the array.

10. The eighteenth line moves the number that TempValue stores to its newly sorted position in the array location that the Count variable specifies.

11. The nineteenth line sets the value of the StopNow variable to 1. This line tells the computer that it's correctly sorted the number that the TempValue variable stores.

12. The twentieth through twenty-third lines print the partially sorted array on-screen so that you can see its progress.

13. The twenty-fourth line is the end of the IF THEN statement that starts on the fourteenth line.

14. The twenty-fifth line increases the value of the Count variable.

15. The twenty-sixth through twenty-eighth lines check to see whether the StopNow variable is equal to one or whether the Count variable is equal to the value that the ArrayPos variable stores. If so, the Time2Stop variable is set to one.

16. The twenty-ninth line is the end of the WHILE loop that begins on the thirteenth line.

17. The thirtieth line is the end of the FOR loop that begins on the eighth line.

18. The thirty-first through thirty-fourth lines print the final sorted array on-screen, along with the message (Sorted array).

19. The thirty-fifth line tells the computer that the program is at an end.

Bubble Sort

The *bubble-sort algorithm* bears that name because individual items in a list appear to "bubble up" to their correct locations. The bubble-sort algorithm examines a list of items repeatedly and sorts adjacent items until it sorts the entire list, as shown in Figure 20-2. Your computer handles a bubble-sort algorithm as follows:

1. It compares the first two items in the list and sorts those two items.

2. It moves to the next item in the list and sorts that item with the last item of the previously sorted pair.

3. It repeats Step 2 for each additional item in the list until the entire list is examined.

4. It repeats Steps 1 through 3 until the entire list is sorted.

Initial list	15	4	78	29	16
	4	15	78	29	16
	4	15	78	29	16
	4	15	29	78	16
	4	15	29	16	78
	4	15	29	16	78
	4	15	29	16	78
	4	15	16	29	78
	4	15	16	29	78

☐ Sorts these two items

Sorted list

Figure 20-2:
The bubble sort examines each item in a list and sorts it in relation to its neighbor.

One drawback to the bubble-sort algorithm is that it often must re-examine a list two or more times before it correctly sorts all items (refer to Figure 20-2).

To see for yourself how the bubble-sort algorithm works, look at the following program:

```
MaxSize = 5
REDIM MyArray(MaxSize)
FOR I = 1 TO MaxSize
  MyArray(I) = INT(RND(1) * 100) + 1
  PRINT MyArray(I); SPACE$(1);
NEXT I
PRINT "(Initial array)"

Pass = 1
Time2Stop = 0
WHILE (Time2Stop = 0)
  NoSwaps = 1
  FOR I = 1 TO (MaxSize - Pass)
    IF MyArray(I) > MyArray(I + 1) THEN
      TempValue = MyArray(I)
MyArray(I) = MyArray(I + 1)
```

```
      MyArray(I + 1) = TempValue
      NoSwaps = 0
      FOR J = 1 TO MaxSize
         PRINT MyArray(J); SPACE$(1);
      NEXT J
      PRINT
    END IF
  NEXT I
  IF NoSwaps = 1 THEN
    Time2Stop = 1
  END IF
WEND

FOR I = 1 TO MaxSize
 PRINT MyArray(I); SPACE$(1);
NEXT I
PRINT "(Sorted array)"
END
```

A typical output for this program looks as follows:

```
5  19  61  26  27  (Initial array)
5  19  26  61  27
5  19  26  27  61
5  19  26  27  61  (Sorted array)
```

The following list breaks down the workings of the bubble-sort program:

1. The first through seventh lines create the variable MaxSize equal to 5, create the array MyArray to hold five integers, create a random number between 1 and 100, store it in the array MyArray, and then print the array on-screen along with the string (Initial array).

2. The eighth line creates the variable Pass and sets its value to 1.

3. The ninth line creates the variable Time2Stop and sets its value to 0.

4. The tenth line starts a WHILE-WEND loop that continues while the value of the Time2Stop variable is equal to zero.

5. The eleventh line creates the variable NoSwaps and sets its value to 0.

6. The twelfth line creates a FOR-NEXT loop that repeats (5 - Pass) times. The first time that the FOR-NEXT loop runs, it repeats four times. The second time, it repeats three times, and so on.

7. The thirteenth line tells the computer, "Check the value of an array item with the item next to it." The first time that this IF THEN statement runs, it checks the first item with the second item in MyArray.

8. The fourteenth through sixteenth lines switch two numbers that MyArray stores next to each other.

9. The seventeenth line sets the value of NoSwaps to zero. This line tells the bubble-sort algorithm that a swap's occurring somewhere in the list, so it must repeat the WHILE-WEND loop again.

10. The eighteenth through twenty-first lines print the array on-screen so that you can see how the computer's sorted the array so far.

11. The twenty-second line marks the end of the IF THEN statement that starts on the twelfth line.

12. The twenty-third line marks the end of the FOR-NEXT loop.

13. The twenty-fourth through twenty-sixth lines use an IF THEN statement to check whether the value of NoSwaps is equal to 1. If so, it sets the value of Time2Stop to one.

14. The twenty-seventh line marks the end of the WHILE-WEND loop. This loop stops looping only after the value of Time2Stop equals 1. This situation occurs only if the list is completely sorted.

15. The twenty-eighth through thirty-first lines print the final sorted array on-screen.

16. The thirty-second line tells the computer that the program is at an end.

For sorting small lists, the bubble-sort algorithm is fairly fast, but it's extremely slow if you need to sort a large number of items. Even worse, the bubble-sort algorithm takes a long time to sort if one or more low values are near the end of the array, which means that the bubble-sort algorithm must run multiple times.

Shell Sort

One problem with insertion-sort and bubble-sort algorithms is that they often must move an item from the far end of a list to the front, an especially serious drawback for the bubble-sort algorithm. The *shell-sort algorithm* presents a simple solution to make sorting faster.

The shell-sort algorithm works by the principle of "divide and conquer." Instead of trying to sort an entire list at a time, the shell-sort algorithm divides a larger list into multiple smaller lists. After it sorts these smaller lists, it combines them into a final sorted list.

The shell-sort algorithm doesn't actually do any sorting; it works with an existing sorting algorithm (such as insert sort or bubble sort) to speed up the overall sorting process.

Basically, the shell sort works as follows:

1. It divides a long list into multiple smaller lists. (Figure 20-3 shows a list divided into three smaller lists. In this case, the shell-sort algorithm is taking every third item in the list to create three separate smaller lists.)

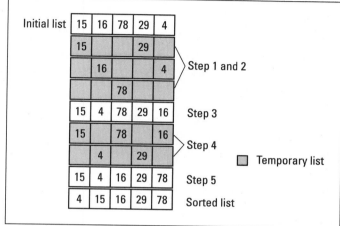

Figure 20-3:
The shell sort breaks a large list into smaller lists and then sorts those smaller lists.

2. It sorts each smaller list by using an algorithm such as insertion sort or bubble sort. In the example shown in Figure 20-3, the first minilist contains the numbers 15 and 29, which don't need sorting. The second minilist contains the numbers 16 and 4, so it sorts their positions. The third minilist contains just the number 78.

3. It smashes all the smaller lists back into a large list. In Figure 20-3, notice that the numbers 4 and 16 are sorted.

4. It divides the long list into multiple smaller lists again but into fewer smaller lists than in Step 1. In Figure 20-3, the shell-sort algorithm divides the list into two small lists, taking every second item to create two smaller lists.

5. It repeats Steps 2 through 4 (if necessary) until a single sorted list remains. Notice that after it sorts the numbers 16 and 78, the entire list is completely sorted.

To see how the shell-sort algorithm works, run the following program, which uses shell sort to initially sort items and then uses the bubble-sort method to actually sort the items in the list:

```
MaxSize = 5
REDIM MyArray(MaxSize)
FOR I = 1 TO MaxSize
  MyArray(I) = INT(RND(1) * 100) + 1
  PRINT MyArray(I); SPACE$(1);
NEXT I
PRINT "(Initial array)"

X = INT(MaxSize / 2)
WHILE X > 0
  Time2Stop = 0
  Limit = MaxSize - X
  WHILE (Time2Stop = 0)
    Switch = 0
    FOR K = 1 TO Limit
      IF MyArray(K) > MyArray(K + X) THEN
        TempX = MyArray(K)
        MyArray(K) = MyArray(K + X)
        MyArray(K + X) = TempX
        Switch = K
      END IF
    NEXT K
    Limit = Switch - X
    IF Switch = 0 THEN
      Time2Stop = 1
    END IF
  WEND

  FOR I = 1 TO MaxSize
    PRINT MyArray(I); SPACE$(1);
  NEXT I
  PRINT
  X = INT(X / 2)
WEND

FOR I = 1 TO MaxSize
  PRINT MyArray(I); SPACE$(1);
NEXT I
PRINT "(Sorted array)"
END
```

A typical output for this program looks like this:

```
94 17 70 90 62 (Initial array)
62 17 70 90 94
17 62 70 90 94
17 62 70 90 94 (Sorted array)
```

The first time that the program runs, the shell-sort algorithm compares the numbers that locations 1, 3, and 5 of the array stores (94, 70, and 62, respectively). After sorting this list, it sorts the numbers in locations 2 and 4 of the array (17 and 90). Then it sorts the entire list.

To see how the shell-sort program works in detail, examine the program line by line, as follows:

1. The first through seventh lines create the variable `MaxSize` equal to 5, create the array `MyArray` to hold five integers, create a random number between 1 and 100, store it in the array `MyArray`, and then print the array on-screen along with the string (`Initial array`).

2. The eighth line creates the variable `X` and divides the total size of the list by 2 and stores the integer value in the `X` variable. In this case, the value of `X` is 2 (`MaxSize / 2 = 2`), so `X` tells the shell-sort algorithm to divide the long list into two smaller lists.

3. The ninth line starts a `WHILE-WEND` loop that continues as long as the value of `X` is greater than 0.

4. The tenth line creates a `Time2Stop` variable and sets its value to zero.

5. The eleventh line creates the variable `Limit` and sets its value to `MaxSize - X`. The first time that this line runs, the value of Limit is `5 - 2`, or 3.

6. The twelfth line is the start of a `WHILE-WEND` loop that continues looping while the value of the `Time2Stop` variable is zero.

7. The thirteenth line creates the variable `Switch` and sets its value to zero.

8. The fourteenth line starts a `FOR-NEXT` loop.

9. The fifteenth line starts an `IF THEN` statement that checks to see whether neighboring items in the array are sorted.

10. The sixteenth through eighteenth lines compare two numbers that the array stores and switch their positions if necessary, which is the bubble-sort algorithm.

11. The nineteenth line sets the value of `Switch` to the value of `K`.

12. The twenty-first line marks the end of the `IF THEN` statement that starts on the fifteenth line.

13. The twenty-second line marks the end of the `FOR-NEXT` loop.

14. The twenty-third line sets the value of `Limit` to `Switch - X`.

15. The twenty-fourth through twenty-sixth lines check to see whether the value of `Switch` equals zero. If so, it then sets the value of `Time2Stop` to one.

16. The twenty-seventh line marks the end of the `WHILE` loop that starts on the twelfth line.

17. The twenty-eighth through thirty-first lines print the partially sorted array on-screen.

18. The thirty-second line divides X by 2 and stores the integer value into the X variable. This tells the shell-sort algorithm how many smaller lists into which to divide the larger list.

19. The thirty-third line marks the end of the WHILE-WEND loop.

20. The thirty-fourth through thirty-seventh lines print the final sorted array on-screen.

21. The thirty-eighth line tells the computer that the program is at an end.

Quicksort

One of the more popular sorting algorithms is known as *Quicksort*. The Quicksort method works by picking a number from the middle of the list and then sorting the remaining numbers to the left or right of the previously picked number, as shown in Figure 20-4.

Figure 20-4:
The Quicksort divides a larger list into small lists based on a number chosen from the middle of that list.

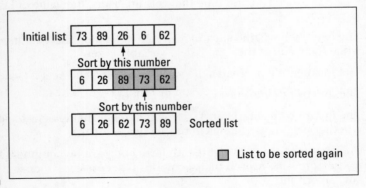

After dividing the initial list in half, the Quicksort algorithm repetitively divides each portion of the list in half again, randomly choosing a number from each list. After the Quicksort algorithm divides a long list into a bunch of smaller ones and sorts each small list, it then combines all the small lists back into a single long list that it sorts.

The Quicksort method works as follows:

1. It picks a number from the middle of the list and uses that number to divide the long list in half. All numbers less than the randomly picked number appear to the left, and all numbers greater than the randomly picked number appear to the right.

2. It repeats Step 1 for each half of the list that a randomly picked number divides until it sorts all items in a bunch of smaller lists.

3. It smashes all the smaller lists back into a large list.

Because the Quicksort algorithm repeats the same steps for smaller and smaller lists, it uses a technique known as *recursion*. Recursion simply means that a subprogram repeatedly runs itself.

Because the Quicksort algorithm needs to use recursion, you must store the actual Quicksort algorithm in a separate subprogram. Thus the complete Quicksort program consists of a main program and a subprogram, as in the following example:

```
MaxSize = 5
REDIM NumArray(MaxSize)
FOR I = 1 TO MaxSize
  NumArray(I) = INT(RND(1)*10) + 1
  PRINT NumArray(I); " ";
NEXT I
PRINT "(Initial array)"

CALL QSort 1, MaxSize

FOR I = 1 TO MaxSize
  PRINT NumArray(I); " ";
NEXT I
PRINT "(Sorted array)"
END
```

The main portion of the Quicksort program works as follows:

1. The first through seventh lines create an array of five random integers and print the array on-screen for you to see.

2. The eighth line calls the QSort subprogram by giving it the front of the list (1) and the maximum size of the list (MaxSize).

3. The ninth through twelfth lines print the final sorted array on-screen.

4. The thirteenth line tells the computer that the program is at an end.

The subprogram QSort looks as follows:

```
SUB QSort Start, Finish
  I = Start
  J = Finish
  X = NumArray(INT((I+J)/2))
  WHILE I <= J
    WHILE NumArray(I) < X
      I = I + 1
    WEND
    WHILE NumArray(J) > X
```

```
        J = J - 1
      WEND
      IF I <= J THEN
        A = NumArray(I)
        NumArray(I) = NumArray(J)
        NumArray(J) = A
        I = I + 1
        J = J - 1
      END IF
    WEND
    FOR K = 1 TO Finish
      PRINT NumArray(K); " ";
    NEXT K
    PRINT
    IF J > Start THEN CALL QSort Start, J
    IF I < Finish THEN CALL QSort I, Finish
  END SUB
```

The QSort subprogram works as follows:

1. The first line defines the name of the subprogram (QSort) and the data that it needs, which includes two integers (Start and Finish).

2. The second and third lines create two variables (I and J) that they set to the same value as the Start and Finish variables. The subprogram needs the variables I and J because their values change as the subprogram runs, but values of Start and Finish remain the same.

3. The fourth line creates the variable X that divides the size of NumArray in half and stores this value as an integer.

4. The fifth line starts a WHILE WEND loop that runs while the value of I is less than or equal to the value of J.

5. The sixth through eighth lines increase the value of I by 1 as long as the number that NumArray stores is less than the value of X.

6. The ninth through eleventh lines decrease the value of J by 1 as long as the number that NumArray stores is greater than the value of X. Here, the program is trying to determine which numbers in the list are less than or greater than the number picked in the middle of the list in the fourth line.

7. The twelfth through eighteenth lines compare the numbers in the list and move them to the left or right of the number chosen in the fourth line.

8. The nineteenth line marks the end of the WHILE WEND loop that starts in the fifth line.

9. The twentieth through twenty-third lines print the partially sorted array on-screen.

10. The twenty-fourth and twenty-fifth lines run the QSort subprogram over and over (recursively), each time feeding it a smaller array of numbers.

11. The twenty-sixth line marks the end of the subprogram.

A typical output for this program looks as follows:

```
27 62 5 79 14 (Initial array)
5 62 27 79 14
5 14 27 79 62
5 14 27 62 79
5 14 27 62 79 (Sorted array)
```

The first time that the program runs, the Quicksort algorithm chooses the third number (5) in the array. Then it sorts the remaining numbers depending on whether they're less than or greater than 5. Because they're all greater than 5, it stores them to the right of the array. Out of the four remaining numbers to the right of 5, the program picks the number 27 and sorts this smaller list, depending on whether the numbers are less than or greater than 27.

Now a third smaller list remains consisting of 79 and 62. The algorithm sorts this short list and then combines it with all the other small lists to make up the entire sorted list.

Sorting Algorithms

The insertion-sort, bubble-sort, shell-sort, and Quicksort algorithms show you the variety of methods that programs can use to sort data. Naturally, computer scientists keep inventing additional sorting algorithms with their own advantages and disadvantages, so choose your sorting algorithms carefully. Pick the right sorting algorithm, and your program can run quickly. Pick the wrong sorting algorithm, and your program may seem unbearably slow to the user.

As a general rule, insertion sort is best for small lists, bubble sort is best for lists that are already almost sorted, and Quicksort is usually fastest for everyday use. To speed up either insertion sort or bubble sort, consider combining the shell-sort algorithm with either insertion sort or bubble sort.

No matter what sorting algorithm you choose, the biggest problem is taking the time to write all the instructions to implement a particular sorting algorithm. To save you time, many programming languages include built-in sorting commands.

While built-in sorting commands may not necessarily be the fastest way to sort data, built-in sorting commands are much easier to use in comparison to writing your own sorting algorithm. In Liberty BASIC, the built-in sorting command is simply SORT, which looks like this:

```
SORT ArrayName, FirstArrayElement, LastArrayElement
```

To use the SORT command, you just have to specify the name of the array you want to sort along with the FirstArrayElement and LastArrayElement to sort. If you want to sort an entire array, the value of FirstArrayElement would be 1, and the value of LastArrayElement would be the length of the array, such as 5.

If you wanted to sort only part of an array, the value of FirstArrayElement would be any number other than 1, such as 4, and the value of LastArrayElement would be any number greater than FirstArrayElement but less than or equal to the total length of the array.

The following example shows how to use the SORT command to sort an array that consists of five (5) elements, as shown in Figure 20-5:

```
MaxSize = 5
REDIM MyArray(MaxSize)
MyArray(1) = INT(RND(1) * 100) + 1
PRINT MyArray(1); SPACE$(1);
FOR I = 2 TO MaxSize
   MyArray(I) = INT(RND(1) * 100) + 1
   PRINT MyArray(I); SPACE$(1);
NEXT I
PRINT

SORT MyArray() 1, MaxSize
PRINT
PRINT "This is the sorted list."
FOR I = 1 TO MaxSize
   PRINT MyArray(I); SPACE$(1);
NEXT
END
```

If your programming language offers a built-in sorting command, use it. If it turns out to be way too slow for your particular data, take the time to write your own sorting algorithm.

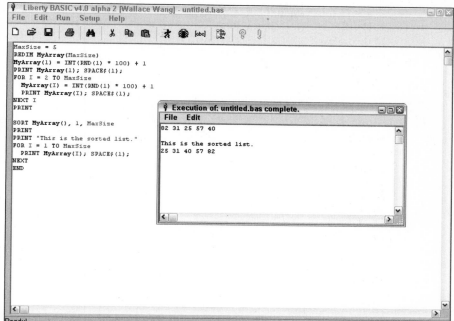

Figure 20-5:
Liberty
BASIC's
built-in
SORT
command
can sort an
array
quickly and
easily with a
minimum
amount of
extra code.

Chapter 21

Searching

Searching for data is the second most common activity (after sorting data) necessary for creating many types of programs. A program that stores names and addresses, for example, needs to sort data and then use a search algorithm to find the data that you want (such as looking for all people who live in Los Angeles and whose last names begin with the letter *M*).

To make searching easier, programs usually sort the data first before trying to search it. For more information about sorting, see Chapter 20.

An *algorithm* is just a fancy way of giving the computer specific types of instructions to accomplish a task. Choosing the right sorting and searching algorithms can make your program run quickly and efficiently. Choose the wrong sorting and searching algorithms and your program may run sluggishly, even for small amounts of data.

Searching Sequentially

A *sequential search* examines every possible item in a data structure (such as an array or linked list) until it finds what it's looking for. This type of search is like looking for your car keys in your apartment by going through room by room, looking in every conceivable location until you find your car keys. Although such a sequential search eventually turns up your car keys (assuming that they're in your apartment in the first place), it may take a long time.

For small lists, a sequential search is simple to use and fast. But if you need to search large amounts of data, the sequential search bogs down rapidly. Imagine the futility of trying to find your car keys somewhere in the city of New York. That's the type of task that a sequential search must face in searching through huge amounts of data.

A sequential search can start at either the beginning or the end of a list. It then proceeds to examine every item in the list until it finds the one item that it's searching for. Then it stops. To see how a sequential search works, try running the following Liberty BASIC program:

```
MaxSize = 5
REDIM MyArray(MaxSize)
MyArray(1) = INT(RND(1) * 10) + 1
PRINT MyArray(1); SPACE$(1);

FOR I = 2 TO MaxSize
   MyArray(I) = MyArray(I - 1) + INT(RND(1) * 10) + 1
   PRINT MyArray(I); SPACE$(1);
NEXT I
PRINT
INPUT "Which number do you want to find: "; FindMe

FoundIt = 0
FOR J = 1 TO MaxSize
   IF FoundIt = 0 THEN
      PRINT "Checking array location "; J
      IF MyArray(J) = FindMe THEN
         FoundIt = 1
      END IF
   END IF
NEXT J

IF FoundIt = 1 THEN
   PRINT "Found it!"
ELSE
   PRINT "The number you want is not in the list."
END IF
END
```

This program works as follows:

1. The first and second lines create the variable MaxSize, set the value of MaxSize to 5, and define the array MyArray, which can hold five (the value of MaxSize) integers.

2. The third through ninth lines create a random number and store it in MyArray. Each additional random number is slightly larger than the previous one to create a sorted array of five integers. Then this group of lines prints the complete array on-screen for you to examine.

3. The tenth line asks the user to type the number to find, which the program stores in the FindMe variable.

4. The eleventh line creates the variable FoundIt and sets its value to 0.

5. The twelfth through nineteenth lines start searching in MyArray for the number that the FindMe variable stores and print each array location that the program checks.

6. The twentieth through twenty-fifth lines print the message Found it! if the program finds the number; if the program doesn't find the number, it prints The number that you want is not in the list.

7. The twenty-sixth line marks the end of the program.

One advantage of a sequential search is that you can use it on both sorted and unsorted lists.

Performing a Binary Search

A sequential search starts from the beginning of a list and keeps trudging through the entire list from start to finish until it finds what it's looking for. But if a list is already sorted, you can shorten the search by using a *binary search*. (See Chapter 20 for more information about sorting data.)

A binary search divides a long (previously sorted) list in half. If the list that you want to sort contains 10 numbers that it arranges from smallest (on the left) to largest (on the right), the computer looks to see which half of the list (5 numbers on the left and 5 numbers on the right) contains the number for which it's searching.

Figure 21-1 shows a binary search trying to find the number 37 in a list containing 10 numbers. First, the binary search algorithm cuts the long list in half and examines the number in the middle of the list. Because the list contains 10 numbers, the binary search examines the fifth number in the list. In this case, the middle (fifth) number is 30, which tells the binary search algorithm that the number that it wants (37) must lie in the right half of the list.

Then the binary search takes the right half of the list (consisting of five numbers) and cuts this list in half, which points to the third number in the list (59). Because 59 is larger than 37 (the number that it's trying to find), the binary-search algorithm determines that the number 37 must lie in the left side of this part of the list.

The left part of this list contains just two numbers, 37 and 45. With two items in a list, the binary search algorithm needs to look at only the first number in this list, which is 37. Fortunately, 37 is the number that the binary search is looking for, and so the search is over.

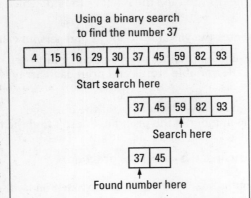

Figure 21-1:
A binary
search cuts
a list in half
until it finds
what it's
looking for.

To see how the binary-search algorithm works, try the following program:

```
MaxSize = 5
REDIM MyArray(MaxSize)
MyArray(1) = INT(RND(1) * 10) + 1
PRINT MyArray(1); SPACE$(1);
FOR I = 2 TO MaxSize
  MyArray(I) = MyArray(I - 1) + INT(RND(1) * 10) + 1
  PRINT MyArray(I); SPACE$(1);
NEXT I
PRINT

INPUT "Which number do you want to find: "; FindMe
Left = 1
Right = MaxSize
Time2Stop = 0
WHILE Time2Stop = 0
  Half = INT((Left + Right) / 2)
  IF FindMe < MyArray(Half) THEN
    Right = Half - 1
  ELSE
    Left = Half + 1
  END IF
  IF (FindMe = MyArray(Half) OR Left > Right) THEN
    Time2Stop = 1
  END IF
WEND
IF FindMe = MyArray(Half) THEN
  PRINT "Found it in location "; Half
ELSE
  PRINT "The number you want is not in the list."
END IF
END
```

The binary search program works as follows:

1. The first and second lines create the variable `MaxSize`, set the value of `MaxSize` to five, and define the array `MyArray`, which can hold five integers (the value of `MaxSize`).

2. The third through ninth lines create a random number and store it in `MyArray`. Each additional random number is slightly larger than the previous one to create a sorted array of five integers. Then this group of lines prints the complete array on-screen for you to examine.

3. The tenth line asks the user to type the number to find which the program stores in the `FindMe` variable.

4. The eleventh line creates the variable `Left` and sets its value to 1.

5. The twelfth line creates the variable `Right` and sets its value to `MaxSize`, the maximum size of the array.

6. The thirteenth line creates the variable `Time2Stop` and sets its value to 0.

7. The fourteenth line is the start of a `WHILE WEND` loop that repeats until the binary search finds the `FindMe` number in the array or until it searches the entire array and can't find the `FindMe` number.

8. The fifteenth line creates the variable `Half`, which divides the list in half and stores the integer result. (So if you divide an odd number, the integer result drops all fractions, so `INT(5 / 2)` equals 2.)

9. The sixteenth through twentieth lines look for the `FindMe` number in the left half of the array. If the `FindMe` number is less than the item that the middle of the array stores, the `Right` variable is set to `Half - 1`. Otherwise, the value of the `Left` variable is set to `Half + 1`. By lowering the value of the `Right` variable and increasing the value of the `Left` variable, the program can keep track after it searches all numbers in the array without finding the number that it's looking for. The moment that the `Left` variable becomes greater than the `Right` variable, the program knows that the number it's searching for isn't anywhere in the array.

10. The twenty-first through twenty-third lines check to see whether it can find the `FindMe` number or until the program determines that the `FindMe` number doesn't exist. If this situation occurs, the value of the `Time2Stop` variable is set to 1.

11. The twenty-fourth line marks the end of the `WHILE-WEND` loop.

12. The twenty-fifth through twenty-ninth lines print the message `Found it in location`, following that message with the array position. If it doesn't find the number in the array, the program prints `The number that you want is not in the list`.

13. The thirtieth line marks the end of the program.

The binary-search algorithm can work only on a sorted list.

Hashing

Finding something is always easier if you know where you stored it last. That's why finding your car keys is easier if they're hanging on a hook by the front door than if you must search the entire house because you can't remember where you put them.

Hashing works on a similar principle. If you want to store an item, hashing first calculates a numeric value (known as a *hash function*) that identifies that item. Then the program uses this numeric value to store the item in a specific location in a data structure (such as an array or a linked list). Now, instead of needing to search an entire array or linked list to find a single item, the program just needs to look in the specific location using the hash function.

Suppose, for example, that you want to store an integer in an array. If you store the integer anywhere in the array, you must search the entire array to find that number again. But if you use hashing, the task is much simpler. First, calculate a hash function by using the following formula:

```
HashValue = Number to store MOD 5
```

This formula tells the computer to take the number that you want to store, divide it by five, and use the remaining value as the hash function. So if you want to store the number 26, the hash function is 1 (`26 / 5 = 5` with a remainder of 1).

`MOD` is a special division command that tells the computer to divide a number and return the remainder. The command `26 MOD 5`, for example, returns the value of 1. Because Liberty BASIC doesn't support the `MOD` command, you need to use the following formula instead, which mimics the `MOD` command that you find in other languages:

```
HashValue = Number to Store - (INT(Number to Store / 5) * 5)
```

No matter what number you choose to store, the hash function calculates one of the following five values — 0, 1, 2, 3, or 4. You can create an array and use the hash function to determine the exact position at which to store an item in the array. Because the hash function of the number 26 equals 1, you can store this integer in array location number 1, as shown in Figure 21-2.

The value of the hash function determines where to store the item in a data structure.

Figure 21-2:
Hashing
calculates
a value to
determine
where to
store data
initially
and where
to find the
data later.

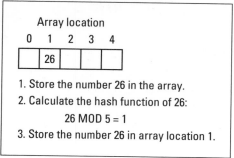

Array location
0   1   2   3   4

| | 26 | | | |

1. Store the number 26 in the array.
2. Calculate the hash function of 26:
        26 MOD 5 = 1
3. Store the number 26 in array location 1.

If you want to find the number 26 in the array again, hashing calculates the same hash function (which calculates to 1), telling the program to look for the number 26 in the first array location. Because hashing doesn't require searching every item in a list, hashing can prove much faster than sequential and binary searching, especially for long lists of data.

Dealing with collisions

Ideally, a hash function calculates a unique value. But a hash function probably calculates the same value for different items. For example, calculating a hash function by using MOD 5 — dividing a number by 5 and using the remainder as the hash function — returns a value of 2 for the numbers 7 and 32.

If you're storing large numbers of items, more than one item is likely to share the same hash function. If two items share the same hash function, programmers say that a *collision* is occurring. To handle collisions, you need to create a data structure that can store multiple items with the same hash function. Figure 21-3 shows two data structures to handle collisions: a two-dimensional array and a one-dimensional array of linked lists. (Chapter 16 contains information about creating and using two-dimensional arrays. Chapter 18 contains information about linked lists. Remember that Liberty BASIC can't create linked lists, but other languages — such as C/C++, C#, Pascal, and Java — can create linked lists.)

In Figure 21-3, the numbers 7 and 32 share the same hash function (which is 2). Because the number 7 is in array element number 2 (which represents the hash function 2), the program must store the number 32 beneath the number 7 underneath the same hash function of 2. Both a two-dimensional array and an array of linked lists enables the program to store multiple numbers underneath the same hash function location of 2.

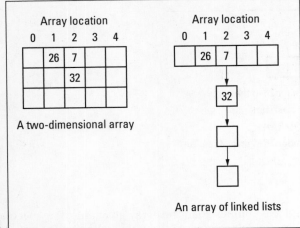

Figure 21-3:
A two-dimensional array or an array of linked lists can handle collisions.

A two-dimensional array

An array of linked lists

Ideally, you want to use a data structure that can expand or shrink to handle items sharing identical hash functions.

Searching by using a hash function

After you store items in a data structure by using hashing, you can search for any of those items by calculating a hash function for the item that you want to find. Then you look for the item in the data structure that stores items sharing the same hash function.

If every item has a unique hash function, the hash function can pinpoint the exact location of an item extremely quickly. Even if multiple items share the same hash function (refer to Figure 21-2), hashing now limits the search to a smaller list of items with identical hash functions. As a result, hashing usually can search faster than sequential or binary searching.

The following Liberty BASIC program creates five random integers — in this case, 41, 50, 57, 75, 67 — and stores them in a two-dimensional array, as shown in Figure 21-4.

If you create an array in Liberty BASIC, the first array location is number one, the second location is number two, and so on. So to mimic an array that holds a hash function of 0 through 4, the following program calculates a hash function and adds one (1) to its value:

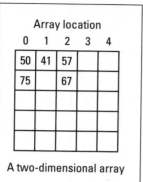

Figure 21-4:
A two-dimensional array can store values that its hash function organizes.

Array location

0	1	2	3	4
50	41	57		
75		67		

A two-dimensional array

```
MaxSize = 5
REDIM MyArray(MaxSize, MaxSize)
FOR I = 1 TO MaxSize ' Vertical
  FOR J = 1 TO MaxSize ' Horizontal
  MyArray(I, J) = 0
  NEXT J
NEXT I

Count = 1
FOR J = 1 TO MaxSize
  StopNow = 0
  StoreMe = INT(RND(1) * 100) + 1
  HashValue = StoreMe - (INT(StoreMe / 5) * 5) + 1
  WHILE StopNow <> 1
    IF MyArray(Count, HashValue) = 0 THEN
      MyArray(Count, HashValue) = StoreMe
      StopNow = 1
    ELSE
      Count = Count + 1
    END IF
  WEND
  PRINT StoreMe; SPACE$(1);
NEXT J

PRINT
PRINT

FOR I = 1 TO MaxSize ' Vertical
  FOR J = 1 TO MaxSize ' Horizontal
    PRINT MyArray(I, J); SPACE$(5);
  NEXT J
  PRINT
NEXT I
END
```

The preceding program uses hashing to store five random numbers in a two-dimensional array, as follows:

1. The first and second lines define the variable `MaxSize` and set its value to 5. Then they create the two-dimensional array `MyArray` that can hold five by five (25) integers.

2. The third through seventh lines fill `MyArray` with zeroes. Notice that the `I` variable defines the row number and the `J` variable defines the column numbers in Figure 21-4. (*Remember:* Because Liberty BASIC arrays always start counting with the number one, the array location that 0 identifies in Figure 21-4 is actually the array location number one in Liberty BASIC; the array location that 1 identifies is actually the array location number two — and so on.)

3. The eighth line creates the variable `Count` and sets its value to one.

4. The ninth line starts a `FOR-NEXT` loop that starts the hash algorithm to store an integer in the two-dimensional array.

5. The tenth line creates the variable `StopNow` and sets its value to zero.

6. The eleventh line creates a random number from 1 to 100 and stores it in the variable `StoreMe`.

7. The twelfth line calculates a hash function and stores it in the variable `HashValue`. `HashValue` is always one of five numbers: 1, 2, 3, 4, or 5.

8. The thirteenth line starts a `WHILE-WEND` loop that tries to determine where to store the `StoreMe` number in `MyArray`.

9. The fourteenth through nineteenth lines try to store the `StoreMe` number in the first row (which the `Count` variable represents) of `MyArray` in the column that the value of `HashValue` represents. If a number is already in the array location, these instructions try to store the number in the next row down until they succeed in finding an empty spot in the array.

10. The twentieth line ends the `WHILE-WEND` loop that starts in the thirteenth line.

11. The twenty-first line prints the five random numbers that the program creates.

12. The twenty-second line represents the end of the `FOR-NEXT` loop that starts in the ninth line.

13. The twenty-third and twenty-fourth lines print two blank lines.

14. The twenty-fifth through thirtieth lines print the entire array so that you can see how hashing sorts the five random numbers that the program creates.

15. The thirty-first line marks the end of the program.

Picking a Searching Algorithm

Sequential searching is the easiest search method to implement and is the fastest for small lists, but for larger lists, sequential searching takes too long. For general use, binary searching is usually faster than sequential searching. The main drawback is that binary searching works only on data that's already sorted.

Hashing is best for large amounts of data, but it's more complicated to implement because you need to calculate a hash function to store each item in a specific location in a data structure. Then you face the additional problem of dealing with collisions (if two items share the same hash function).

As a general rule, use sequential searching for small lists or unsorted lists; binary searching for larger, sorted lists; and hashing if you don't mind calculating hash functions for each item.

Chapter 22

Optimizing Your Code

· ·

In This Chapter

▶ Choosing the right data structure

▶ Choosing the right algorithm

▶ Fine-tuning the source code

▶ Using a faster language

▶ Optimizing your compiler

· ·

*G*etting a program to work correctly is often a miracle in itself. But after you do get a program to work and eliminate as many bugs as possible, the next question is whether to use (or release) the program right away or take some time to optimize it.

Optimization means trying to meet the following three goals (without introducing bugs into the program in the process):

▸ Make the program faster.

▸ Make the program smaller.

▸ Make the program require less memory to run.

As a general rule, software companies rush the new version (such as version 1.0 or version 4.0) of any program out the door just to grab market share. Within a few months, companies usually release slightly modified versions (such as version 1.01 or version 4.1), which fix some bugs (and usually introduce some new ones as well) and optimize the program in some way. In the commercial software market, optimization is usually a luxury, which is why so many programs are known as *bloatware* — they require globs of memory and hard drive space.

Choosing the Right Data Structure

Every program needs to store data, so you need to choose the right data structure for holding information in your program. An array may seem easy to create, but you must know the number of items that the array needs to hold ahead of time. Make an array too small and your program runs out of space to store additional data, possibly crashing your program. Make an array too large and you risk allocating space for storage that you don't need, which can cause your program to gobble up more memory than necessary.

More important, the data structure that you choose can affect the efficiency of the sorting and searching algorithms in your program. Compared with sorting items in an array, a sorting algorithm runs much faster rearranging pointers in a linked list.

To find out more about different types of data structures, see Chapters 16 through 19. To learn more about pointers and linked lists, see Chapter 18.

Choosing the Right Algorithm

An algorithm tells the computer how to accomplish a specific task. Think, for example, about all the different ways you can tell your friends to get to your house from downtown. You can tell them to take the highway, which is easier but may take longer. Or you can tell them to take a variety of side streets that ultimately make the trip shorter but make your directions harder to follow.

Deciding which set of directions to give to someone is much like deciding which algorithm to use in your program. If you need to sort a list containing 30,000 names, for example, the bubble-sort algorithm sorts that list much slower than the Quicksort algorithm sorts the same list. (See Chapter 20 for explanations on the bubble-sort and Quicksort algorithms.) After you sort 30,000 names, using a sequential-search algorithm to find a name is much slower than using a binary-search algorithm. (See Chapter 21 for explanations on sequential- and binary-search algorithms.)

For another example of choosing the right algorithm, think of a video game that displays the ten highest scores. Before anyone plays the game, the ten highest scores are all zero. The first time that a person plays the game, the video game lists that person's score as number one. Each time that someone plays the game again, the video game must sort the scores to display the highest to the lowest ten scores.

For this video game example, the insertion-sort algorithm is most efficient. After the video game shows two scores, the insertion-sort algorithm sorts those two scores from highest to lowest. The third time that someone plays the video game, the insertion-sort algorithm compares the third score with the previous two scores and inserts the third score in its correct place. Each additional time that someone plays the video game, the insertion-sort algorithm compares the new score with the previous high scores to determine where to insert the new score in the top-ten list of scores (assuming that it ranks that high, that is).

If you use a bubble-sort algorithm to sort the top-ten scores, the bubble-sort algorithm needs to examine the list multiple times and compare each score with its neighbor — taking more time than the insert-sort algorithm as a result. In this particular case, you can see how the insert sort-algorithm is more efficient than the bubble-sort algorithm.

As you write your own programs, remember that different algorithms are available for you to use to accomplish identical tasks for your program. Choose the algorithm that runs the fastest for your program.

Fine-Tuning the Source Code

Even if you choose data structures and algorithms with care, you can still optimize your program by fine-tuning the source code. This phrase means that you rewrite portions of your program to make it run faster or require less memory.

Put the condition most likely to be false first

When you use the AND operator in an IF THEN statement, you combine two or more conditions, as follows:

```
IF (Boolean expression 1) AND (Boolean expression 2) THEN
  ' Follow one or more instructions listed here
END IF
```

See Chapter 9 for more information about Boolean expressions.

This IF THEN statement runs only after the computer takes time to verify that both Boolean expression 1 and Boolean expression 2 are true. If either one of these Boolean expressions is false, the instructions inside the IF THEN statement don't run.

So if you intend to use the AND operator, put the expression that's most likely false in the first part of the AND operation. For example, if Boolean expression 1 is false, the computer doesn't bother checking to see whether Boolean expression 2 is true because one false Boolean expression always makes the entire AND operation false.

The moment that the computer determines that the first Boolean expression in an AND operation is false, it doesn't check the second Boolean expression, thus saving time and helping make your program run just a little bit faster.

Put the condition most likely to be true first

The IF THEN ELSEIF and SELECT CASE statements often need to check several conditions to make a decision, as the following code shows:

```
IF (Boolean expression 1) THEN
  ' Follow one or more instructions listed here
ELSEIF (Boolean expression 2) THEN
  ' Follow one or more instructions listed here
END IF
```

In this IF THEN ELSEIF statement, the computer first checks to see whether Boolean expression 1 is true. If not, it checks to see whether Boolean expression 2 is true.

But what if Boolean expression 1 is false most of the time and Boolean expression 2 is true most of the time? Then the program wastes time always checking Boolean expression 1 (which is usually false) before it can get to Boolean expression 2 (which is usually true).

To keep your program from wasting time checking a Boolean expression that's usually false, put the Boolean expression that's most likely true at the front and the Boolean expression that's least likely true at the end of the IF THEN ELSEIF statement, as follows:

```
IF (Boolean expression 2) THEN
  ' Follow one or more instructions listed here
ELSEIF (Boolean expression 1) THEN
  ' Follow one or more instructions listed here
END IF
```

By placing the Boolean expression that's most likely true at the beginning, you save the computer from wasting time checking one or more additional Boolean expressions that's usually going to prove false anyway.

Liberty BASIC doesn't support the IF THEN ELSEIF statement.

This technique also works for SELECT CASE statements, as in the following example:

```
SELECT CASE Variable
CASE Value1
  ' Follow these instructions if the Variable = Value1
CASE Value2
  ' Follow these instructions if the Variable = Value2
END SELECT
```

SELECT CASE statements check to see whether a variable equals one value (such as Value1). If you put the values most likely to match the SELECT CASE variable up front, you avoid forcing the computer to check a long list of values that are least likely to match anyway.

Although the technique of putting the conditions that are most likely true first may seem trivial, every little bit of time that you save can add up to make a faster and more responsive program.

Don't run a FOR-NEXT loop needlessly

Loops can gobble up time, so make sure that you choose the right loop. If you're using a sequential search to find an item in an array, for example, you can use a FOR-NEXT loop. The FOR-NEXT loop can count to make the computer check every position in the array to look for a specific item.

The FOR-NEXT loop runs a specific number of times. What do you think happens if it finds the item that it's looking for on the first try? The FOR-NEXT loop doesn't care; it continues looping a fixed number of times anyway, thereby wasting time.

If you use a FOR-NEXT loop, make sure that you absolutely need the program to loop a fixed number of times; otherwise, use the EXIT FOR command to exit the FOR-NEXT loop as soon as possible.

The following BASIC example uses the EXIT FOR command to exit from the FOR NEXT loop at the moment that it finds what it's looking for. Without the EXIT FOR command, the FOR-NEXT loop always repeats itself 30 times, regardless of whether it needs to loop all 30 times, as the following code shows:

```
FoundIt = 0
FOR J = 1 TO 30
  PRINT "Checking array location"; J
  IF MyArray(J) = FindMe THEN
    FoundIt = 1
    EXIT FOR
  END IF
NEXT J
```

Clean out your loops

You must absolutely place all instructions that you cram inside a loop . . . well, inside the loop. If you put an instruction inside a loop that serves no purpose in the loop, you force the computer to keep running that instruction repeatedly, thereby slowing down your loop and ultimately your program as well.

Consider, for example, the following loop:

```
FOR J = 1 TO 5000
  I = 0
  IF MyArray(J) = 55 THEN
    PRINT MyArray(J)
  END IF
NEXT J
```

The preceding FOR-NEXT loop repeats itself 5,000 times, but the program never uses the I = 0 instruction inside the FOR-NEXT loop. It forces the computer to run the I = 0 instruction 5,000 times for no reason. To avoid this problem, simply remove the I = 0 instruction from the loop, as follows:

```
I = 0
FOR J = 1 TO 5000
  IF MyArray(J) = 55 THEN
    PRINT MyArray(J)
  END IF
NEXT J
```

In the programming world, *nesting* occurs if you cram one type of control or loop structure inside another one. In the preceding Liberty BASIC program example, an IF THEN statement nests inside a FOR-NEXT loop.

Be especially wary of nested loops. If you nest one loop inside the other, the inner loop runs more often than the outer loop. By ridding the inner loop of any instructions that don't need to be inside that loop, you avoid forcing the computer to repeat an instruction needlessly.

Use the correct data types

To save memory, use the correct data types. Many versions of BASIC, such as Visual Basic, enable you to declare your variables as integers (as in DIM Num AS INTEGER) or as long integers (as in DIM Num AS LONG). Long integers can range in value from −2,147,483,648 to 2,147,483,647; ordinary integers can range in value only from −32,768 to 32,767.

A long integer variable, however, gobbles up more memory if you need to stuff a really large number into it, such as 2,147,483,647. If your variables never need to hold such a large number, a smaller data type (such as an integer) works just as well and requires less memory.

TECHNICAL STUFF

Why C/C++ programs can be hard to understand

Programs that you write in C/C++ usually run faster and more efficiently than identical programs written in other languages, such as Pascal or BASIC. But C/C++ has developed a well-deserved reputation for allowing programmers to create cryptic code. One reason is that C/C++ allows a variety of shortcuts that can make your program run faster — but at the sacrifice of readability.

Rather than type `x = x + 5` or `y = y - 23`, for example, C/C++ enables you to use shortcuts, as in the following examples:

```
x += 5; /* equivalent to x = x
   + 5 */
y -= 23; /* equivalent to y = y
   - 23 */
```

C/C++ also includes something called a prefix or postfix operator that can increment or decrement a variable by one. The following are examples of postfix operators:

```
x++; /* equivalent to x = x + 1
   */
y--; /* equivalent to y = y - 1
   */
```

The prefix operators that are equivalent to the preceding postfix operators are as follows:

```
++x; /* equivalent to x = x + 1
   */
--y; /* equivalent to y = y - 1
   */
```

If you think they look and act alike, you're almost right. The big difference occurs if you combine postfix or prefix operators into a formula, as follows:

```
x = y + z++
```

The preceding formula is actually equivalent to the following two instructions:

```
x = y + z
z = z + 1
```

You can use the following prefix operator instead:

```
a = b + --c
```

This line is equivalent to the following two instructions:

```
c = c - 1
a = b + c
```

C/C++ even offers a strange shortcut for an IF ELSE statement that uses a combination of a question mark and a colon, as follows:

```
printf("This number is bigger =
   %d\n", (x > y) ? x : y);
```

This line is equivalent to the following normal-looking IF ELSE statement:

```
if (x > y)
   printf("This number is bigger
      = %d\n", x);
else
   printf("This number is bigger
      = %d\n", y);
```

The shorter, more cryptic version of the IF ELSE statement may take up less space and run faster, but it's harder to understand at first glance. In using shortcuts, be aware that they can make your program harder to read.

Use built-in commands whenever possible

Nearly every programming language includes special built-in commands that run faster than equivalent commands that you type yourself. If you have a variable (MyNumber) that you want to increment by 1, for example, you can use the following command:

```
MyNumber = MyNumber + 1
```

Nothing is wrong with this command, but other languages offer shortcuts for incrementing a variable by 1. In C/C++, you can use a shortcut as shown in the following example:

```
mynumber++
```

If you want to increment a variable in Delphi (which is based on the Pascal language), you can use the following bit of code:

```
Inc(MyNumber)
```

If you use built-in commands, you risk making your code more cryptic and harder to understand. That's because not all programmers know all the built-in commands (shortcuts) that a particular language may offer. If a programmer encounters a built-in command, he may not understand how that particular command actually works.

Using a Faster Language

The fastest possible language in which you can write a program is machine code, followed by assembly language and C/C++, with the other languages (such as Pascal and BASIC) trailing slightly behind. If you want to speed up your program, consider switching to a different programming language.

Many programmers use a simpler language such as Visual Basic to develop a prototype program that they can show to a client and to design the user interface. After you create a prototype program, you have two choices. Your first choice is to dump the entire prototype program and rewrite the whole thing from scratch using a faster language, such as C/C++. Naturally, this process can take a long time and doesn't guarantee that the program works right (but at least it probably looks good). Your second choice is to use the prototype of the program as the basis for your actual working program. But instead of writing the entire program in a single language, you can write the parts of the program that you expect people to use most often in a faster language.

If you use two or more languages to create a single program, you can take advantage of each language's strengths. The drawback of this strategy is trying to make two or three different programming languages cooperate with one another.

Many people create a program by using a simple language, such as Visual Basic, and then, with each revision, they gradually rewrite parts of the program in a faster language, such as C/C++ or assembly language. The entire program may start out in one language, but eventually you completely rewrite in a different language.

Optimizing Your Compiler

As an alternative to using a faster language, you can use a faster compiler. If you put the identical program through different compilers, each compiler creates the same program, but one compiler's program may run faster than another compiler's program. Unfortunately, if you write a program in C++ for one compiler (such as Microsoft Visual C++), the program may not run at all in another C++ compiler (such as Borland C++ Builder) without extensive modifications.

To give you more control over your program, most compilers offer options for changing the way that the compiler works. You can change these options to fine-tune your compiler for your particular program, as shown in Figure 22-1.

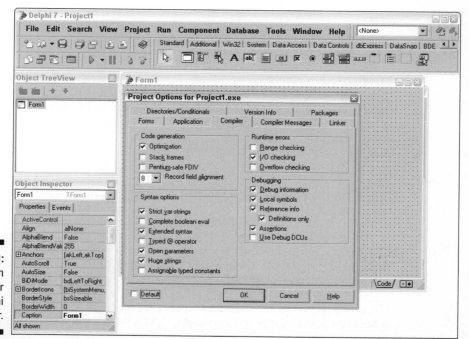

Figure 22-1: Optimization settings for the Delphi compiler.

Make sure that you know what you're doing before you change any of your compiler optimization settings. Most of these optimization settings can make your program run faster but at the expense of turning off the compiler's built-in error-checking feature, which can help you spot bugs in your program. If you turn off your compiler's error-checking capabilities, your program runs faster, but it may crash more often as a result.

Part VI

Internet Programming

The 5th Wave   By Rich Tennant

Tarzan - Lord of the Web

"... and then one day it hit Tarzan,
Lord of Jungle - where future in that?"

In this part . . .

Programming a computer once meant running a set of instructions on a single computer. If another computer wanted to run the same program, you needed to make a copy of the program and then run each copy on a different computer.

But with the growing popularity of the Internet, a new variation of programming has appeared. Instead of writing a single program to run on a single computer, you can write a single program that can run on a variety of different computers across the Internet. Theoretically, what you create on your computer another user can see on another computer anywhere in the world.

This part of the book introduces you to the wonderful world of Internet programming languages. Programs that you write in Internet languages exist as source code on a single computer. If another computer accesses this source code, that computer runs the program and interprets the results.

The most common Internet programming language is known as *HTML*, which is a special language for designing Web pages. Other popular languages for creating more interactive Web sites include *Java* and *JavaScript*. If you ever wanted to create your own Web pages that can interact with the user, this part is the place to start.

Chapter 23

Playing with HTML

· ·

· ·

*T*he World Wide Web adds a graphical user interface to the Internet. You can use the Internet without using the World Wide Web, but you can't use the World Wide Web without using the Internet.

Initially, the World Wide Web consisted solely of text, but the World Wide Web also allowed something called *hyperlinks* (text references that point to other documents stored on the World Wide Web). Because plain old text looks boring, eventually people added pictures to make the World Wide Web easier and prettier to use.

Because the Internet consists of a variety of computers, programmers needed to make the graphical interface of the World Wide Web a standard that can run on any computer. Every computer can understand ASCII codes, so programmers created an ASCII-based language that they dubbed *HyperText Markup Language*, or *HTML*.

To create a Web site, you type HTML codes and store them in an ASCII file, which usually ends with the file extension .htm or .html. If another computer wants to view your Web site, it uses a special program known as a *browser* that translates the HTML code into a pretty graphical interface.

Grasping the Basics of HTML

HTML code defines the way that text and graphics appear in a browser. A Web page actually consists of HTML code that you store in an ASCII file, usually with the HTM or HTML file extension. HTML code consists of something known as *tags*, which appear in brackets. Most (but not all) tags appear in pairs, where the first tag defines the start of something and the second tag defines the end of something, such as defining italic text or a heading, as in the following example:

```
<I>This text appears in italics.</I>
```

An ASCII file contains nothing but characters without any formatting such as fonts or underlining. Because all computers can understand characters (such as letters, numbers, and symbols that you can type from a keyboard), you can transfer text from one computer to another using ASCII files.

Ending tags always use a slash character: </I> or </BODY>.

You can enclose tags within other tags, as in the following line:

```
<B>This <I>text</I> appears in bold.</B>
```

The preceding two tags display the entire line in bold and display the word *text* in both bold and italics, which looks as follows:

This *text* appears in bold.

Tags act as containers for holding text. Think of tags as marking the beginning and ending of a container. Make sure that you don't mix up your tags, or you may get unpredictable formatting of text, as in the following example:

```
<B>This <I>text appears</B> in bold. </I>
```

If you used the above mixed up tags, your text looks as follows:

This *text appears* in bold.

Ideally, you want to locate tags completely inside the beginning and ending of other tags, as shown in Figure 23-1.

HTML codes can look cryptic if you cram them together, so feel free to use plenty of blank lines and spaces to make your HTML code look halfway readable. Remember that when a browser interprets your HTML code into a Web page, it ignores blank lines or spaces.

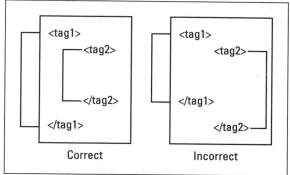

Figure 23-1:
The correct
(left) and
incorrect
(right) ways
to use
HTML tags.

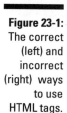

You can write HTML code in any text editor, such as Windows Notepad or even the Liberty BASIC editor. Just remember to save your file with the HTM or HTML file extension. After you create a file by using HTML codes, you can load that file into your browser by choosing File⇨Open from the browser's menu bar.

Grasping the most important HTML tags

The following are the first HTML tags that every Web page needs:

```
<HTML>
</HTML>
```

These two tags simply define a blank Web page. Anything that appears inside these two tags appears on the Web page. Nothing should appear before the <HTML> tag or after the </HTML> tag. If anything does appear in these locations in your text editor, it doesn't appear on-screen if you view the page in a Web browser.

Creating a header and title

Next, you need to define anything that you want to appear in the header (the top) of your Web page by using the <HEAD> tag, which looks as follows:

```
<HTML>
<HEAD>
</HEAD>
</HTML>
```

The most common item to place between the `<HEAD>` and `</HEAD>` tags is a title. If someone decides to bookmark your Web page, the title is the text that the browser stores in that person's bookmark list. Without a title, the user's bookmark list contains the actual filename, which is often cryptic and confusing. After all, what's easier to read in a bookmark listing — an actual Web-page name, such as `Web Site Containing American Nuclear Secrets` or a filename, such as `NK1999.HTM`?

To define a title for your Web page, you shove the title tags between the header tags, as follows:

```
<HTML>
<HEAD>
 <TITLE>Document title</TITLE>
</HEAD>
</HTML>
```

A Web page needs only one title.

Defining the bulk of your Web page

After you define a header and title for your Web page, you need to define the remainder of your page by using the `<BODY>` and `</BODY>` tags, as follows:

```
<HTML>
<HEAD>
 <TITLE>Document title</TITLE>
</HEAD>
<BODY>
</BODY>
</HTML>
```

Adding comments

In Liberty BASIC and other programming languages, you can insert comments that explain what your program is doing, when you last changed the program, and who last modified the program. As you're writing HTML code, you can also add comments to your Web pages.

Comments don't appear in a browser; they appear only if you're viewing the HTML code. A comment must appear inside brackets as follows:

```
<!-- This is a comment: Your mother is ugly and so are you.
     -->
```

The `<!--` marks the beginning of the comment tag, and the `-->` marks the end of the comment tag.

Defining Text with Tags

The basic HTML tags define your Web page as a whole, but you need to add text to provide something useful for viewers to read. HTML provides special tags for creating the following elements:

- *Headings* separate sections of text and categorize blocks of text under a single topic (similar to the way that headings in this chapter separate and categorize text).
- *Paragraphs* are blocks of text consisting of one or more sentences.
- *Quotes* are similar to paragraphs, but the HTML tags for quotes indent and surround them with more space than ordinary paragraphs.
- *Text emphasis* displays text in a certain format or style to highlight the text.

The following sections describe each of these different text tags.

Making a heading

HTML enables you to choose among six heading styles. Heading 1 signifies the most important heading, and Heading 6 signifies the least important heading. Figure 23-2 shows an example of each type of heading.

To create one of these six headings, use one of the following sets of HTML tags:

```
<H1>Heading 1</H1>
<H2>Heading 2</H2>
<H3>Heading 3</H3>
<H4>Heading 4</H4>
<H5>Heading 5</H5>
<H6>Heading 6</H6>
```

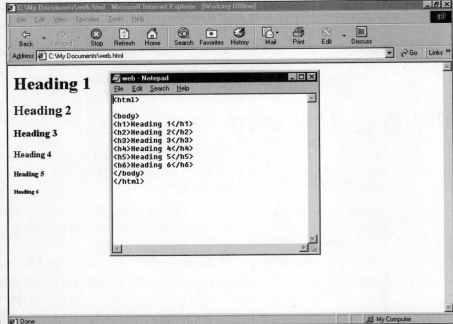

Figure 23-2:
The six
types of
headings
that you
can create
by using
HTML tags.

Usually, you want at least two subheadings under each heading. You want, for example, two or three Heading 2s under a single Heading 1. Or you want two or three Heading 6s under a single Heading 5.

Defining a paragraph

A paragraph is a chunk of text that you separate from the surrounding text by a blank line (just as with the paragraphs that you see on this page). To define the start of a paragraph, you use the <P> tag, and to define the end of the paragraph, you use the </P> tag, as follows:

```
<P>
This text you can consider a paragraph.
</P>
```

If you type text inside a pair of paragraph tags, the entire paragraph can exist on a single line, extending from the left margin of the screen to beyond the right margin of the screen. The paragraph tags automatically take care of displaying text within the margins of the screen.

To make your paragraph text easier to read, you may want to press Enter to make paragraph lines appear on multiple lines instead of on a single line.

If you want to insert a line break in the middle of a paragraph, you can use a special line-break tag — the `<BR>` tag. Unlike other tags, the line-break tag appears by itself. Figure 23-3 shows how the paragraph tag `<P>` and the line-break tag `<BR>` can create a blank line between paragraphs.

Highlighting a quote

If you want to make a paragraph stand out from the rest of your text, you can define it as a quote this way:

```
<BLOCKQUOTE>
This text appears indented.
</BLOCKQUOTE>
```

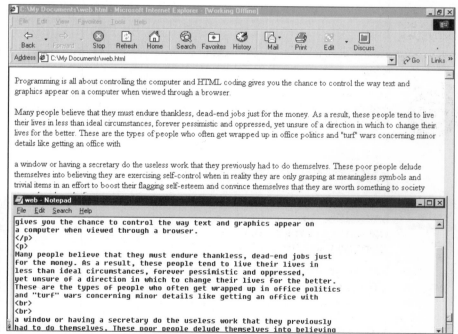

Figure 23-3:
How a paragraph looks if you display it in a Web browser.

Adding emphasis to text

Paragraph tags can separate your text into paragraphs (automatically inserting blank lines before and after the paragraph), and block quotes can indent your text. But you may want to highlight specific words or phrases. To do so, you can use the following pairs of HTML tags:

- <B> and </B> display text in bold.
- <I> and </I> display text in italics.
- <U> and </U> display text underlined.
- <TT> and </TT> display text as if you're printing it from a typewriter.
- <HR> displays a horizontal line. (Notice that the <HR> tag is another tag that doesn't appear in a pair.)

Figure 23-4 shows a Web page that uses all these special ways to emphasize text within a browser.

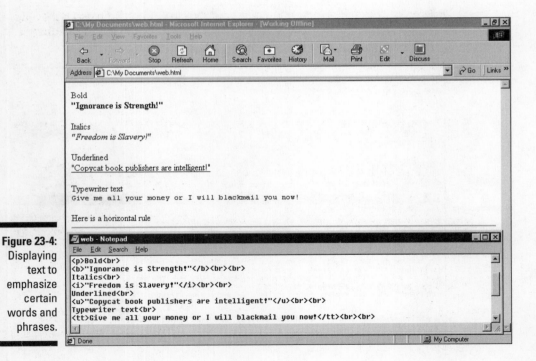

Figure 23-4: Displaying text to emphasize certain words and phrases.

Using Tag Attributes

To truly enhance the appearance of your text, you can use attributes. An *attribute* is a special command that you bury inside an HTML tag. An attribute modifies the appearance of any text that tag defines. The following are some common attributes:

- ALIGN aligns paragraph or heading text to the right, center, or left.
- BGCOLOR changes the background color of a Web page.
- TEXT changes the color of text.
- LINK changes the color of hyperlinks.
- VLINK changes the color of hyperlinks that a user has already visited.

Aligning text

You normally left-align headings and paragraphs, but you can also right-align or center-align them by using the ALIGN attribute inside the first heading or paragraph tag, as in the following example:

```
<P ALIGN="center">
This text appears centered.
</P>
```

To center-align text, you just need to use the word "center" with the ALIGN attribute.

To align text to the right or left, use the word "right" or "left" with the ALIGN attribute, as follows:

```
<H1 ALIGN="right">
This text appears right-aligned.
</H1>
```

Playing with colors

To define the background and text colors, you must set the BGCOLOR and TEXT attributes to the color that you want to use. The latest versions of most browsers allow you to define colors by using names such as `red`, `blue`, or `yellow` as shown below:

```
<BODY BGCOLOR="white"> (white background)
<BODY TEXT="black"> (black text)
```

For greater flexibility, you can use a six-digit (hexadecimal) number that represents the *RGB* (*Red-Green-Blue*) value. An RGB value defines how much red, green, and blue appears. By altering the amount of red, green, or blue, you can create a variety of different colors such as purple, white, orange, yellow, and so on. The following code is just one example:

```
<BODY BGCOLOR="FFFFFF"> (white background)
<BODY TEXT="000000"> (black text)
```

You define RGB colors by using hexadecimal numbers, which range from 0 to F (0, 1, 2, 3, 4, 5, 6, 7, 8, 9, A, B, C, D, E, F). A zero (0) represents the absence of a color, whereas an F represents the maximum amount of a color. You can vary the values for red, blue, and green to create other colors.

The first two digits in the `BGCOLOR` and `TEXT` attributes represent the amount of red (R), the second two digits represent the amount of green (G), and the last two digits represent the amount of blue (B) in the color. If you want a completely red background, use the following command:

```
<BODY BGCOLOR="FF0000">
```

For a completely green background, use the following command:

```
<BODY BGCOLOR="00FF00">
```

And for a totally blue background, use the following command:

```
<BODY BGCOLOR="0000FF">
```

Coloring your hyperlinks

You may also want to adjust the colors for your hyperlinks. Most Web pages display hyperlinks in a bright color to make them obvious. After a user visits a hyperlink, that hyperlink can change colors to show the user that he's already been to that Web page. To change colors for your hyperlinks, use one of the following tags:

```
<BODY LINK="#hexadecimal_here">
<BODY VLINK="#hexadecimal_here">
```

If you want to use both the LINK and VLINK attributes, you can do so as follows:

```
<BODY LINK="#hexadecimal_here" VLINK="#hexadecimal_here">
```

The LINK attribute uses the same hexadecimal numbers as for text and backgrounds to define the color for a hyperlink. The VLINK attribute similarly defines the color to display a hyperlink that the user's already visited.

Making a List

Creating a Web page to inform people about something is like creating an attention-grabbing television advertisement. In both cases, you want to show the viewer as much information as possible in an attractive and easily digestible way. Many people find large chunks of text intimidating and hard to read, so consider separating your text into lists.

HTML provides the following three types of lists (and I'm using a list to show you those lists):

- *Unordered lists* display text with bullets in front of each line, such as the list of which this text is a part.

- *Ordered lists* number each line of text.

- *Definition lists* indent each line of text.

Unordered lists

To create an unordered list, you need to use two types of HTML tags. The first HTML tags are <UL> and </UL>, which define the unordered list. The second tag, <LI> (which stands for List Item), marks each bulleted item. Following is an example:

```
<UL>
<LI>Take out the trash.
<LI>Develop a nuclear weapon.
<LI>Borrow an expensive appliance from the neighbor.
</UL>
```

The `<LI>` tag doesn't require an ending tag. You can use `<LI>` by itself, if desired, or you can use `</LI>` as the ending tag.

You can also create a *nested* unordered list as follows:

```
<UL>
<LI>Take out the trash.
<LI>Develop a nuclear weapon.
 <UL>
 <LI>Steal secrets from the United States.
 <LI>Bomb our own embassy.
 <LI>Export more MSG to our enemies.
 </UL>
<LI>Borrow an expensive appliance from the neighbor.
</UL>
```

Figure 23-5 shows how the preceding HTML code creates a nested, unordered list. Notice that the nested unordered list uses unique bullets to differentiate it from the outer unordered list.

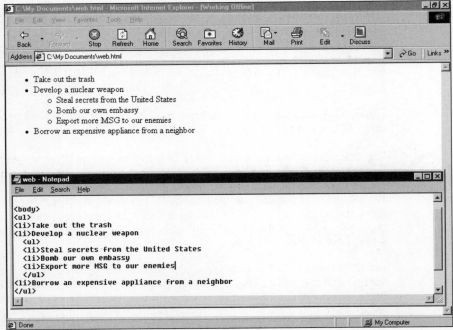

Figure 23-5:
Creating
a nested
unordered
list.

Ordered lists

Whereas an unordered list displays items with bullets, an ordered list displays items with numbers. The first list item is number 1; the second is number 2; and so on.

To create an ordered list, you use the HTML tags `<OL>` and `</OL>` to define the ordered list. Then you use the `<LI>` tag to mark each numbered item. Following is an example:

```
<OL>
<LI>Turn left at the traffic light.
<LI>Drive five blocks.
<LI>Throw a rotten egg at the front door.
</OL>
```

You can also create a *nested* ordered list as follows:

```
<OL>
<LI>Turn left at the traffic light.
<LI>Drive five blocks.
 <OL>
 <LI>Go past a burned down house.
 <LI>Drive through the next three traffic lights.
 <LI>Look for the house with toilet paper in the trees.
 </OL>
<LI>Throw a rotten egg at the front door.
</OL>
```

Figure 23-6 shows a nested, ordered list. Notice that the nested ordered list uses different numbering from the outer ordered list.

You can nest ordered and unordered lists inside one another, instead of nesting two unordered lists or two ordered lists. That way, you can have a bulleted list inside a numbered list or vice versa.

Definition lists

Definition lists get their name from the fact that people often use them in glossaries, where one line lists a term and a second line lists the definition of that term. To create a definition list, you need to use the following three types of HTML tags:

✔ The `<DL>` and `</DL>` tags define the start and end of a definition list.

✔ The `<DT>` tag displays a line of text, such as a single word or term.

✔ The `<DD>` tag displays a definition for the word or term that the preceding `<DT>` tag defines.

To see how to create a definition list, look at the following code and then take a look at Figure 23-7, which shows how the following HTML code looks in a browser:

```
<DL>
<DT>Cat
<DD>An animal that enslaves its owners.
<DT>Flashlight
<DD>A case for holding dead batteries.
<DT>Morons
<DD>A boss or someone who doesn't know how to do anything but
            pretends to be important.
</DL>
```

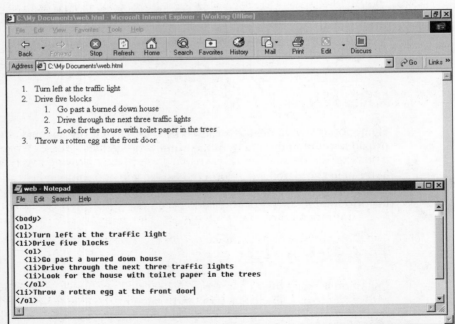

Figure 23-6:
Creating
a nested
ordered list.

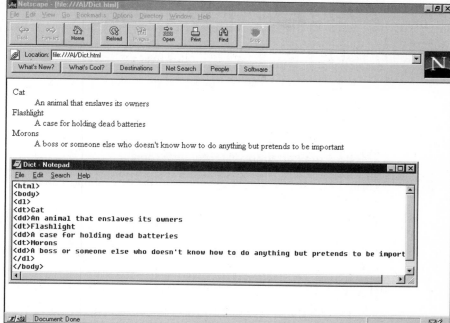

File Edit View Go Bookmarks Options Directory Window Help

Back Forward Home Reload Images Open Print Find Stop

Location: file:///Al/Dict.html

What's New? What's Cool? Destinations Net Search People Software

Cat
    An animal that enslaves its owners
Flashlight
    A case for holding dead batteries
Morons
    A boss or someone else who doesn't know how to do anything but pretends to be important

Dict - Notepad

File Edit Search Help

```
<html>
<body>
<dl>
<dt>Cat
<dd>An animal that enslaves its owners
<dt>Flashlight
<dd>A case for holding dead batteries
<dt>Morons
<dd>A boss or someone else who doesn't know how to do anything but pretends to be import
</dl>
</body>
```

Document: Done

Figure 23-7:
A definition
list as it
appears
in a Web
browser.

Creating Hyperlinks

Every good Web page needs two items: *information* (usually text) that
provides some useful content and *hyperlinks* that link your Web page to
a related Web page. A Web page usually offers the following two types of
hyperlinks:

- ✔ *External hyperlinks* are links to other Web pages that typically reside on
  another computer (and often in another geographical location).

- ✔ *Internal hyperlinks* are links to different pages of your own Web site or to
  a different part of the same Web page.

To create a hyperlink, you must use a pair of anchor tags, such as <A> and
</A>. Inside the first anchor tag, you must specify either an external or inter-
nal hyperlink. Between the two anchor tags, you type the text or graphics that
act as the hyperlink.

Making external hyperlinks

In defining an external hyperlink, the HREF (which stands for *H*ypertext *REF*erence) attribute defines the following two items:

- ✔ The external hyperlink address, which appears in a form similar to the following example:

  `http://www.someaddress.com.`

- ✔ The text or graphic that acts as the hyperlink, which is what the user clicks to jump to the external hyperlink.

To use the HREF attribute, you must put it inside the first anchor tag, as shown in the following example:

```
<A HREF="http://www.dummies.com">Dummies Web page</A>
```

In this example, the words `Dummies Web page` are the text the viewer sees as the hyperlink. Clicking the hyperlink takes users to the `www.dummies.com` Web site.

External hyperlinks are completely out of your control, so if a Web site to which you link goes down, your Web page's hyperlink leads viewers to a dead end.

Making internal hyperlinks

To make a hyperlink to another Web page on your own site, use the HREF attribute — but instead of listing another Web site address, just type the file-name of the Web page to which you want to link, as in the following example:

```
<A HREF="index.html">Index</A>
```

This creates a hyperlink of the word `Index`. After users click this hyperlink, their browsers display the Web page that you store in the `index.html` file.

Linking to a specific spot on a Web page

One problem with linking to another Web page is that the user may need to scroll down the page to find specific information. To avoid this problem, you can create a hyperlink to a specific spot on a Web page, such as the middle or the bottom of the Web page. That way, the hyperlink directs the viewer to the exact information that you want to display.

Creating a hyperlink that connects to a particular spot on another Web page is a two-step process, as the following steps describe:

1. **Create an anchor in the spot on the Web page that you want a hyperlink to display.**

    If you want a hyperlink to direct a viewer to the bottom of a Web page, for example, you place an anchor at the bottom of that particular page.

2. **Create a hyperlink that directs a viewer to an anchor that you define.**

To create an anchor, you must use the NAME attribute, as follows:

```
<A NAME="TOC">Table of Contents</A>
```

This example displays the text Table of Contents on the Web page and assigns it the name "TOC". After you create an anchor, the next step is to create a hyperlink that points to that particular anchor.

Anchors are *case-sensitive*, which means that an anchor that you name TOC is completely different from an anchor that you name toc. If you forget this difference, your anchors won't work at all.

To make a hyperlink point to a predefined anchor, use the HREF attribute and include the Web-page filename, and the anchor name, separated from the Web page filename with the # character as follows:

```
<A HREF="index.html#TOC">Go to Page One</A>
```

The preceding code displays the hyperlink Go to Page One on-screen. After the user clicks this hyperlink, the browser jumps to the index.html page and displays the anchor that the name "TOC" defines. In this case, the browser displays the Table of Contents at the top of the page, regardless of whether the words Table of Contents appear in the middle or at the bottom of the
Web page.

Displaying Graphics

Just displaying text on a Web page can get pretty boring, so HTML enables you to display graphic images on your Web pages to make everything look prettier. Graphics can appear as part of the Web page or in the background.

The only picture files that you can use for Web pages are *GIF* (*G*raphical *I*nterchange *F*ormat) and *JPG* (also spelled *JPEG*, which stands for *J*oint *P*hotographic *E*xperts *G*roup) files because these are the two graphic file formats that every computer can display.

Putting a picture on a Web page

To display a picture on a Web page, you must use the image tag <IMG> and the source (SRC) attribute to tell the computer the specific filename of the graphic image that you want to display. Following is an example:

```
<IMG SRC="filename.gif">
```

To give you greater control over the placement of a picture in relation to any text that appears next to the picture, you can use the ALIGN attribute. This attribute defines whether text appears at the top, at the bottom, or to either side of the image, as follows:

```
<IMG SRC="filename.gif" ALIGN=middle>
```

Figure 23-8 shows examples of text aligning with graphic images in a browser.

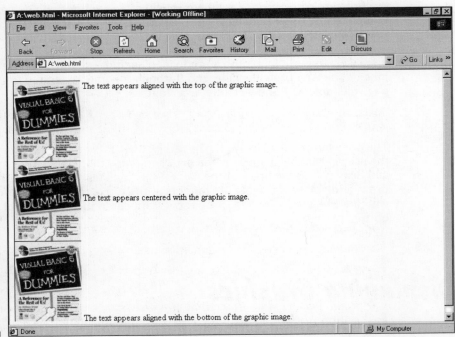

Figure 23-8:
The three positions for aligning text with a graphic image.

Adding a background picture

In addition to adding colors to a Web page, you may also want to display a picture in the background. To add a picture to a Web page, use the BACKGROUND attribute inside the BODY tag, as in the following example:

```
<BODY BACKGROUND ="filename.GIF">
```

Creating a User Interface on a Form

Although you can use HTML to display text on-screen, you may want to create something more flexible — what's known as a *form*. A form enables you to display *text boxes*, *command buttons*, and *check boxes* on-screen. To define a form, you use the `<FORM>` and `</FORM>` tags, which you sandwich between the `<BODY>` and `</BODY>` tags, as follows:

```
<HTML>
<BODY>
<FORM>
</FORM>
</BODY>
</HTML>
```

Make sure that you sandwich the `<FORM>` and `</FORM>` tags inside the `<BODY>` and `</BODY>` tags; otherwise, your form doesn't appear on-screen.

Of course, the `<FORM>` and `</FORM>` tags simply define a form, so you still must add your user interface items on the form, as shown in Figure 23-9. The following are some common user interface items that you may want to include on a form:

✔ *Text boxes* are boxes in which users can type data.

✔ *Buttons* are command buttons that users can click.

✔ *Check boxes* are boxes that users can check or clear to choose or remove an option.

✔ *Radio buttons* are buttons that users can check or clear to choose an option. You can select only one radio button at a time.

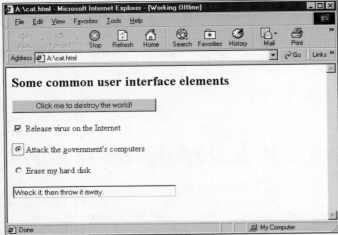

Figure 23-9:
Common
user
interface
elements
that you
can display
on a form.

Handling events

Every user interface element can respond to the user. Any time that the user does something to a user interface item, such as clicking on a command button, this action is known as an *event*.

After an event occurs on a specific user interface item, such as a command button, your form can respond by displaying text, opening a window, and so on. The following are the HTML codes for some common events:

- ✔ onAbort occurs after the user stops loading an image, either by clicking a link or clicking the Stop button.

- ✔ onBlur occurs after an item, such as a text box or command button, loses focus. This event usually occurs after the user clicks another item.

- ✔ onChange occurs after the contents of an item, such as a text box, change.

- ✔ onClick occurs after the user clicks a specific item, such as a radio button or a command button.

- ✔ onFocus occurs after the user clicks an object or highlights an object by using the Tab key.

- ✔ onMouseOut occurs after the mouse pointer no longer appears over a certain item.

- ✔ onMouseOver occurs after the mouse pointer moves over a certain item.

- ✔ onSelect occurs after the user selects text within a text box.

Events link to a specific user interface item, such as a command button or a check box. A single user interface item can respond to more than one type of event.

Creating a text box

A text box can display text and enable the user to type text. To create a text box, type the following command inside the `<FORM>` and `</FORM>` tags:

```
<FORM>
<INPUT
 TYPE=text
 NAME="textboxName"
 VALUE="Text inside the text box"
 SIZE=integer
 [onBlur="command"]
 [onChange="command"]
 [onFocus="command"]
 [onSelect="command"]>
</FORM>
```

The `TYPE=text` command tells the computer to create a text box on-screen. The `NAME` command assigns any name that you choose to represent your text box. The `VALUE` command displays text inside your text box. The `SIZE` command defines how many characters the text box can display without scrolling.

A text box can respond to four different events: `onBlur`, `onChange`, `onFocus`, and `onSelect`. The following shows how to create a text box that displays the message `"Ow! You click too hard!"` after you click inside the text box:

```
<HTML>
<BODY>
<FORM>
<INPUT
 TYPE=text
 NAME="textboxName"
 VALUE="This appears inside the text box"
 SIZE=30
 onFocus="textboxName.value='Ow! You click too hard!'">
</FORM>
</BODY>
</HTML>
```

Notice the use of single and double quotation marks following the onFocus event. The double quotation marks enclose the entire command that you want the computer to follow after the onFocus event occurs. Any command inside the double quotation marks must use single quotation marks or the entire command won't work.

Creating a command button

A command button displays a button that the user can click to perform a specific action. To create a command button, use the following code inside the <FORM> and </FORM> tags:

```
<FORM>
<INPUT
 TYPE=button
 NAME="buttonName"
 VALUE="Text that appears on the button"
 [onBlur="handlerText"]
 [onClick="handlerText"]
 [onFocus="handlerText"]>
</FORM>
```

The TYPE=button command creates a command button on-screen. The NAME command assigns a name to represent your command button. The VALUE command displays the text that appears inside the command button, such as OK or Click Me.

Command buttons can respond to three different events: onBlur, onClick, and onFocus. The following example shows how to create two command buttons — one that opens a window to display the Web page that you store in the index.html file and one that closes the window:

```
<HTML>
<BODY>
<FORM>
<INPUT
 TYPE=button
 NAME="open"
 VALUE="Open window"
 onClick="mywindow=window.open('index.html')">
<INPUT
 TYPE=button
 NAME="close"
 VALUE="Close window"
 onClick="mywindow.close()">
</FORM>
</BODY>
</HTML>
```

REMEMBER

Notice that the command that the `onClick` event defines uses double quotation marks to enclose the entire command. Anything that appears inside must use single quotation marks or the entire command won't work.

Creating a check box

Check boxes display options that the user can choose by clicking the check box to add or remove a check mark. To make a check box, put the following command inside the `<FORM>` and `</FORM>` tags:

```
<FORM>
<INPUT
 TYPE=checkbox
 NAME="checkboxName"
 VALUE="checkboxValue"
 [CHECKED]
 [onBlur="handlerText"]
 [onClick="handlerText"]
 [onFocus="handlerText"]>
 textToDisplay
 </FORM>
```

The `TYPE=checkbox` command creates a check box on-screen. The `NAME` command assigns a name to represent that check box. The `VALUE` command specifies a number or string that the check box represents if the user chooses it. The `CHECKED` command displays a check mark in the check box. The `text ToDisplay` variable represents any text that you want to display next to the check box.

A check box can respond to three different events: `onBlur`, `onClick`, and `onFocus`. The following example creates three check boxes:

```
<HTML>
<BODY>
<H2>Where do you want your computer to go today?</H2>
<FORM>
<INPUT
 TYPE = checkbox
 NAME="check1"
 VALUE=99
 onClick="litterbox.value='Throw the computer in the
          trash.'">
 In the trash can
<BR>
<INPUT
 TYPE = checkbox
 NAME="check2"
 VALUE=99
```

```
onClick="litterbox.value='Toss the computer outside.'">
 Out the window
<BR>
<INPUT
 TYPE = checkbox
 NAME="check3"
 VALUE=99
 onClick="litterbox.value='Wreck it, and then throw it
         away.'">
 Smash it to pieces
<BR>
<INPUT
 TYPE = text
 NAME="litterbox"
 VALUE=""
 SIZE = 40>
</FORM>
</BODY>
</HTML>
```

After you click a check box, a message appears in a text box below it, as shown in Figure 23-10.

If you type text to appear next to a check box, you don't need to enclose it in quotation marks. If you do enclose the text inside quotation marks, the quotation marks appear on-screen as well.

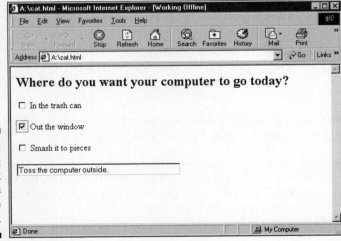

Figure 23-10:
Creating
three check
boxes
and one
text box.

Creating a radio button

A radio button works much like a check box, except that you can choose only one radio button at any given time. Radio buttons enable users to answer questions for which only one answer is possible, as in the following example:

```
What is your current marital status?
```

To answer this question, you need radio buttons for the following three responses:

- ✔ Single
- ✔ Married
- ✔ Divorced

The user can choose only one of the responses. If the user clicks the Single radio button, changes his mind, and then clicks the Divorced radio button, a dot appears in the Divorced radio button to show that the user's choosing it, and the Single radio button becomes empty to show that it's no longer chosen.

To see how to create a radio button, look at the following code:

```
<FORM>
<INPUT
 TYPE=radio
 NAME="radioName"
 VALUE="buttonValue"
 [CHECKED]
 [onBlur="handlerText"]
 [onClick="handlerText"]
 [onFocus="handlerText"]>
 textToDisplay
 </FORM>
```

The TYPE=radio command creates a radio button on-screen. The NAME command assigns a name to represent that radio button.

If you want only one radio button to appear chosen within a group of radio buttons, you must give all radio buttons exactly the same name. When radio buttons share the same name, the computer makes sure that only one radio button can be selected at a time.

The VALUE command specifies a number or string that the radio button represents if the user chooses it. The CHECKED command displays the radio button as chosen as it first appears on-screen. The textToDisplay variable represents any text that you want to appear next to the radio button.

A radio button can respond to three different events: onBlur, onClick, and onFocus. After you click a radio button, a message appears in a text box below the button. The following example shows how to create three radio buttons:

```
<HTML>
<BODY>
<H2>Where do you want your computer to go today?</H2>
<FORM>
<INPUT
 TYPE = radio
 NAME="group1"
 VALUE=99
 onClick="litterbox.value='Throw the computer in the
            trash.'">
 In the trash can
<BR>
<INPUT
 TYPE = radio
 NAME="group1"
 VALUE=99
 onClick="litterbox.value='Toss the computer outside.'">
 Out the window
<BR>
<INPUT
 TYPE = radio
 NAME="group1"
 VALUE=99
 onClick="litterbox.value='Wreck it, and then throw it
            away.'">
 Smash it to pieces
<BR>
<INPUT
 TYPE = text
 NAME="litterbox"
 VALUE=""
 SIZE = 40>
</FORM>
</BODY>
</HTML>
```

Notice that all radio buttons in the preceding example share the same name, which is `"group1"`. That way, the computer makes sure that only one radio button at a time can be selected by the user.

Deciding to Use Additional HTML Features

The basic HTML codes described in the preceding sections of this chapter provide the fundamental elements that you need to know to create and edit simple Web pages. But newer versions of HTML offer additional features for creating tables, displaying fonts, or dividing a Web page into frames.

Frames enable you to divide a Web browser screen into two or more parts, where each part (frame) can display a different Web page or a different part of the same Web page.

Although these features may seem useful and fun, keep in mind that they don't always work with all versions of browsers. If you want to ensure that all users can view your Web page, stick with the basic HTML tags described in this chapter.

Chapter 24

Making Interactive Web Pages with JavaScript

*H*TML code can produce pretty — but ultimately static — pages that resemble billboards or magazine advertisements. Although these Web pages are functional, many people want to take fuller advantage of the computer and create miniprograms on their Web pages so that people can interact with the Web page by playing games or analyzing their stock portfolio.

So to create more interactive Web pages, programmers created specialized Web-page programming languages, such as *JavaScript* and *VBScript*. If you write miniature programs in either JavaScript or VBScript, you can create your own programs just for running on your Web site.

Despite the name similarities, JavaScript bears only a superficial resemblance to Java. JavaScript uses simple commands, and JavaScript programs can run only inside a browser. Java uses more complicated commands and can create separate applications.

To practice writing JavaScript programs, use a text editor (such as Windows Notepad or the Liberty BASIC editor) and save your files with the HTML file extension. Then load your browser, choose File⇨Open, and choose the file that you just saved with the HTML file extension to see how your browser interprets your JavaScript programs.

Netscape created JavaScript; to compete against JavaScript, Microsoft created a similar language that it dubbed VBScript. VBScript isn't as popular as JavaScript, but it's still easy to use because it's based on the Visual Basic language. Just remember that any time you write a JavaScript or VBScript program in your Web page, the program may not run on an older version of a browser (which are often found running on Internet appliances such as Internet kiosks and WebTV devices).

For another way to make your Web pages flashier and interesting, consider using a program called Flash (www.macromedia.com). Professional Web designers use Flash to create pull-down menus or show animated cartoons. If you're planning to design Web pages professionally, learning Flash is an absolute must. (For more information about Flash, pick up a copy of *Macromedia Flash MX For Dummies* by Gurdy Leete and Ellen Finkelstein, published by Wiley Publishing, Inc.)

Understanding the Basics of JavaScript

To define the start and end of a JavaScript program, you use just two tags, which look similar to HTML tags. Following is an example:

```
<script language = "JavaScript">
</script>
```

You can insert a JavaScript program between the <BODY> and </BODY> HTML tags, as in the following example:

```
<HTML>
<HEAD>
 <TITLE>Document title</TITLE>
</HEAD>
<BODY>
<script language = "JavaScript">
</script>
</BODY>
</HTML>
```

Because older browsers may not understand JavaScript commands, insert two additional lines immediately after the <script> tag and immediately before the </script> tag, as follows:

```
<script language = "JavaScript">
<!--
//-->
</script>
```

The middle two lines tell older browsers to treat any JavaScript commands as comments, essentially making the browser ignore JavaScript altogether. Newer browsers that can understand JavaScript simply run the JavaScript commands.

Objects and JavaScript

JavaScript is based on *objects*. (See Chapter 19 for more information about objects.) Objects include three characteristics: *properties, methods*, and *events*.

Properties define the appearance of the object, such as its color. Methods define actions that you can make the object perform. One of the most common objects is a `document` object, and its most common method is the `write` command. Events are occurrences that the object can respond to, such as a mouse clicking an object.

You can still use JavaScript without knowing much about objects, but knowing how objects work can help you better understand JavaScript. For now, just keep in mind that JavaScript is based on objects, so if you see strange JavaScript commands — such as `document.write("Hello, there!")` — you can recognize that this command is telling a `document` object to write something on-screen.

As an alternative to typing JavaScript code directly into an HTML file, you can store your JavaScript code in a separate file. Then to load and run the code in your JavaScript file, you can use the SRC attribute, as in the following example:

```
<script language = "JavaScript" SRC="program.js">
</script>
```

This example tells the computer to load and run the JavaScript program stored in the file PROGRAM.JS.

Displaying text

JavaScript includes a `document.write` command for printing text on-screen: To see how this command works, look at the following example:

```
document.write("Text to print goes here.")
```

If you want to get fancy, you can include ordinary HTML tags inside the parentheses to format the text. To display text in boldface, for example, just shove in the HTML bold tag, as in the following example:

```
document.write("<B>", "This text appears bold.", "</B>")
```

The `document.write` command can also smash strings together by using the plus (+) sign, as follows:

```
document.write("<B>", "This text appears bold.", "</B>" + "
          And this text appears as normal text.")
```

The preceding command creates the following display:

```
This text appears bold. And this text appears as normal text.
```

Creating variables

In the `document.write` example in the preceding section, the plus sign (+) links strings and variables that represent strings. In JavaScript, you can declare a variable by using the magical `var` command, as follows:

```
var variablename
```

In JavaScript, you don't need to declare a variable data type; you just declare a variable name. Then you can set a variable to represent a string and use the plus sign (+) to link a string to a variable representing a string, as in the following example:

```
<script language = "JavaScript">
<!--
var mymessage
mymessage = "A goldfish."
document.write("What animal has a near death experience every
          time you flush the toilet? Answer: " + mymessage)
//-->
</script>
```

This JavaScript program tells the computer to do the following:

1. The first and second lines tells the computer, "Anything that you see between the `<script>` and the `</script>` tags is a JavaScript program."

2. The third line creates the variable `mymessage`.

3. The fourth line assigns the string `A goldfish` to the `mymessage` variable.

4. The fifth line writes the string, `What animal has a near death experience every time you flush the toilet? Answer: A goldfish.`

5. The sixth and seventh lines tell the computer that the JavaScript program is at an end.

Making dialog boxes

The `document.write` command can come in handy for displaying text on-screen. But JavaScript can go much farther than displaying text by creating dialog boxes. JavaScript can create the following types of dialog boxes:

- ✔ An alert dialog box
- ✔ A confirmation dialog box
- ✔ A prompt dialog box

Making an alert dialog box

One type of dialog box that programs use fairly often is an *alert dialog box*. An alert dialog box usually pops up on-screen to alert the user that something important has just happened or is about to happen, as shown in Figure 24-1. To create this alert dialog box, you use the following `alert` command:

```
alert("Nuclear meltdown has occurred. Time to evacuate!")
```

Figure 24-1:
An alert
dialog box
created with
the `alert`
JavaScript
command.

The `alert` command displays a dialog box that stays visible on-screen until the user clicks the OK button to make it go away.

Making a confirmation dialog box

A *confirmation dialog box* displays a message and gives the user a choice of two buttons — OK and Cancel. If the user clicks OK, the value of the `confirm` command is true. If the user clicks Cancel, the value of the `confirm` command is false. The following program creates a confirmation dialog box that looks like the one shown in Figure 24-2:

```
if (confirm("Do you want to erase your hard drive now?"))
  document.write("Now erasing your hard drive.")
else
  document.write("Then wait until Windows crashes, and that
          will erase your hard drive for you.")
```

Figure 24-2:
A combi-
nation
dialog box
offers the
user a
choice.

If the user clicks the OK button, the program displays the string, `"Now erasing your hard drive."` If the user clicks the Cancel button, the program displays the string, `"Then wait until Windows crashes, and that will erase your hard drive for you."`

Making a prompt dialog box

To prod the user into typing some data into the computer, many programs use a *prompt dialog box*, similar to the one shown in Figure 24-3. A prompt dialog box asks the user for input by using the prompt command, as follows:

```
prompt("How many times has your computer crashed on you
       today?")
```

Figure 24-3:
A prompt
dialog box
with a
default
value of 98.

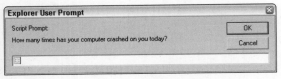

If you want to provide a default value that the user can choose without typing anything (as shown in the dialog box in Figure 24-3), you can add the default value after the message text, as in the following code:

```
prompt("How many times has your computer crashed on you
       today?", 98)
```

REMEMBER

If you don't define a default value, the prompt dialog box simply displays the word Undefined.

Because the prompt dialog box asks the user for input, you need to create a variable to hold the data that the user types into the prompt dialog box. After creating a variable, you need to set the variable equal to the prompt command, as in the following example:

```
<script language = "JavaScript">
<!--
var userdata
userdata = prompt("How many times has your computer crashed
          on you today?", 98)
document.write("This is what the user typed in = ", userdata)
//-->
</script>
```

This JavaScript program tells the computer to do the following:

1. The first and second lines tell the computer, "Anything that you see within the `<script>` and `</script>` tags is a JavaScript program."

2. The third line creates the variable `userdata`.

3. The fourth line displays a prompt dialog box with the message How many times has your computer crashed on you today? In the text box, it displays a default value of 98. Any data that appears in the text box after the user clicks the OK button the program stores in the `userdata` variable.

4. The fifth line prints This is what the user typed in = on-screen, following it with the data that the program's storing in the `userdata` variable.

5. The sixth and seventh lines tell the computer that the JavaScript program is at an end.

Playing with Functions

Rather than create one massive JavaScript program, you can create subprograms known as *functions*.

A function consists of the following four parts:

- **The function keyword:** This part identifies your function as a legitimate JavaScript subprogram.

- **A function name:** This part is the name that your JavaScript uses to "call" the function and make it run. In the following example, the function name is `square`:

```
function square(number) {
  return number * number
}
```

- **A list of arguments (data) that the function requires:** The data can be numbers or strings, but you must separate items by commas. In the example following the preceding bulleted item, the only data that the function requires is a number.

✔ **Curly brackets enclosing the function instructions:** The instructions that the curly brackets trap inside themselves tell the function how to work. In the preceding example, the function accepts a number, multiplies that number by itself, and returns the value of this multiplication.

A typical function may look as follows:

```
function FunctionName(Data) {
 // one or more instructions
}
```

To create a function, you must choose a function name, what type of data the function needs, and how the function works. The following function, square, for example, accepts a single number and multiplies that number by itself:

```
function square(number) {
 return number * number
}
```

If you don't want the function to return a value, omit the return keyword.

To see how functions can work in a real-life JavaScript program, type the following code into an editor (such as Windows Notepad) and save it with the HTML file extension:

```
<html>
<body>
<script language = "JavaScript">
<!--
function square (number) {
 return number * number
}
function printbig (headlevel, headtext) {
 document.write("<H", headlevel, ">", headtext, "</H",
         headlevel, ">")
}
var myvalue, longstring
myvalue = prompt ("How many times has your computer crashed
         on you today?", 98)
longstring = " This is how many more times your computer will
         crash = " + square(myvalue)
printbig (2, longstring)
//-->
</script>
</body>
</html>
```

Starting with the line that begins with the script tag <script language>, this JavaScript program tells the computer to do the following:

1. The `<script language = "JavaScript">` line tells the computer, "Anything that you see within the `<script>` and `</script>` tags is a JavaScript program."

2. The next line tells the computer that everything sandwiched in between the `<!--` and `//→` tags should be treated as a comment for older browsers that don't understand JavaScript.

3. The third line defines the function `square`, which accepts one chunk of data that the program stores in the variable `number`.

4. The fourth line tells the `square` function to multiply the number that the variable `number` stores and to return the multiplication result to the main JavaScript program.

5. The fifth line marks the end of the JavaScript function `square`.

6. The sixth line defines the function `printbig`, which accepts two chunks of data that the program stores in the variables `headlevel` and `headtext`.

7. The seventh line creates an HTML tag for defining a heading level and for displaying text in that heading level.

8. The eighth line marks the end of the JavaScript function `printbig`.

9. The ninth line creates two variables, `myvalue` and `longstring`.

10. The tenth line displays a prompt dialog box that asks, `"How many times has your computer crashed on you today?"` For a default value, the prompt dialog box displays the number 98. After the user clicks the OK button, the program stores the value appearing in the prompt dialog box in the `myvalue` variable.

11. The eleventh line calls the `square` function by using the value that the `myvalue` variable stores. It takes this result and tacks it onto the end of the string, `"This is how many more times your computer will crash = "`. Then it assigns the entire string, plus the value of `square(myvalue)`, to the variable `longstring`.

12. The twelfth line calls the `printbig` function and feeds it the number 2 and the data that the `longstring` variable stores. In this case, the `printbig` function creates a heading 2 and displays the text that the `longstring` variable stores as a heading 2 on-screen.

Opening and Closing a Window

Although your browser may normally display only one window at a time, you can open two or more windows on-screen to display different Web pages.

(Web sites often open multiple windows to display those annoying pop-up or pop-under advertisements.)

Opening a window

To open a window, sandwich the `open` command between the `<script>` and `</script>` tags, as in the following example:

```
<script language = "JavaScript" SRC="program.js">
<!--
 WindowName = window.open(web page or address)
//-->
</script>
```

You can also use the `window.open` command with a user interface item such as a button. Chapter 23 provides more information about using commands with user interface items.

You must define the `WindowName`, which can be any name you want. You also must define what the window displays. If you want the window to display a specific Web page, you must type the filename of that Web page, as in the following example:

```
MyWindow = window.open("index.html")
```

This command opens a new window, `MyWindow`, and displays the Web page that the file `index.html` stores. If you want the window to display a Web site, you must type the entire Web-site address, as follows:

```
MyWindow = window.open("http://www.dummies.com")
```

Defining a window's appearance

To give you more control over a window's appearance, you can define the size and appearance of a window. If you define a window's appearance, you must give the window a second name, following it with any attributes that you want, as in the following example:

```
MyWindow = window.open("index.html", "secondname",
           "toolbar=no, resizable=yes")
```

This opens a window that displays the `index.html` Web page. This window doesn't have toolbars, but you can resize the window. You use the second name of the window (in this example, `"secondname"`) if you want to refer to this window from another window, such as through a hyperlink.

Attributes can modify the appearance of a window, such as by adding a toolbar and a menu bar. The following list explains those attributes that you can define for any window that you open:

- ✔ `toolbar[=yes|no]|[=1|0]`: Displays a toolbar at the top of the window with buttons such as Back, Forward, and Stop.
- ✔ `location[=yes|no]|[=1|0]`: Creates a text box displaying the current Web page or Web address.
- ✔ `directories[=yes|no]|[=1|0]`: Displays directory buttons at the top of the window.
- ✔ `status[=yes|no]|[=1|0]`: Displays a status bar at the bottom of the window.
- ✔ `menubar[=yes|no]|[=1|0]`: Displays menus at the top of the window.
- ✔ `scrollbars[=yes|no]|[=1|0]`: Creates horizontal and vertical scrollbars if the document is larger than the window dimensions.
- ✔ `resizable[=yes|no]|[=1|0]`: Enables the user to resize the window.
- ✔ `width=pixels`: Specifies the width of the window, measuring it in pixels.
- ✔ `height=pixels`: Specifies the height of the window, measuring it in pixels.

If you want to open a window but hide the toolbar, for example, you can set the toolbar attribute to either `yes/no` or `0/1`, as in the following example (using `yes/no`):

```
MyWindow = window.open("index.html", "secondname",
           "toolbar=no")
```

Or you can use the following example (with `1/0`) for the same task:

```
MyWindow = window.open("index.html", "secondname",
           "toolbar=0")
```

Closing a window

After you open a window, you may want to close it. To close a window, you must use the `close` command, as in the following example:

```
WindowName.close()
```

This command closes a window that you identify as `WindowName`. If you want to close a window that you call `adWindow`, you use the following command:

```
adWindow.close()
```

The name of the window that you use with the `close` command is the same name that you use to open the window. You open a window with the following command:

```
WeirdStuff = window.open("index.html")
```

You close the same window with the following command:

```
WeirdStuff.close()
```

JavaScript is a full-blown programming language, far too complex to cover completely in this chapter. For more information about JavaScript, pick up a copy of *JavaScript For Dummies,* 3rd Edition, by Emily A. Vander Veer (published by Wiley Publishing).

Chapter 25

Using Java Applets on Web Pages

*J*ava can create two types of programs: full-blown applications (such as word processors or Web browsers) and smaller applets that can run only when viewed through a browser. (This chapter is concerned only with using Java to write applets, rather than complete applications.)

When you write applets in Java, you can add more sophisticated features to your Web pages. (If you'd rather not write your own Java applets, you can always use applets that someone else has written for you, as long as you trust that the applet works correctly.)

Writing Java applets can get extremely detailed and time-consuming, depending on how much work you want to put into your applet. For specific instructions on how to write programs in Java, pick up a copy of *Beginning Programming with Java For Dummies* by Barry Burd (Wiley Publishing).

How Java Applets Work

A Java applet is a miniature program written in the Java programming language. Unlike C++ (which compiles programs into machine code), Java applets get converted from source code into a special byte code format.

Byte code format (also known as p-code) is a special file format that needs a special Java run-time file known as a *virtual machine* or VM. As long as you have an operating system with a Java VM on it (such as Windows, Linux, or OS X), you can run Java programs on your computer.

Java versus JavaScript

Although both Java and JavaScript enable you to create interactive Web pages that ordinary HTML code can't offer, they're actually two completely different languages. But when should you use Java, and when should you use JavaScript?

JavaScript is easier than Java to learn and use, so it's a much faster method for creating interactive Web pages. On the other hand, Java is a much more powerful and flexible programming language that enables you to create features that would be cumbersome, difficult, or impossible to duplicate in JavaScript.

As a general rule, use JavaScript for short, simple tasks, and use Java for more complicated tasks. Of course, you can use both JavaScript and Java together on the same Web page to get the best of both worlds.

The source code of a Java program is stored in an ASCII file with the file extension of `.java`, such as `Virus.java`. When you compile a Java program into byte code format, you create a separate file with the file extension of `.class`, such as `Virus.class`.

Because computers understand only machine code, no computer in the world knows how to run a Java program saved in byte code format. If you want to run a Java program stored in byte code format, you have to use a special (and free) program called a Java Virtual Machine (VM). (Chances are good that if you have a browser such as Internet Explorer or Netscape Navigator, you already have a copy of the Java VM on your computer.)

Java programs can run on any computer that has a copy of the Java VM, including Windows, the Macintosh, and UNIX. If you compile your Java programs into byte code format, you can run them on a variety of computers and operating systems without any modifications whatsoever.

To show you what a Java applet looks like (don't worry about understanding how the code actually works), here's a simple Java applet that displays the message `"Stop staring at me!"` on-screen:

```
import java.awt.*;
import java.applet.Applet;
public class TrivialApplet extends Applet
{
  Font f = new Font("TimesRoman", Font.BOLD, 24);
```

```
public void init() {
repaint();
}
public void paint( Graphics g ) {
g.setFont(f);
g.setColor(Color.blue);
g.drawString( "Stop staring at me!", 15, 75 );
}
}
```

Figure 25-1 shows the output of the preceding Java program.

You can type a Java program using any text editor (such as Liberty BASIC's editor or the Windows Notepad). To compile your Java program into byte code format, you need to use a Java compiler, such as the free Sun Microsystems (java.sun.com) Java compiler or a commercial Java compiler such as JBuilder from Borland (www.borland.com) or CodeWarrior (www.metrowerks.com) from Metrowerks.

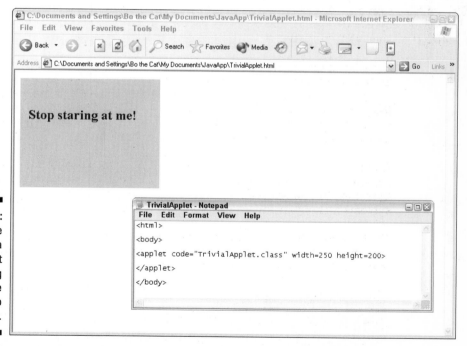

Figure 25-1:
The source code to a Java applet running inside a Web browser.

Limiting the power of Java applets

Java applets are miniature programs, which means that they have the potential to erase files or mess up your computer if someone writes a virus or Trojan Horse in Java. To prevent malicious Java applets from attacking your computer, Java restricts Java applets from performing certain tasks such as deleting files, reading the contents of a hard drive, renaming files, creating directories, or running any external programs.

Naturally, since Java's introduction, people have found numerous holes in Java's defenses. Although none of these weaknesses has yet allowed a malicious hacker to exploit these holes and threaten the world, these flaws do serve to remind programmers that Java presents opportunities to attack your computer, given enough creativity and persistence on the part of a malicious Java programmer.

Adding a Java Applet to a Web Page

When you have a Java applet compiled into byte code format, you're ready to use HTML tags to run that Java applet on a Web page. Adding a Java applet to a Web page involves using two tags, sandwiched between the `<BODY>` and `</BODY>` tags:

```
<APPLET CODE = "JavaAppletName">
Text to display if the Java applet can't run
</APPLET>
```

The `JavaAppletName` variable is the actual name of the Java applet that you want to run. If you want to run a Java applet named `Message.class`, the HTML applet tag would look like this:

```
<APPLET CODE = "Message.class">
Text to display if the Java applet can't run
</APPLET>
```

One or more lines of text can be sandwiched between the `<APPLET>` and `</APPLET>` tags. This text appears only if the Java applet can't run within a particular browser. So rather than display a blank image on-screen, the text appears in order to explain to the user that the Java applet can't run.

Defining the size of a Java applet window

For additional fun, you can define the size of the area that your Java applet appears in by using the `WIDTH` and `HEIGHT` attributes, as in the following example:

```
<APPLET CODE = "Message.class" WIDTH = 250 HEIGHT = 100>
Text to display if the Java applet can't run
</APPLET>
```

This example defines a width of 250 pixels and a height of 100 pixels for the applet.

Aligning the location of a Java applet window

When an applet appears on a Web page, you may want to use the ALIGN command to define how text appears next to the applet. You can use the following three ALIGN attributes:

- ALIGN=TOP aligns the text with the top of the applet.
- ALIGN=MIDDLE aligns the text in the middle of the applet.
- ALIGN=BOTTOM aligns the text with the bottom of the applet.

Figure 25-2 shows how text appears when aligned with an applet in three ways.

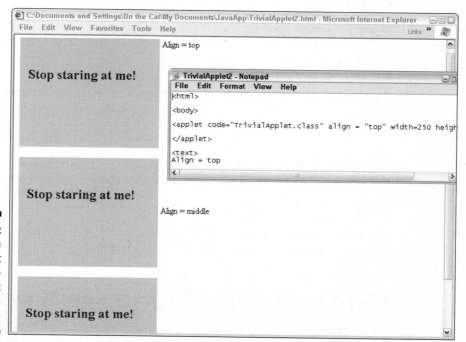

Figure 25-2: Three different ways to align text with a Java applet.

If Java is free, why buy a Java compiler?

In an effort to make Java as widespread and universal as possible, Sun Microsystems provides a free Java compiler, source code, and tools that you can download for free from the Sun Microsystems Java Web site (java.sun.com). But if you can get a free Java compiler, why should you buy a commercial Java compiler?

First, the Sun Microsystems Java compiler provides the bare necessities for writing and compiling a Java program. Using the free Sun Microsystems Java compiler is a lot like walking from New York to Los Angeles: You could do it, but paying extra to take a plane would be easier, faster, and more convenient.

Second, a commercial Java compiler offers additional benefits that the free Sun Microsystems Java compiler can't offer. For example, JBuilder (from Borland) allows you to graphically design your Java program's user interface and appearance so that you don't have to write Java code to create the user interface yourself. So feel free to try programming in Java using Sun Microsystem's free tools, but when you're ready to start creating larger programs on a regular basis, seriously consider buying a Java compiler instead. You'll be glad you did.

Defining space around a Java applet

To keep your text from appearing too close to an applet on a Web page, you can define the amount of horizontal and vertical space to put between the applet and the text. Use the following HSPACE and VSPACE attributes to define this spacing:

```
<APPLET CODE = "Message.class" WIDTH = 250 HEIGHT = 100
        VSPACE = 25 HSPACE = 15>
Text to display if the Java applet can't run
</APPLET>
```

The preceding code defines a vertical space of 25 pixels between text and the applet and a horizontal space of 15 pixels between text and the applet. Figure 25-3 shows what appears when you view the following code in your browser:

```
<html>
<body>

<applet code="TrivialApplet.class" align = "middle" width=250
        height=200>
</applet>
```

```
<text>
The value of HSPACE = 0
</text>

<p>
This paragraph appears smashed near the Java applet since the
        value of VSPACE = 0
</p>

<applet code="TrivialApplet.class" align = "middle" width=250
        height=200 vspace = 45 hspace = 55>
</applet>

<text>
The value of HSPACE = 55
</text>

<p>
This paragraph appears at a distance from the Java applet
        since VSPACE = 45
</p>
</body>
```

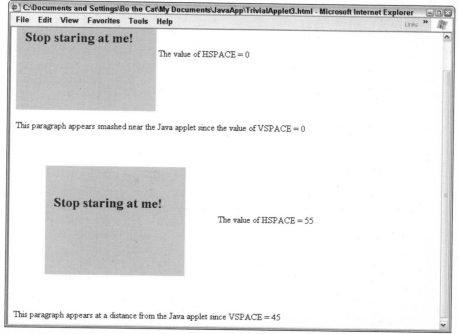

Figure 25-3:
The
HSPACE
and
VSPACE
commands
can keep
text away
from the
edges of a
Java applet.

Finding Free Java Applets

If you want to write your own Java applets, you have to spend some time studying Java programming. Java can be a challenging language for beginners to master on their own. Until you master Java (or instead of mastering Java), you may prefer to use Java applets written by other people.

You can paste other people's ready-made applets into your Web pages. Or if the source code is available, you can modify the applet and recompile it yourself, which often helps you understand the Java code more quickly.

To find a list of Web sites that offer Java applets, visit your favorite Internet search engine, such as Hotbot (www.hotbot.com) or Google (www.google.com), and search for the string "Java applet." Or you can visit Yahoo! (www.yahoo.com) and click the links labeled Computers and Internet, Programming and Development, Languages, Java, and Applets. These links take you to a list of dozens of Web sites where you can download free Java applets and source code.

Part VII
The Part of Tens

In this part . . .

Once you learn the fundamentals of programming, most books, classes, and schools push you out the door, wish you luck, and force you to figure out what to do with your programming skills. But this book doesn't abandon you without giving you some directions on where to go with your skills. To avoid feeling aimless and lost, you can use this part of the book to get some ideas for applying and profiting from your programming abilities.

As a programmer, you possess unique skills, so don't settle for an ordinary job in an ordinary company doing ordinary work that ultimately gives you an ordinary (and boring) life. Instead, browse through this part of the book to see all the different ways that people are using their programming skills at fun, exciting, and unusual jobs that you can get, too. This part also provides guidance for helping you finding your next language compiler and offers some tips for playing games to sharpen your programming skills.

Chapter 26

Ten Cool Programming Careers

*A*sk most high school or college guidance counselors what you can do with your programming skills, and they're likely to steer you in the direction of sterile job titles such as programmer analyst or data-entry operator. To help stimulate your imagination so that you can get a really cool job playing around with computers all day, this chapter lists some unusual programming jobs that you may want to consider so that you can actually have fun with your life and your job at the same time.

Programming Computer Games for Fun and Profit

Of all the programming topics in the world, none is more popular than game programming. Besides the obvious job of designing computer games (and getting paid to do it), game programming offers a wide variety of related jobs that can prove just as much fun as game designing but don't get as much publicity.

Most computer games are team designs. One team may design the game rules; another team does the actual programming; another creates the graphic backgrounds and animation; and still another gets paid to play the latest games to look for bugs and offer suggestions for making the games more exciting (and, hence, more profitable for the publisher).

If you want to write computer games, you need to learn C/C++ and a little bit of assembly language because games need to be as small and as fast as possible. Metrowerks (at www.metrowerks.com) sells special versions of its CodeWarrior compiler for writing computer games in C/C++ for Sony PlayStation and Nintendo game consoles.

If you'd rather exercise your graphic skills, you need to learn animation, which means studying a lot of math (which you use to calculate the best ways to make objects move around the screen).

To start writing your own games, consider using a game engine — a special program that provides instructions to tell the computer how to move animated objects around on-screen. You then spend your time designing your game, not worrying about the details of controlling animated characters on-screen.

For a free game engine that runs on Windows, Linux, and the Macintosh, download the Crystal Space game engine from the official Crystal Space Web site (at http://crystal.sourceforge.net/drupal). Using Crystal Space (and other game engines), you can create 3D triangle mesh sprites with frame animation or transparent and semitransparent textures for creating see-through water surfaces and windows.

If none of this stuff makes any sense to you, imagine trying to create a game and, at the same time, needing to learn all these technical terms and how to program them yourself. That's why many people use game engines to help them make new games. Without a game engine, making a game can prove as complicated as making your own word processor just so that you can write a letter.

To find out more about game programming, visit one of the following Web sites (and start on your new career as a professional game programmer today!):

- ✔ **International Game Developer's Association** (at www.igda.org) is the granddaddy of computer-gaming organizations that promotes and protects the computer-gaming industry as well as provides conferences to bring computer gaming professionals together.

- ✔ **Game Developer** (at www.gdmag.com) is a special online magazine devoted exclusively to covering the latest game-programming techniques and game-programming industry news.

✔ **Game Programmer** (at `gameprogrammer.com`) is a Web site that provides information and links to the multitude of game programming resources all across the Internet.

✔ **DigiPen** (at `www.digipen.edu`) is the site of one of the first schools (with close ties to Nintendo) devoted to training game-programming professionals and awarding them with real college degrees.

✔ **GameJobs** (at `www.gamejobs.com`) is a site that provides information, tips, and contacts to help you find a job in the computer-gaming industry.

Creating Computer Animation

Computer animation isn't just for creating animated characters to shoot or blow up in video games. Programmers also use computer animation in virtual reality, training simulators, and Hollywood special effects (because blowing up a computer-animated building is easier than building a mock-up of an existing building to blow up).

Computer animation can range from creating lifelike images for TV and movies to creating multimedia presentations for business, to making cartoons and animated films. If you like to draw but want to become more than just an artist, combine your knowledge of graphics with programming and help design new graphics-animation programs, create virtual-reality simulators, or work on the next Hollywood blockbuster's special effects.

To learn more about the wonderfully weird world of computer animation, browse through these Web sites and see what sparks your imagination:

✔ **Pixar Animation Studios** (at `www.pixar.com`) is a leading Hollywood animation studio responsible for animating movies such as *Toy Story*, *Finding Nemo*, and *A Bug's Life*.

✔ **MIT Computer Graphics Society** (at `www.mit.edu/activities/cgs/mitcgs.html`) is an MIT club dedicated to studying computer graphics as an artistic medium.

✔ **International Animated Film Society** (at `www.asifa-hollywood.org`) grants awards (similar to the Academy Awards) for the best computer-animation short films.

✔ **Animation Magazine** (at `www.animationmagazine.net`) provides news and information for the entire animation industry.

✔ **National Centre for Computer Animation** (at `ncca.bournemouth.ac.uk`) is the United Kingdom's leading research and training institution for computer animation and digital media.

✔ **Computer Graphics World Online** (at `http://cgw.pennnet.com/home/home.cfm`) is a magazine covering all the tools, news, and conferences that professional computer graphics artists may need to know about.

Making (And Breaking) Encryption

Ever since nations decided to play the game of war and send their people into battle for their own political reasons, armies have used secret codes to communicate with their commanders without revealing information to their enemies.

Because war isn't likely to disappear anytime soon, every country in the world continues to develop encryption techniques for creating codes and breaking the codes of others. If the world of James Bond, espionage, and cloak-and-dagger spies appeals to your sense of adventure, consider a career in encryption.

Encryption is the art of converting plain-text information into unreadable garbage (which often resembles tax forms or legal documents) so that no one but your intended recipient can read it. Then, by using a secret password or code phrase, the recipient of your encrypted message can unscramble and read it.

The art of encrypting data involves plenty of math (usually focusing on prime numbers). If you plan to pursue a career in encryption, earn some graduate degrees in advanced mathematics and practice your C/C++ programming skills. Then get a job working for the military, a defense contractor, a software encryption publisher, or a security agency such as the National Security Agency (at `www.nsa.gov`).

The National Security Agency (open to U.S. citizens only) is the premier code-making and code-breaking agency in the world, housing the most supercomputers in one location. If you know programming, advanced math, or any foreign language, you can use your abilities to read intercepted messages, track enemy submarine acoustic signatures in the Atlantic Ocean, or search through databases to spot the movements and operations of international terrorists.

If you find encryption fascinating but you'd rather not help your country prepare for war, consider putting your encryption skills to use in the international banking and financial world, where encryption protects electronic transactions worth billions of dollars every day.

For more information about encryption, visit one of the following Web sites. Many of these sites offer C/C++ source code to various encryption algorithms, so you can practice both your programming and encryption skills at the same time.

- ✔ **CypherNet** (at www.cypher.net) is a grass-roots organization dedicated to helping individuals use encryption to protect themselves against their own governments.

- ✔ **Central Intelligence Agency** (at www.cia.gov) is the most famous intelligence agency in the world, responsible for spying on other countries.

- ✔ **North American Cryptography Archives** (at www.cryptography.org) offers plenty of encryption programs and encryption algorithm source code to help you learn as much as possible about encryption.

- ✔ **International PGP Home Page** (at www.pgpi.com) is the home of the most famous personal encryption program in the world, Pretty Good Privacy (PGP).

- ✔ **RSA** (at www.rsasecurity.com), the name of which derives from the first names of its founders, Rivest, Shamir, and Adleman, is the number-one encryption company providing encryption technology for many programs that rely on the Internet.

Internet Programming

Besides Internet companies gobbling up programmers, many old-fashioned companies also need programmers to help them create interactive Web sites. With so much activity revolving around the Internet, the increasing demand for Internet programmers is no surprise.

To get involved in this field, spend some time mastering the intricacies of HTML so that you know the basics of designing Web pages. (A little bit of training in graphic design and layout doesn't hurt either.)

Although HTML can create pretty Web pages, companies really want to take advantage of the Internet to sell products online. To create interactive Web sites, programmers use a variety of languages, including Java, XML, JavaScript, VBScript, Perl, C#, and Python.

To get a start in Internet programming, teach yourself HTML; start playing around with an Internet programming language (such as JavaScript); sharpen your Windows XP, Linux, or Unix operating system skills; learn more about accessing databases by using SQL; and play with Web servers such as Apache (which often comes free with Linux).

(Coincidentally, Wiley publishes many books about the preceding topics, including Java and Linux. To learn more about these books, visit www. dummies.com.)

Visit one of the following Web sites to see how quickly you can start working (and earning a lot of money) in an Internet programming position:

- **Career Moves** (at www.computerweekly.com/careermoves) lists various Internet programming jobs, along with advice to help you find the best job for you.

- **GeekFinder** (at www.geekfinder.com) provides plenty of jobs for a wide variety fo computer-related jobs all around the world.

- **Web Jobs USA** (at www.webjobsusa.com) is dedicated to helping Internet professionals find jobs practicing their Web-page and Internet-programming skills.

- **Java Jobs** (at javajobs.com) provides tutorials, training, and Java-related job listings.

Fighting Computer Viruses and Worms

Every month, malicious programmers release hundreds of new computer viruses into the wild. Fortunately, many of these computer viruses contain bugs that keep them from working correctly: They don't spread; they're too easy to detect; they don't do anything other than take up space . . . and so on.

Still, every year, a few new computer viruses manage to cause immense headaches to computer users throughout the world. Some of the more infamous superviruses that made headlines include the Slammer worm, the CIH virus, the Melissa virus, and the LoveBug worm.

Although most virus writers create viruses for their own amusement and entertainment, a small minority actively write destructive viruses as an intellectual challenge. Because malicious programmers, such as virus writers, are always around, programmers who can create and update antivirus programs can always find work.

To learn more about computer viruses, study assembly language along with VBA (Visual Basic for Applications), the macro programming language that Microsoft uses in its Office suite. Most viruses and antivirus programs use assembly language to create small, fast programs that can directly access the actual computer hardware. To learn more about different antivirus companies and what type of positions they have available, visit any of the following Web sites:

- ✔ **Network Associates** (at www.nai.com) publishes the popular VirusScan antivirus program.

- ✔ **Sophos** (at www.sophos.com) publishes the popular Sophos AntiVirus program.

- ✔ **Symantec** (at www.symantec.com) publishes the popular Norton AntiVirus program.

- ✔ **Trend Micro** (at www.trend.com) publishes the popular PC-cillin AntiVirus program.

- ✔ **F-Secure** (at www.datafellows.com) publishes the well-regarded F-Prot antivirus program.

Hacking for Hire

Hackers are often extremely skilled (or extremely patient) people who enjoy the technical challenge of breaking into computers. Although breaking into computers is technically illegal, your chances of getting caught increase immensely the moment that you start causing damage.

Rather than risk getting thrown in jail because you can't resist playing around with computers, consider the alternative challenge of trying to outwit the hackers themselves. As a computer-security expert, you can work for the government to help track down malicious hackers, or you can work for a corporation and help keep hackers out of a company's computers.

By working as a "good" hacker, you get to face all the technical challenges of hacking while getting paid. Plus you get to experience the thrill of working on the side of law-enforcement agencies to track down hackers around the world.

To learn more about using your hacking skills on the side of law enforcement, visit the following Web sites:

- ✔ **Federal Bureau of Investigation** (at www.fbi.gov) is the agency in charge of United States law enforcement on a national level, including investigating and prosecuting computer hackers.

- ✔ **AntiOnline** (at www.antionline.com) provides news and hacking tools, along with a network of computers on which hackers can safely and legally expand their skills.

- ✔ **2600** (at www.2600.com) is a quarterly hacker magazine that provides hacking-related articles and information.

- ✔ **BlackCode** (at www.blackcode.com) provides the latest news about computer hacking.

Participating in an Open-Source Project

To get a job, you need job experience, but you can't get job experience unless you have a job. Given this paradox, the most reliable way to solve this problem is to demonstrate your abilities by working for free.

To get valuable programming experience that impresses big companies, consider participating in an open-source project. The whole idea behind an open-source project is to get programmers to contribute to the development of a single project, such as the Linux operating system or the GNOME user interface for Linux.

Working on an open source project not only gives you instant credibility (providing that you actually contribute something useful), but it also gives you valuable experience in working with a real-life programming project. While other programmers may get shuffled into entry-level positions working on boring projects that nobody really cares about, you get to work on something that can give you pride and a sense of accomplishment.

The prestige of contributing to an open-source project can later help you find a better-paying job, or it can serve as an amusing hobby. Either way, open-source projects give you a chance to prove to the world what you can actually accomplish with your programming skills.

To get involved with an open source project, visit one of the following Web sites and start programming:

- ✔ **Open Source** (at www.opensource.org) provides news and information about the value of open source projects.

- ✔ **Free Software Foundation** (at www.fsf.org) offers information about open-source projects in general and the GNU C compiler in particular.

- ✔ **Perl** (at www.perl.com) is the home page of the Perl programming language, which is quickly becoming the most popular programming language for the Internet.

- ✔ **Apple Open Source** (at http://developer.apple.com/darwin) is the place for information about Apple Computer's open-source operating-system projects.

- ✔ **GNOME project** (at www.gnome.org) guides the development of the GNOME interface, which aims to put a friendly graphical user interface on Linux.

- ✔ **Mozilla** (at www.mozilla.org) is the open-source project for Netscape Navigator, the second most popular Web browser in the universe.

- ✔ **Linux** (at www.linux.org) is the premier Unix-clone operating system that worries even Microsoft.

Niche-Market Programming

One problem with programming classes is that they teach you how to write programs, but they don't teach you how to put your skills to practical use. Most companies use computers, so try to combine your knowledge of programming with another field.

Who's better qualified to design and write medical software, for example, than a programmer with a medical background (or a medical professional with a programming background)? Sports fanatics combine programming skills with enthusiasm for sports to design horse race-handicapping software; health professionals design nutrition and diet software; and lawyers create special legal software.

Practically every field faces unique needs that general-purpose software (such as spreadsheets or databases) can't solve. That's why professionals hire programmers to develop custom software.

Best of all, niche markets are so small that you never need to worry about monolithic companies such as Microsoft competing against you and wiping out your business. In addition, only a handful of programmers can even possibly write programs for certain niche markets — how many programmers have experience in hotel management, for example? — which means that you face less competition and a market practically begging for your software.

If you ever wanted to take advantage of your previous job experience and combine it with your new programming skills, consider developing a program that solves a specific problem in a niche market. Who knows? With your programming skills, you can perhaps find new opportunities in a field that may have seemed a dead end.

Teaching Others about Computers

Become an expert in any field, and you can teach others your unique skills. In addition to the obvious teaching positions in schools, training others to use popular programs such as Microsoft Word, Lotus Notes, or C++ programming is a lucrative business.

Training professionals travel around the world, conducting classes for corporations who want to train their workers to use a variety of programs in hopes that they become more productive. As a trainer, you get to see the world, meet people, and see for yourself how many different ways Holiday Inns can design the inside of a hotel room.

If you like dealing with people, enjoy traveling, and love sharing your knowledge of computers with others, this sort of job may prove the perfect position for you.

Selling Your Own Software

There's no cheaper way to go into business for yourself than to develop and sell your own software. Unlike restaurants or bookstores, you don't need a large amount of space or an extensive inventory. You simply write a program and sell it electronically across the Internet.

The most popular way to test-market a program is through shareware distribution: You give away copies of your software and ask that people send you money if they find it useful. To encourage more people to send money, your program must prove useful and work reliably.

Despite the seemingly bizarre business logic of giving away your product and trusting that people actually pay you for it, many shareware authors earn hundreds (and sometimes millions) of dollars for their programs over the years. (One of the most successful shareware programs is WinZip, which you can download at www.winzip.com.) Distributing programs as shareware can make you rich or earn you a little bit of extra spending money.

If you ever wanted to start your own business but didn't want to take out a loan, starting a shareware business is the easiest and cheapest solution. All it takes is a good idea, some decent programming skills, and a little bit of marketing know-how to launch your business.

If your program doesn't appeal to the average computer user, try selling it to a niche market instead. In addition to niche markets for stock brokers, law-enforcement agencies, or restaurant owners, you can also find niche markets that target specific computers, such as the Palm or PocketPC handheld computers.

You can turn your programming skills into your own business with the right computer program. And if you like programming, what other job lets you stay home all day, play around with your computer, and still get paid for it in a business all your own?

Chapter 27

Ten Additional Programming Resources

. . . .

In This Chapter

▶ Commercial compilers

▶ Finding shareware and freeware compilers

▶ Using proprietary languages

▶ Buying from mail-order houses

▶ Finding sources for source code

▶ Joining a user group

▶ Browsing Usenet newsgroups

▶ Playing Core War

▶ Building battling robots

▶ Playing with Lego Mindstorms

. . . .

*I*f Liberty BASIC is your first foray into the wonderfully wacky world of computer programming, you may be curious about where to go from here. Although you can continue practicing with Liberty BASIC and even use Liberty BASIC to create programs that you can sell to others, you may want to learn what other programming languages you can use as well.

If you're serious about programming as a career, the next logical choice is to learn C/C++, C#, or Java. Of course, this step means learning the arcane syntax of C/C++, C#, or Java, so you may want to consider a simpler (but still powerful) alternative such as Visual Basic.

Then again, why limit yourself to C, C++, Java, or any version of BASIC if you can choose from literally hundreds of different programming languages with oddball names such as Modula-2, LISP, LOGO, Scheme, Prolog, ICON, APL, COBOL, FORTRAN, Ada, and Perl?

Because programming can often get frustrating and downright troublesome, this chapter also includes resources where you can find additional help from real-life people — for example, at computer user groups in your area or Usenet newsgroups on the Internet.

To save you money, this chapter also points you to mail-order houses where you can find a wide variety of programming tools at steep discounts. If you get tired of practicing programming, this chapter also directs you to various programming games that you can play to sharpen your programming skills and have fun at the same time.

Just remember that no matter what language you use or where you find additional programming help, ultimately your own skills determine whether you finish your programming project on time and it works or is so buggy and unreliable that users abandon it.

Trying Commercial Compilers

The most important tool for any programmer is a *language compiler*. (See Chapter 4 for information on what a compiler does and why you'd want one.) Although you can find plenty of free language compilers, most programmers rely on commercial compilers that offer support and regular updates. Most commercial compilers cost several hundred dollars (which doesn't matter if your company is paying for them), but you can often buy special beginner or standard editions of compilers that cost much less (typically ranging in price from $50 to $150).

Windows programming

Like it or not, Microsoft Windows is the dominant operating system on the planet (although Linux is quickly gaining momentum). If you plan to write a program to sell to people, the largest and most profitable market is the Windows market.

The standard language for writing Windows programs is Visual C++ .NET, which the friendly folks at Microsoft (at www.microsoft.com) produce. Despite the addition of the term "Visual," Visual C++ .NET is a fairly complex C/C++ programming environment that even professional programmers have trouble mastering. Still, if you want to write Windows programs, you can't go wrong by picking up a copy of Visual C++ .NET.

Despite the popularity of C++, the future for Windows programming lies in Microsoft's newest language, C# (pronounced *C-sharp*). Their Visual C# .NET compiler combines the best features of C++ and Visual Basic to create a friendlier language that also protects you from making the majority of horrendous mistakes that plague C++ programs.

Because few people want to devote half their lives to learning the cryptic structure of C/C++ or C#, many programmers choose the second most popular programming tool: Visual Basic .NET.

Unlike Visual C++ .NET or Visual C# .NET, Visual Basic .NET is much easier to learn since the BASIC language more closely resembles English than C++ or C#. If you want to preserve your knowledge of Liberty BASIC, learning Visual Basic .NET is the next logical step in any programmer's quest to dominate the programming world.

Because of the growing popularity of Java, you may want to take a look at JBuilder by Borland (at www.borland.com). Borland has a long history of providing quality programming tools and also sells two other popular rapid-application development tools, C++Builder and Delphi. Like JBuilder, C++Builder and Delphi let you design the user interface visually, and then write code in either Java, Pascal, or C++ to make the program actually work.

A *rapid-application development (RAD)* tool enables you to build the user interface quickly. (For more information about RAD tools, see Chapter 2.)

If you have any interest in creating cross-platform applications (programs that can run on different operating systems such as Windows, Linux, and the Macintosh), a popular choice is Metrowerks CodeWarrior (at www.metrowerks.com). Unlike most of its competitors, such as Visual C++ .NET or C++ Builder, CodeWarrior runs on such different operating systems as Windows, Solaris, Linux, and the Macintosh, so you can (theoretically) copy your source code from the Windows version of CodeWarrior to the Linux version of CodeWarrior and compile your program for another operating system with little or no modifications.

To help you choose the best compiler for your needs, Table 27-1 lists several popular Windows compilers.

Table 27-1	Popular Windows Compilers	
Compiler Name	*Language Used*	*Web Site*
Visual C++ .NET	C, C++	www.microsoft.com
Visual Basic .NET	BASIC	www.microsoft.com
Visual C# .NET	C#	www.microsoft.com
CodeWarrior	C, C++, Java	www.metrowerks.com
RealBasic	BASIC	www.realbasic.com

(continued)

Table 27-1 *(continued)*

Compiler Name	Language Used	Web Site
JBuilder	Java	www.borland.com
C++ Builder	C, C++	www.borland.com
Delphi	Pascal	www.borland.com

Macintosh and Palm OS programming

The Macintosh easily maintains its reputation as one of the easiest computers in the world to use — and one of the hardest to program. Fortunately, the latest Macintosh programming tools make Macintosh programming much easier.

The premier Macintosh programming tool is CodeWarrior (which many often credit with saving the Macintosh, because it was the only reliable programming tool available at one time). CodeWarrior, by Metrowerks (at www.metrowerks.com), enables you to write programs in three different languages: C, C++, and Java. So rather than buy three separate compilers, you get everything that you need in one package.

Best of all, Metrowerks sells special versions of CodeWarrior so that you can write programs for Windows (including Windows 98/Me/NT/2000/XP and Windows CE), Solaris, Linux, Sony PlayStation game consoles, Nintendo game consoles, and the most popular handheld computer in the world, the Palm handheld computer. If you plan to write programs for the Macintosh, the Palm handheld, or game consoles such as Nintendo or Sony PlayStation, CodeWarrior is your first (and probably only) choice.

Of course, CodeWarrior doesn't support BASIC, so if you want to program a Macintosh by using BASIC, you have only two choices: Future Basic and RealBasic.

Future Basic (at www.stazsoftware.com) closely resembles Liberty BASIC but runs entirely on the Macintosh.

RealBasic (at www.realbasic.com) is another BASIC programming language that closely resembles Visual Basic. As with Visual Basic, you can design the user interface of your program and then write BASIC code to make your program work.

RealBasic even goes one step farther and enables you to convert Visual Basic source code to run on the Macintosh. If you have any Visual Basic programs that you need to turn into Macintosh programs, you can do so by using RealBasic.

Of course, converting Visual Basic programs into RealBasic isn't 100 percent accurate, which means that you may need to modify the programs slightly. So if you really need to create both Macintosh and Windows programs, write your program in RealBasic and have RealBasic turn it into Macintosh and Windows programs at the same time.

Table 27-2 lists the most popular Macintosh compilers for writing programs for the Mac.

Table 27-2	Popular Macintosh Compilers	
Compiler Name	*Language Used*	*Web Site*
CodeWarrior	C, C++, Java	www.metrowerks.com
RealBasic	BASIC	www.realbasic.com
Future Basic	BASIC	www.stazsoftware.com

Linux programming

If any operating system can break the Microsoft stranglehold on the personal computer market, Linux looks like the best choice. Linux is surging in popularity, and many companies and programmers are quickly porting their programs to run under Linux.

Several commercial vendors have released Linux versions of their compilers (such as CodeWarrior, JBuilder, and Kylix, which is a Linux version of Delphi), but you may be pleased to know that Linux also offers a rich assortment of language compilers that you can use for free.

Depending on your version of Linux (RedHat, SUSE, or Debian, for example), you may already have a language compiler such as GNU C (a C language compiler) or EGCS (a C++ compiler).

Although Linux doesn't offer as many popular applications as Windows or the Macintosh, plenty of Linux compilers are available for a variety of languages, including Ada, Pascal, FORTRAN, and BASIC. For more information about many popular Linux compilers, visit www.gnu.ai.mit.edu/software/gcc/gcc.html.

Programming a handheld computer

Microsoft created a stripped-down version of Windows known as *Windows CE* for use in handheld and palm-size computers (often known as *PocketPC computers*). Unfortunately, programs that you write for Windows 98/Me/NT/2000/XP can't run on Windows CE. So if you want to write programs for Windows CE, you must use a special Windows CE compiler. Microsoft developed Windows CE, so naturally Microsoft offers Windows CE programming toolkits so that you can write programs for Windows CE/PocketPC computers by using either Visual C++ or Visual Basic.

Two other programming languages for writing Windows CE/PocketPC programs include Pocket C (at www.orbworks.com) and NSBASIC (at www.nsbasic.com). Pocket C uses a stripped-down version of the C programming language, and NSBASIC uses a stripped-down version of the BASIC programming language. Pocket C and NSBASIC aren't quite as powerful as Visual C++ and Visual Basic, but they still enable you to create commercial-quality programs for a Windows CE/PocketPC computer.

Both Pocket C and NSBASIC also come in versions that run under the Palm OS, so you can also write programs for the Palm handheld computer. Because the Palm OS and Windows CE/Pocket PC are drastically different computers, you can't run your programs on both the Palm OS and Windows CE/Pocket PC without extensive modification.

Testing the Shareware and Freeware Compilers

Choosing a programming language can often prove as emotional and subjective as choosing someone to marry. Rather than buy a handful of commercial compilers only to find out that you don't like any of them or the programming languages that they use, take some time to download a shareware or freeware compiler instead.

As you test shareware or freeware compilers, you can practice using different programming languages such as C++ or Java. If you find a programming language that you like, consider buying the shareware or a similar commercial compiler. For a list of free compilers for a variety of different programming languages, visit the Catalog of Free Compilers and Interpreters Web page at www.idiom.com/free-compilers.

BASIC compilers

For a BASIC compiler that can create MS-DOS and Windows programs, consider PowerBasic (at www.powerbasic.com). For writing MS-DOS programs, the company offers their FirstBasic and PowerBasic shareware compilers. For writing Windows programs, try the PowerBasic for Windows compiler.

If you have a Macintosh, you can download the freeware Chipmunk Basic interpreter (not a compiler) from www.nicholson.com/rhn/basic.

One of the more challenging tasks for any programmer is writing 3D computer animated games. Although most programmers use C/C++ to write computer video games, you may want to use your knowledge of BASIC to write your own computer games for Windows by using a special game-creation language known as *DarkBASIC* (at http://darkbasic.thegamecreators.com).

C/C++ and Java compilers

C and C++ are powerful languages, but they can prove intimidating to many people. Rather than spend lots of money buying a commercial C/C++ compiler, spend some time playing with shareware and freeware C/C++ compilers first.

The most popular C compiler for Linux is the GNU C compiler, so that same compiler was ported to Windows and renamed the Cygwin compiler (at http://sources.redhat.com/cygwin).

For those who want to tackle Java programming, download the free Java software development kit direct from Sun Microsystems (at java.sun.com), the inventors of Java. This bare-bones Java programming tool can help you learn Java.

To help spread the popularity of their C++ and Java compilers, Borland International offers free versions of their C++ Builder and JBuilder compilers. The idea is that if you like using the free versions, you might want to buy their more advanced versions later.

Pascal compilers

Although Pascal has faded in popularity in North America, it's still popular among a small group of programming die-hards. For a free Pascal compiler for MS-DOS, Windows, and Linux, download Free Pascal from www.freepascal.org. If you always wanted to dig into the guts of a compiler, visit the Bloodshed Software Web site (at www.bloodshed.net), where you can join an ongoing effort to create and develop a Pascal compiler for Windows.

Currently the most well-known Pascal compiler is Delphi, a Visual Basic-like compiler developed by Borland International. To help spread the popularity of Delphi, Borland offers a free version of Delphi (and Kylix, their Linux

Pascal compiler) for personal use. Just visit www.borland.com to grab your free copy and start programming your Windows or Linux computer in Pascal today.

Oddball language compilers and interpreters

Not everyone likes the idea of following the pack and learning traditional languages such as C/C++ or BASIC. For you rebels out there, consider some of the oddball free language compilers or interpreters that give you a chance to play with some obscure programming languages.

Prolog has gained a loyal following as one of the more popular languages with which to learn about artificial intelligence. If you want to understand all the excitement about artificial intelligence languages in general, and Prolog in particular, download a free copy of Strawberry Prolog from www.dobrev.com, which runs on Both Windows and Linux. For another free Prolog compiler for Windows, download a copy of Visual Prolog from www.visual-prolog.com.

Back in the early 1980s, the Department of Defense tried to force the Ada programming language into full-scale use for all military projects. Unfortunately for the Pentagon, by the time Ada compilers were available, most of the rest of the world had already switched to C/C++ and left Ada behind. Still, Ada has its supporters, and if you want to experiment with a language that tried to become the best programming language in the world, grab a copy of GNAT Ada from ftp://cs.nyu.edu/pub/gnat.

Although BASIC was designed to teach beginners how to program computers, another language, LOGO, was specifically designed to teach kids how to program computers. If you want to program Windows by using the LOGO language, get a free copy of MSW Logo from Softronics (at www.softronix.com).

Using a Proprietary Language

A wide variety of books, magazines, newsletters, source code, and users around the world can provide help and advice for solving specific problems with programming languages such as C/C++ and Java. Unfortunately, popular programming languages are designed to solve a wide variety of different problems, which means that they usually can't solve any single problem quickly and easily.

As an alternative to popular programming languages, consider using a *proprietary programming language*. A single company usually develops proprietary programming languages to perform a specific type of task, such as creating multimedia presentations or artificially intelligent programs. Proprietary programming languages have the following advantages:

- Proprietary languages are generally easier to learn than popular languages.

- Proprietary language programs are often smaller and faster to create because the languages are designed to perform a specific task.

Although proprietary programming languages can prove easier to learn and enable you to create fancy applications with a minimum amount of programming, they have their own disadvantages, as I describe in the following list, which may make you wary of using them for critical projects:

- You don't find as much third-party support (such as books or magazines) for proprietary languages as you do for popular languages.

- Proprietary languages may run on only certain operating systems (meaning that porting the program to another operating system may prove virtually impossible).

- You're dependent on a single company for support. If the company that makes your proprietary language goes out of business, your program may prove difficult or next to impossible to update.

- Buying a proprietary language may prove extremely expensive compared to buying general-purpose language compilers.

- Proprietary language programs often run slower than programs that you create in a general-purpose language.

HyperCard

One of the most famous (and ultimately most ignored) proprietary programming languages comes from Apple Computer's *HyperCard* program. HyperCard was originally designed to enable nonprogrammers to write programs by using an index card metaphor.

An entire HyperCard program is meant to resemble a stack of index cards, with one card at a time appearing on-screen. Text and pictures appear on each card, and cards can provide hyperlinks to other cards. By using a simplified programming language known as *HyperTalk*, you can write programs to make your HyperCard stack calculate results or display information.

Although most consider HyperCard the forerunner of hypertext and visual programming (long before the popularity of the World Wide Web and Visual Basic), the HyperCard programs often ran too slowly and were limited to running only on the Macintosh.

Apple Computer no longer gives away free copies of HyperCard with every Macintosh, and the company has pretty much let HyperCard drift farther into the background of neglect. Still, HyperCard's latest claim to fame was that the designers of the best-selling game, Myst, used it to create their product, which shows that imagination is ultimately more important than the programming language you choose.

To discover more about HyperCard, visit www.apple.com.

Revolution

In the wake of HyperCard's initial popularity, many companies offered HyperCard-clone programs. Following HyperCard's steady decline into obscurity, most of these HyperCard-clone programs also died.

One of the few remaining HyperCard clones is *Revolution*, which not only runs HyperCard stacks, but also runs them on a variety of different operating systems including the Macintosh, Windows, and Linux/Unix. So if you write any programs by using HyperCard and want to preserve your programs while enabling them to run on different computers, consider using Revolution (www.runrev.com).

PowerBuilder

One of the more popular database development languages is *PowerBuilder*, which enables you to visually design a database application with a minimum of coding. Whether you need to share data with big mainframe computers or minicomputers, PowerBuilder may prove the product to use for making your next application. To find out more about PowerBuilder, visit www.sybase.com.

Shopping by Mail Order

You can buy language compilers directly from the publishers, but unless they're offering a special discounted price, you're better off buying from a mail-order house. Mail-order houses sell products at a discount — and they often don't charge you sales tax.

In addition to offering a wide variety of commercial compilers at discounted prices, mail-order houses often stock a variety of programming tools that you may never find anywhere else, such as special programming editors, code analyzers, language utilities to make programming easier, copy-protection kits, and installation programs.

The following mail-order houses specialize in programming tools:

- **Programmer's Paradise** (at www.pparadise.com) offers a variety of programming tools for a variety of languages.
- **VBXtras** (at www.vbxtras.com) specializes in Visual Basic add-ons and programming aids.

Getting Your Hands on Source Code

Because one of the best ways to learn anything is to learn from someone else, many programmers voluntarily share their source code so that others can benefit from their work. The Linux operating system is the ultimate example of people sharing source code.

If you can get the source code to another program, you can include its features in your own program, thus saving you time. Many companies sell programming utilities (such as miniature word processors, spreadsheets, or graphics-charting programs) that you can paste together into your own programs. As a bonus, some of these companies also include the source code so that you can modify the program for your needs.

You can often find the source code to small programs scattered around the Internet for free. These small programs typically solve simple problems, but one of those problems may prove exactly what you need.

To find source code for your favorite language, use a search engine to search for the string **"C source code"**. This search string likely turns up a long list of useless Web sites and an occasional useful Web site that offers source code that you can download for free.

To help narrow your search for source code, try visiting one of the following Web sites:

- **Code Guru** (at www.codeguru.com) offers source code snippets to a variety of popular languages, including C/C++, Visual Basic, and Java.
- **Planet Source Code** (at www.planet-source-code.com) provides Visual Basic and Java source code.

- ✔ **The Delphi Source** (at www.delphisource.com/) features source code just for Delphi programmers.
- ✔ **ABC: All BASIC Code** (at www.allbasiccode.com/) provides source code for nearly all varieties of BASIC, including Liberty BASIC, QBASIC, QuickBasic, and Visual Basic.
- ✔ **The JavaScript Source** (at http://javascript.internet.com/) offers loads of free source code for programming in JavaScript.
- ✔ **The cprogramming.com site** (at www.cprogramming.com) offers lots of source code for C/C++ programmers to use and enjoy.

Joining a Local User Group

Programming can prove lonely and difficult in isolation. If you're lucky (or unlucky, depending on your point of view) enough to live in a big city, you can perhaps find a local programming user group.

User groups meet regularly — usually weekly or monthly — and enable programmers to share tips and information with one another concerning their favorite language, such as C/C++, Java, Visual Basic, or Delphi.

Many user groups advertise in local computer magazines and newsletters, which you can often find in your favorite computer store. For another way to find a user group in your area, visit the Web site of your favorite compiler company (such as www.microsoft.com or www.borland.com). Company Web sites often list user group meetings in different cities.

Frequenting Usenet Newsgroups

Learning anything can prove much easier if you have some friends to help you out. If you don't have any knowledgeable programming friends nearby, use the next best resource — a Usenet newsgroup.

Newsgroups act as electronic bulletin boards, where anyone can leave a message asking for help. Complete strangers from all around the world can give you advice or information to answer your question. If you browse through newsgroups long enough, you can often respond to other people's messages and give them some help as well.

Nearly every programming language has a newsgroup where loyal programmers gather and swap tips, tricks, and news. Check out the following newsgroups:

✔ comp.lang is a general-purpose programming newsgroup.

✔ comp.lang.basic is a newsgroup for BASIC programming enthusiasts.

✔ comp.lang.c is for C programming fanatics and followers.

✔ comp.lang.c++ enables you to learn C++ from this newsgroup.

✔ comp.lang.delphi enables you to band together with other Delphi programmers.

✔ comp.lang.java.help is a great place for getting help with programming and using Java.

✔ comp.lang.pascal covers Pascal programming, including some Delphi programming news and information.

This list is just a short sampling of available programming newsgroups. With a little bit of searching, you can find newsgroups for other programming languages and specific compilers such as Visual Basic, C++Builder, and RealBasic.

Playing Core War

People tend to learn faster and more effectively if they're having fun (which is a lesson that public schools and copycat book publishers still haven't figured out yet). Although writing a program that can calculate a second-order differential equation may improve your programming skills, it may also make you think that programming is extremely boring.

So to keep you from getting bored and to show you that programming can actually prove a lot of fun, you can play one of many programming games available for free (or for a nominal price). The purpose of programming games is to help sharpen your programming skills. If you want to win, you must learn to write the smallest, fastest, and most efficient programs — just as in real life.

The granddaddy of all programming games is *Core War*. In the old days, computers didn't use floppy or hard disks. Instead, they stored data on a magnetically-charged doughnut-shaped device called *core memory* or just *core* for short.

The idea behind Core War is to write a program that you "store" in the core memory of an imaginary mainframe computer. To play Core War, each player must write a program by using a simplified version of assembly language, dubbed Red Code. Each program must search for enemy programs and erase them from the computer's core memory. The winner is the player whose program is the last surviving program in core memory.

Although Core War is popular, it's not a very visually exciting game to watch. All you see are the various programs stalking one another in core memory and trying to erase the instructions of enemy programs, which often looks no more interesting than watching a visual depiction of defragmenting your hard disk.

For more information about Core War, visit one of the following sites:

- ✔ `www.ecst.csuchico.edu/~pizza/koth`
- ✔ `www.koth.org`
- ✔ `ftp.csua.berkeley.edu/pub/corewar`

To exchange messages with other Core War fanatics, visit the `news:rec.games.corewar` newsgroup, where you can learn about the latest Core War tournaments and start writing your own killer programs.

Programming a Battling Robot

The Core War programming game (described in the preceding section) doesn't offer great graphics to hold a player's attention. To satisfy the players' need for visual appeal, rival programming games incorporate more adventurous graphics. And, of course, what can prove any more appealing than war and gladiatorial combat? Instead of sending human gladiators into an arena to fight to the death, however, some programming games provide an imaginary arena where battling robots fight to the death.

Each robot incorporates identical capabilities to move, search, and shoot. But the way that each player programs his robot determines the actual actions of each robot. To program a robot, you must write a miniature program by using a simplified version of the C, C++, or Pascal language.

The challenge is not only to write a program that runs correctly, but also to provide your robot with instructions that create an optimum defensive and offensive strategy for surviving, stalking, and killing enemy robots at the same time.

Write a large program that gives your robot limited choices, and your robot probably gets blown up within seconds. Write a small program that runs quickly and provides your robot with enough intelligence to avoid damage while pummeling its opponents as often as possible, and your robot is likely to survive any battle.

In addition to providing a more visually appealing way to see whose programming is better, battling robot games also give you a chance to practice writing programs in your favorite language, such as C, C++, or Pascal. After you master how to control a robot using C or Pascal, you can transfer your robot programming skills to real-life programs.

Most battling robot programs run only on MS-DOS. If that's okay with you, download a free copy of a battling-robots game from one of the following Web sites:

- ✔ **The C++ Robots game** is at `www.gamerz.net/c++robots/`.

- ✔ **The C-Robots and P-Robots game** is at `www.informatik.uni-frankfurt.de/~hbecker/pcroth.html`.

Toying with Lego Mindstorms

Nearly every kid's had the chance to play with Lego building blocks (and plenty of parents have had the chance to step on a Lego building block in their bare feet). Because so many kids love playing with computers, the fine people controlling the Lego empire decided to combine Legos with computers, and the result is something known as *Lego Mindstorms* (at `http://mindstorms.lego.com`).

By using Lego Mindstorms, you can use Lego bricks to build a robot and then program it by using a simplified, graphically oriented programming language. Of course, if you find this simplified programming language too tame, the Lego Mindstorms Web site offers a free software developer's toolkit that enables you to program a Lego robot by using Visual Basic. Programming a Lego robot involves pasting together blocks of instructions, similar to snapping together Lego building blocks.

For hardcore programmers who'd rather use a language tougher than Visual Basic, visit the legOS Web site (at `www.noga.de/legOS`) and download tools that enable you to control your Lego Mindstorms robots by using assembly language, C, C++, Pascal, or practically any programming language that you choose.

By using a copy of Lego Mindstorms and any of the free programming toolkits available, you can create your own robots out of Legos and program them to attack one another, chase your dog around the house, or run berserk and protect your house against prowlers. After you practice your programming skills with Lego Mindstorms, you can create almost anything that you want within the safe, friendly environment of Legos.

Appendix

About the CD

Here's just some of the stuff available on the *Beginning Programming For Dummies,* Third Edition, CD-ROM:

- ✔ **Liberty BASIC:** a shareware program for writing Windows programs using BASIC

- ✔ **NS Basic:** a trial program that allows you to write BASIC programs for either the PalmOS or the PocketPC handheld computer

- ✔ **REALbasic:** a demo that allows you to create Macintosh and Windows programs by drawing your user interface and then writing BASIC code to make it work

- ✔ **Dev-C++:** a freeware and open source C++ compiler that allows you to see how a compiler works and write C/C++ programs for Windows

- ✔ **Revolution:** a cross-platform trial program that lets you write programs for Windows, the Macintosh, and Linux

- ✔ **pMARS:** a freeware game program in which players write programs that stalk each other through the memory of an imaginary computer

System Requirements

Make sure that your computer meets the minimum system requirements that I give in the following list. If your computer doesn't match up to most of these requirements, you may experience problems in using the contents of the CD.

- ✔ A PC with a Pentium (or similar processor such as a Duron, K6, Celeron, or Athlon) or faster processor or a Mac OS computer with a PowerPC processor.

- ✔ Microsoft Windows 98 or later or Mac OS system software 8.6 or later.

> ✔ At least 32MB total RAM on your computer.
>
> ✔ A CD-ROM drive.

If you need more information on the basics, check out *PCs For Dummies,* 7th Edition, by Dan Gookin; *Macs For Dummies,* 7th Edition, by David Pogue; *iMac For Dummies*, by David Pogue; or *Windows Me Millennium Edition For Dummies, Windows 98 For Dummies,* or *Windows XP For Dummies,* 2nd Edition, all by Andy Rathbone (all published by Wiley Publishing).

Using the CD with Microsoft Windows

To install from the CD to your hard drive, follow these steps:

1. **Insert the CD into your computer's CD-ROM drive.**

2. **Click the Start button and choose Run from the menu.**

3. **Type D:\ where *D* is the letter of your CD-ROM drive.**

4. **Double-click the file called License.txt.**

   This file contains the end-user license that you agree to by using the CD. When you are done reading the license, close the program, most likely NotePad, that displayed the file.

5. **Double click the file called Readme.txt.**

   This file contains instructions about installing the software from this CD. It might be helpful to leave this text file open while you are using the CD.

6. **Double-click the folder for the software you are interested in.**

   Be sure to read the descriptions of the programs in the next section of this appendix (much of this information also shows up in the Readme file). These descriptions will give you more precise information about the programs' folder names, and about finding and running the installer program.

7. **Find the file called Setup.exe, or Install.exe, or something similar, and double-click on that file.**

   The program's installer will walk you through the process of setting up your new software.

To run some of the programs on the *Beginning Programming For Dummies* CD-ROM, you may need to keep the CD inside your CD-ROM drive. This requirement is a good thing. Otherwise, you may need to install a very large chunk of the program to your hard drive, which can possibly keep you from installing other software.

Using the CD with Mac OS

To install the items from the CD to your Mac's hard drive, follow these steps:

1. **Insert the CD into your computer's CD-ROM drive.**

   In a moment, an icon representing the CD you just inserted appears on your Mac desktop. The icon probably looks like a CD-ROM.

2. **Double-click the CD icon to show the CD's contents.**

3. **Double-click the License Agreement icon.**

4. **Double-click the Read Me First icon.**

   The Read Me First text file contains information about the CD's programs and any last-minute instructions that you may need to correctly install them.

5. **To install most programs, open the program folder and double-click the Install (or Installer) icon.**

   Sometimes the installers are actually self-extracting archives, which just means that the program files are bundled up into an archive, and this self-extractor unbundles the files and places them on your hard drive. This kind of program is often known as a SEA file. Double-click anything with SEA in the title, and it runs just like an installer.

6. **For those programs don't come with installers, just drag the program's folder from the CD window and drop it onto your hard drive icon.**

   After you install the programs that you want, you can eject the CD. Carefully place it back in the plastic jacket of the book for safekeeping.

Using the CD with Linux

To install the items from the CD to your hard drive, follow these steps:

1. **Log in as root.**

2. **Insert the CD into your computer's CD-ROM drive.**

3. **If your computer has Auto-Mount enabled, wait for the CD to mount. Otherwise, follow these steps:**

   a. Command line instructions:

   At the command prompt type:

   ```
   mount /dev/cdrom /mnt/cdrom
   ```

(This mounts the *cdrom* device to the `mnt/cdrom` directory. If your device has a different name, change *cdrom* to that device name — for example, *cdrom1*.)

b. Graphical: Right-click the CD-ROM icon on the desktop and choose Mount CD-ROM. This mounts your CD-ROM.

4. **Browse the CD and follow the individual installation instructions for the products listed below.**

5. **To remove the CD from your CD-ROM drive, follow these steps:**

a. Command line instructions:

At the command prompt type:

```
umount /mnt/cdrom
```

b. Graphical: Right-click the CD-ROM icon on the desktop and choose UMount CD-ROM. This un-mounts your CD-ROM.

When you have installed the programs that you want, you can eject the CD. Carefully place it back in the plastic jacket of the book for safekeeping.

What You'll Find

This CD is crammed with a variety of different programming languages so that you can experiment and explore different languages from the comfort and convenience of your own computer. Just as studying different foreign languages can give you a broader understanding of human communication, so can studying a range of computer programming languages give you a broader understanding of computer programming in general.

Software

Adobe Acrobat, from Adobe (`www.adobe.com`). Adobe Acrobat enables you to read Acrobat PDF files on a Windows or Macintosh computer.

BBedit, from Bare Bones Software (`www.barebones.com`), BBEdit is a text editor for the Macintosh, which lets you write any type of programs including HTML code to design your own web pages.

C++ Builder, from Borland International (`www.borland.com`). C++ Builder allows you to visually design your user interface and then use the C++ programming language to make it work. Borland plans to make C++ Builder into a cross-platform compiler so you can write programs for both Windows and Linux.

C++ Robots, a game where you program a battling robot using the C++ programming language. Well-written programs survive awhile poorly written programs (those that don't work right or run too slowly) get wiped out on the battlefield. (http://www.gamerz.net/rrognlie/projects.html)

C# Builder Personal, from Borland International (www.borland.com). C# Builder allows you to use Microsoft's newest C# programming language to create Windows programs.

Delphi, from Borland International (www.borland.com). Delphi is a rapid-application development tool based on the Pascal programming language. By copying source code between Linux and Delphi, you can create applications for both Windows and Linux.

Dev-C++, from Bloodshed Software (at www.bloodshed.net). Dev-C++ is a complete C/C++ programming environment for creating Windows programs.

Free Pascal, from Free Pascal.org (at www.freepascal.org). Free Pascal is a Pascal compiler that closely follows the syntax of Borland Pascal version 7.0 and Delphi.

Future BASIC[3], from Staz Software (at www.stazsoftware.com). Future BASIC[3] enables you to write applications for the Macintosh by using the BASIC programming language.

IBM® Robocode V1.0.6, battling robot game from IBM, which lets you program a robot in Java (http://robocode.alphaworks.ibm.com/home/home.html). Poorly written programs get killed while well-written programs wipe out the competition and survive.

JBuilder, from Borland International (www.borland.com). JBuilder is a rapid-application development tool for writing programs using the Java programming language. Because Java programs can run on different operating systems, JBuilder programs can as well, including Windows and Linux.

Kylix, from Borland International (www.borland.com). Kylix is the Linux version of Delphi, which allows you to use Pascal to write Linux applications. By copying source code between Linux and Delphi, you can create applications for both Windows and Linux.

Liberty BASIC, from ShopTalk Systems (at www.libertybasic.com). Liberty BASIC offers a BASIC compiler for Windows capable of creating complete Windows applications.

MacPerl, a Macintosh version of the popular Perl programming language, often used to program web sites but also capable of creating general purpose programs too (www.macperl.com).

NS Basic, from the NSBasic Corporation (www.nsbasic.com). This demo version allows you to write BASIC programs for the handheld PocketPC operating system.

Perl, a popular programming language, derived from the C language, often used to create programs for web sites. If you're going to create web sites that do more than just display text and graphics, you'll probably need to use Perl. (www.perl.com).

pMARS, from KOTH.org (at www.koth.org). Core Wars programming game where contestants write their own programs that try to wipe other competing programs from an imaginary computer's memory.

"Programming in Python" bonus chapter. A short chapter, stored in an Adobe Acrobat PDF file, that explains the Python programming language.

Python, from the Python Consortium (at www.python.org). Python is an object-oriented scripting language that people often use for creating Internet applications. Programmers often compare Python to languages such as Perl and Java.

REALbasic, from REAL Software (at www.realbasic.com). REALbasic enables you to draw your user interface and write BASIC code to create applications for the Macintosh, Linux, or Windows.

Revolution, from Runtime Revolution (at www.runrev.com). Revolution is a cross-platform, HyperCard clone that enables you to create stacks of graphics and text that you can link together to create your own programs.

Ruby, a free programming language designed to teach the principles of object-oriented programming. (www.ruby-lang.org/en). Ruby programs can run on a wide variety of operating systems including Windows, Linux, Macintosh, and even OS/2.

TextPad, simple, yet powerful text editor for Windows to let you write programs or HTML code to design your own web pages. (www.textpad.com)

WinAce, a trial version of a file-compression program used to smash multiple files into a single file and compress their size to make it easier to transfer data from one computer to another. (www.winace.com)

WinRAR, a trial version of another file-compression program used to smash multiple files into a single file and compress their size to make it easier to transfer data from one computer to another. (www.rarlabs.com)

Shareware programs are fully functional, free, trial versions of copyrighted programs. If you like particular programs, register with their authors for a nominal fee and receive licenses, enhanced versions, and technical support.

Freeware programs are free, copyrighted games, applications, and utilities. You can copy them to as many PCs as you like — free — but they have no technical support.

GNU software is governed by its own license, which you find inside the folder of the GNU software. You face no restrictions on distribution of this software. See the GNU license for more details.

Trial, demo, or evaluation versions are usually limited either by time or functionality (such as an inability to save projects).

If You've Got Problems (Of the CD Kind)

I tried my best to compile programs that work on most computers with the minimum system requirements. Alas, your computer may differ, and some programs may not work correctly for some reason.

The two likeliest problems are that your machine doesn't have enough memory (RAM) for the programs that you want to use or that you have other programs running that are affecting installation or running of a program. If you get error messages such as `Not enough memory` or `Setup cannot continue`, try one or more of the following methods and then try using the software again:

- **Turn off any antivirus software that's on your computer.** Installers sometimes mimic virus activity and may make your computer incorrectly believe that a virus is infecting it.

- **Close all running programs.** The more programs that you're running, the less memory is available to other programs. Installers also typically update files and programs; if you keep other programs running, installation may not work correctly.

- **In Windows, close the CD interface and run demos or installations directly from Windows Explorer.** The interface itself can tie up system memory or even conflict with certain kinds of interactive demos. Use Windows Explorer to browse the files on the CD and launch installers or demos.

- **Have your local computer store add more RAM to your computer.** This course is, admittedly, a drastic and somewhat expensive step. If you have a Windows 95 PC or a Mac OS computer with a PowerPC chip, however, adding more memory can really help the speed of your computer and enable more programs to run at the same time.

If you still have trouble with the CD-ROM, please call the Wiley Product Technical Support phone number: (800) 762-2974. Outside the United States, call 1(317) 572-3994. You can also contact Wiley Product Technical Support through the internet at: www.wiley.com/techsupport. Wiley Publishing will provide technical support only for installation and other general quality control items; for technical support on the applications themselves, consult the program's vendor or author.

To place additional orders or to request information about other Wiley products, please call (800) 225-5945.

Index

Wiley Publishing, Inc.
End-User License Agreement

READ THIS. You should carefully read these terms and conditions before opening the software packet(s) included with this book "Book". This is a license agreement "Agreement" between you and Wiley Publishing, Inc.,"WPI". By opening the accompanying software packet(s), you acknowledge that you have read and accept the following terms and conditions. If you do not agree and do not want to be bound by such terms and conditions, promptly return the Book and the unopened software packet(s) to the place you obtained them for a full refund.

1. **License Grant.** WPI grants to you (either an individual or entity) a nonexclusive license to use one copy of the enclosed software program(s) (collectively, the "Software" solely for your own personal or business purposes on a single computer (whether a standard computer or a workstation component of a multi-user network). The Software is in use on a computer when it is loaded into temporary memory (RAM) or installed into permanent memory (hard disk, CD-ROM, or other storage device). WPI reserves all rights not expressly granted herein.

2. **Ownership.** WPI is the owner of all right, title, and interest, including copyright, in and to the compilation of the Software recorded on the disk(s) or CD-ROM "Software Media". Copyright to the individual programs recorded on the Software Media is owned by the author or other authorized copyright owner of each program. Ownership of the Software and all proprietary rights relating thereto remain with WPI and its licensers.

3. **Restrictions On Use and Transfer.**

    (a) You may only (i) make one copy of the Software for backup or archival purposes, or (ii) transfer the Software to a single hard disk, provided that you keep the original for backup or archival purposes. You may not (i) rent or lease the Software, (ii) copy or reproduce the Software through a LAN or other network system or through any computer subscriber system or bulletin- board system, or (iii) modify, adapt, or create derivative works based on the Software.

    (b) You may not reverse engineer, decompile, or disassemble the Software. You may transfer the Software and user documentation on a permanent basis, provided that the transferee agrees to accept the terms and conditions of this Agreement and you retain no copies. If the Software is an update or has been updated, any transfer must include the most recent update and all prior versions.

4. **Restrictions on Use of Individual Programs.** You must follow the individual requirements and restrictions detailed for each individual program in the About the CD-ROM appendix of this Book. These limitations are also contained in the individual license agreements recorded on the Software Media. These limitations may include a requirement that after using the program for a specified period of time, the user must pay a registration fee or discontinue use. By opening the Software packet(s), you will be agreeing to abide by the licenses and restrictions for these individual programs that are detailed in the About the CD-ROM appendix and on the Software Media. None of the material on this Software Media or listed in this Book may ever be redistributed, in original or modified form, for commercial purposes.

5. **Limited Warranty.**

    (a) WPI warrants that the Software and Software Media are free from defects in materials and workmanship under normal use for a period of sixty (60) days from the date of purchase of this Book. If WPI receives notification within the warranty period of defects in materials or workmanship, WPI will replace the defective Software Media.

    (b) WPI AND THE AUTHOR OF THE BOOK DISCLAIM ALL OTHER WARRANTIES, EXPRESS OR IMPLIED, INCLUDING WITHOUT LIMITATION IMPLIED WARRANTIES OF MERCHANTABILITY AND FITNESS FOR A PARTICULAR PURPOSE, WITH RESPECT TO THE SOFTWARE, THE PROGRAMS, THE SOURCE CODE CONTAINED THEREIN, AND/OR THE TECHNIQUES DESCRIBED IN THIS BOOK. WPI DOES NOT WARRANT THAT THE FUNCTIONS CONTAINED IN THE SOFTWARE WILL MEET YOUR REQUIREMENTS OR THAT THE OPERATION OF THE SOFTWARE WILL BE ERROR FREE.

    (c) This limited warranty gives you specific legal rights, and you may have other rights that vary from jurisdiction to jurisdiction.

6. **Remedies.**

    (a) WPI's entire liability and your exclusive remedy for defects in materials and workmanship shall be limited to replacement of the Software Media, which may be returned to WPI with a copy of your receipt at the following address: Software Media Fulfillment Department, Attn.: *Beginning Programming For Dummies,* 3rd Edition, Wiley Publishing, Inc., 10475 Crosspoint Blvd., Indianapolis, IN 46256, or call 1-800-762-2974. Please allow four to six weeks for delivery. This Limited Warranty is void if failure of the Software Media has resulted from accident, abuse, or misapplication. Any replacement Software Media will be warranted for the remainder of the original warranty period or thirty (30) days, whichever is longer.

    (b) In no event shall WPI or the author be liable for any damages whatsoever (including without limitation damages for loss of business profits, business interruption, loss of business information, or any other pecuniary loss) arising from the use of or inability to use the Book or the Software, even if WPI has been advised of the possibility of such damages.

    (c) Because some jurisdictions do not allow the exclusion or limitation of liability for consequential or incidental damages, the above limitation or exclusion may not apply to you.

7. **U.S. Government Restricted Rights.** Use, duplication, or disclosure of the Software for or on behalf of the United States of America, its agencies and/or instrumentalities "U.S. Government" is subject to restrictions as stated in paragraph (c)(1)(ii) of the Rights in Technical Data and Computer Software clause of DFARS 252.227-7013, or subparagraphs (c) (1) and (2) of the Commercial Computer Software - Restricted Rights clause at FAR 52.227-19, and in similar clauses in the NASA FAR supplement, as applicable.

8. **General.** This Agreement constitutes the entire understanding of the parties and revokes and supersedes all prior agreements, oral or written, between them and may not be modified or amended except in a writing signed by both parties hereto that specifically refers to this Agreement. This Agreement shall take precedence over any other documents that may be in conflict herewith. If any one or more provisions contained in this Agreement are held by any court or tribunal to be invalid, illegal, or otherwise unenforceable, each and every other provision shall remain in full force and effect.